The Mechanics of Modernity in Europe and East Asia

This book provides a new answer to the old question of the 'rise of the west.' Why, from the eighteenth century onwards, did some countries embark on a path of sustained economic growth while others stagnated? For instance, European powers such as Great Britain and Germany emerged, whilst the likes of China failed to fulfil their potential.

Ringmar concludes that, for sustained development to be possible, change must be institutionalised. The implications of this are brought to bear on issues facing the developing world today – with particular emphasis on Asia.

Erik Ringmar teaches in the government department at the London School of Economics. He is the author of *How We Survived Capitalism and Remained Almost Human* (Anthem Books, 2005).

Routledge explorations in economic history

The Mechanics of Modernity in Europe and East Asia

The institutional origins of social change and stagnation

Erik Ringmar

Routledge
Taylor & Francis Group

LONDON AND NEW YORK

First published 2005
by Routledge
2 Park Square, Milton Park, Abingdon, Oxon OX14 4RN

Simultaneously published in the USA and Canada
by Routledge
270 Madison Ave, New York, NY 10016

Routledge is an imprint of the Taylor & Francis Group

Typeset in Goudy by Wearset Ltd, Boldon, Tyne and Wear
Printed and bound in Great Britain by MPG Books Ltd, Bodmin

British Library Cataloguing in Publication Data
A catalogue record for this book is available from the British Library

Library of Congress Cataloging in Publication Data
A catalog record for this book has been requested

ISBN 0-415-34254-6

Contents

Acknowledgements

The best ideas in this book were originally developed in conversations with Professor V. M. Sergeev of MGIMO, Moscow.

Part I
The logic

1 The nature and origin of modern society

For most of their existence there was nothing particularly unique about European societies. In medieval Europe, everybody, next to everybody, was a peasant, poor and illiterate with a life expectancy at birth of perhaps 35 years. The few tools that existed in peasant society required a heavy input of manpower; productivity was low and the occasional surplus was quickly gobbled up by a small, oppressive, elite. What passed for science was, even among the educated, hopelessly confused with superstition and most aspects of life were heavily influenced by custom and by an all-pervasive Church. Medieval society was not static to be sure, but changes when they occurred were *ad hoc* and coincidental; stability was the social norm if not always a social reality.

Then something happened that in a comparatively short time made European societies radically different both from previous versions of themselves and from other societies. Agriculture became more productive; people moved to cities to work in factories where production took place according to increasingly sophisticated techniques; people's life expectancy and level of education went up and science made rapid and amazing progress. Instead of being slaves to nature, the Europeans became nature's masters, and instead of living side by side with other cultures, they set off to conquer the world. No longer *ad hoc* and coincidental, change became continuous and progressive. This restless, ruthless, expanding and ever-changing world is the modern, Western, world. This is modernity as we still know it.

Compare East Asia. Countries such as China and Japan were always at least as 'sophisticated' and 'advanced' as the countries of Europe. In the sixteenth century the first European visitors to this part of the world acknowledged as much and were profoundly impressed with the power and wealth of East Asian rulers and with the good manners and discipline of their subjects.[1] And yet history took quite a different turn in this part of the world. When the West began changing rapidly, especially in the nineteenth century, East Asia seemed to remain much as before. This 'failure' to emulate European examples was immediately noticed by observers as diverse as John Stuart Mill and G. W. F. Hegel. Looking at their own part of the world, the Europeans saw change everywhere; looking at the East, they saw nothing but 'stagnation' and 'the despotism of custom.'

Although we today are unlikely to endorse these particular conclusions, the puzzle itself remains. The differences between East Asia and Europe did indeed increase dramatically in the course of the nineteenth century. The most obvious indicator of this sudden gap is perhaps the new style of European imperialism. When sustained contacts with East Asia first were established in the sixteenth century, the European presence was limited. Foreigners were banned from Japanese soil between 1639 and 1868 and in China they were strictly controlled by the authorities. In the nineteenth century, however, the Europeans returned with far more ambitious plans and with the troops and gunboats to back them up. And while neither China nor Japan ever formally was colonised, from this time onward elites in both countries began struggling hard to somehow 'catch up' with the technically proficient barbarians.[2]

This contrast between Europe and East Asia gives rise to a number of questions. The most obvious ones concern why and how. Why was Europe suddenly able to develop so rapidly and how did the transformation happen? Which conjunction of factors made it possible for this particular part of the world to break so radically with its past and to become so different from other societies? And why did the transformation not first take place in China or Japan which by all accounts were at least as well positioned for a similar take-off? Put slightly differently, these historical questions concern the nature and origin of what has come to be called a 'modern' society. The question is what it is that makes a society modern and why some societies have been able to modernise more quickly and more effortlessly than others.[3] The aim of this book is to answer these questions.

'Modernity' and 'the modern'

More needs to be said about the idea of the modern. In the history of ideas, references to 'the modern,' or a 'modern age,' first appear in the work of Humanist scholars of the Renaissance, and their use of the term was almost always polemical.[4] The aim behind the phrase was to draw as sharp a contrast as possible between the activities of the Humanists themselves and the traditional, Scholastic, philosophers associated with the universities and the Church.[5] The Humanists were people who admired the achievements of classical Greece and Rome and who were highly critical of the ignorance and superstition of contemporary Europeans. Yet things could improve if only the glories of the ancients somehow could be revived. By modelling the future on Antiquity, the intervening period – what came to be known as the 'middle ages' – could be dismissed as an embarrassing age of darkness. The people who devoted themselves to this subversive antiquarianism were known as 'the moderns.'

Yet the more the Humanists learnt about the classical civilisations, the more multifaceted and realistic their picture of them became. As some of the moderns came to realise, there were actually a large number of things that the ancients did not know, could not do or had not discovered. Notably, as the English philosopher Francis Bacon pointed out in the early seventeenth century, the

Greeks and the Romans knew nothing about gunpowder, the compass and the printing press.[6] All three were instead recent inventions, achievements of the modern age. This ability to invent new, previously unheard of, things, gradually came to change the relationship with the ancient world. As Bacon explained, antiquity 'deserves that reverence, that man should make a stand thereupon, and discover what is the best way; but when the discovery is well taken, then to make progression.'[7] From the seventeenth century onwards, the future became far more important than the past and the Europeans increasingly looked forward rather than backward.

In the course of the eighteenth century this forward-looking optimism was translated into a new account of history.[8] According to the Enlightenment philosophers the past should not be understood as a disparate collection of stories about assorted peoples and events, but instead as a single, unified, account of the constant improvement of mankind. To be a human being is to be a part of this universal history of progress. Through the Enlightenment, according to Immanuel Kant, man had liberated himself from his 'self-imposed immaturity'; the free use of reason had replaced the slavish reliance on instinct, superstition and dogma.[9] Through the French Revolution, according to G. W. F. Hegel, man had for the first time become his own master, and through the state – particularly through the Prussian state – man had found a place where he could develop his full potential.[10] Sharing the same basic outline, the modern story of progress was soon developed in a number of competing versions. Liberals followed Kant and saw continuous progress in the development of human rights, in political and bureaucratic rationalism, and in constant economic growth. Socialists followed Hegel, but saw history as a question of material, not spiritual, development, and identified the end of history with communism, not with the Prussian state.

This contemporary – this modern – understanding of modernity is never better expressed than through the idea of a 'revolution.' Before the Enlightenment revolutions were understood as movements that took a society back in time to an original, and better, era.[11] The relevant metaphor was astrological: just as the revolutions of the stars always followed the same paths, the history of a society unfolded in a circular pattern. Hence the rationale of the Glorious Revolution in England in 1688 was to restore Protestantism and a notion of limited kingship, and the rationale of the American revolution of 1776 was similarly to restore the 'ancient rights of all Englishmen.'[12] In intent, if not in their effects, these revolutions were reactionary.

Modern revolutions, however, are not reactionary but progressive. The aim of all revolutionaries from 1789 onward has not been to restore something old but on the contrary to create something new, different and better.[13] The whole point is to break with the past, its traditions and injustices, and remake the world in accordance with our own preferred design. In this bold aim the French revolutionaries were followed by twentieth-century revolutionaries in Russia, China, and a host of other countries, often with the most disastrous of consequences.

Yet in modern societies, revolutions are not only taking place in politics but in all walks of life: in social and economic conditions, in music, fashion and the arts.[14] To be modern is to constantly create – or to believe that one constantly is creating – everything anew. To be modern is to always be different from what one is; it is to be up-to-date; in touch with the latest developments; at the forefront, or the cutting edge, of that which is best, most current, sophisticated and advanced. Hence our current obsession with economic growth. The steady improvement in economic indicators has a value in itself since it gives the impression that the past is ever more remote and the future is ever closer. Every day things are getting just a little bit better, and every improvement confirms our faith in the progressive movement of time. In modern society, where the future is god, economic change becomes our daily act of worship.

The irony – and the fundamental predicament of all modern societies – is that none of us ever will be able to reach this final destination. The future is our god, but since the future is unknown, so are necessarily the truths we believe in. All we have for now are instead preliminary theses and best guesses.[15] In the end the object of our worship is at least as remote as ever the gods of previous civilisations. The future, just as Jesus Christ, will never actually come.

The poverty of economic theorising

The question is why it was that certain societies in Europe suddenly began changing in this relentless and ever-progressive fashion. Why did the future suddenly become something to look forward to as something different from the past, and why did people feel they had the power to influence it? And, on a more concrete and practical level, how is it possible to organise a society in such a way that it is able to undergo continuous social, political and cultural changes?

Economists have a simple and powerful way of answering all such questions. It is, they say, all a result of the development of capitalism. The development of capitalism is what makes all other aspects of society change. This was famously the view of Karl Marx who saw economic relationships as the 'base' on which the 'superstructure' of political, social and cultural life was founded. In Marx's own life-time capitalism was making 'all that is solid melt into air,' as it undermined traditional authorities and created new wealth and new misery.[16] And many classically trained, non-Marxist, economists have drawn much the same conclusions. The capitalist outlook, according to Joseph Schumpeter,

> starts upon its conqueror's career subjugating – rationalizing – man's tools and philosophies, his medical practice, his picture of the cosmos, his outlook on life, everything in fact including his concepts of beauty and justice and his spiritual ambitions.[17]

As both Marx and Schumpeter would have it, if Western societies have been in a perpetual state of change over the last couple of centuries it is because capitalism perpetually has changed them.

As a moment's reflection makes obvious, however, capitalism cannot possibly be the original cause of all the changes that take place in modern society. The reason is that capitalist development itself has causes. Capitalist economies are not, after all, growing automatically and by themselves; capitalism is not a *primum mobile*, an 'unmoved mover.' Indeed, as we know from history, sustained economic growth is a relatively rare phenomenon and most societies have yet to experience much of it even at the beginning of the twenty-first century. Without in any way denying the importance of capitalism and its potentially world transforming powers, the question still has to be asked what it is that makes capitalist development possible in the first place.[18]

On the most general level, this question is easy enough to answer. Economies develop for basically two reasons: either because they come to employ more resources or because they come to employ existing resources more efficiently.[19] When more resources are mobilised – more land, more people, more machinery – more can be produced. But production increases also if the resources are used more productively: if land is made more fertile, if people are better educated or if the machinery is operating more quickly or accurately. The first kind of growth we could call 'input-led growth' and the second could be called 'productivity-led growth.'

These two forms of growth in turn refer to two different notions of efficiency: what we could refer to as 'allocative' and 'adaptive' efficiency.[20] Allocative efficiency is improved when things are moved around in an economy to places where they are more productively employed. Allocative efficiency is essentially a function of the invisible hand of the market. As Adam Smith famously and powerfully argued, the most efficient allocation of resources is achieved where supply and demand are allowed to interact freely.[21] But allocative efficiency also depends on the size of the market. Everything else equal, the larger the market, the more people are able to specialise on those particular tasks which they are relatively better at performing. The larger the market, the smaller pieces labour can be divided into, and the more extensive the division of labour, the higher the rates of growth.

While acknowledging the validity of Smith's insights, later generations of economists also noticed their limits.[22] Sooner or later, they pointed out, the productive resources of society would be as well allocated as they ever could be and labour would be divided into its smallest possible units. When this point is reached the factors that go into the process of production – labour, capital and land – would necessarily start to yield declining returns.[23] Most dramatically, Thomas Malthus argued, increases in income will result in more births which in turn will lower the income per capita.[24] Thus, as Karl Marx concluded, once capitalism has exhausted its potential, it has to be replaced by a new and superior system. And even those economists who were less keen on revolutionary action than Marx suspected that the long-term prospects for economic growth were bleak.[25]

However, what none of these nineteenth-century economists sufficiently had considered was the possibility of improvements in productivity.[26] Productivity-led growth takes place through the introduction of new management techniques, through improvements in education and training, or even through social or cultural change. What is taken to be important above all, however, are changes in technology. Radically new inventions such as the railroad, electricity, the automobile or the computer constitute technological quantum leaps that move the economy as a whole onto a new growth path. It is the ability of contemporary societies to constantly experience such leaps which up to now has made it possible to avoid the bleak predictions of the nineteenth-century economists. Thanks to continuous improvements in technology we are never running up against the limits of what it is possible to produce.

What is at stake here is not allocative but instead adaptive efficiency. Merely reallocating resources within a market will never make it possible to sustain growth over the long term. What matters is rather whether enough resources are devoted to increasing the productive potential of society.[27] This the market mechanism alone cannot necessarily guarantee. The forces of supply and demand may operate with textbook-like ferocity – allowing people to perfectly satisfy their preferences – but a society where this is the case may still grow more slowly than another society in which market forces are less efficient but where resources are more obviously geared towards long-term growth.

If Adam Smith provided the best analysis of how output-led growth takes place, Joseph Schumpeter provided the best analysis of productivity-led growth.[28] According to Schumpeter, economies grow not by following their established paths but instead by breaking with them. Entrepreneurs are the ones who are responsible for these breaks. Entrepreneurs are people who constantly look for new things to sell and for new ways in which to sell them. In the process they introduce the kinds of innovations on which the economy ultimately depends for its development. The entrepreneur, according to Schumpeter, is the person who is responsible both for destroying the old and for creating the new.[29]

When looking at empirical series of growth rates for a country such as the United States economists have found that the vastly larger proportion of growth can be attributed to increases in productivity.[30] Only around 12 per cent of growth between 1909 and 1949 can, for example, be explained by the expansion of capital per worker. The remainder – commonly referred to as 'the residual' – accounts for the remaining 88 per cent. Since it cannot directly be attributed to any factor of production it is not immediately obvious what it refers to, but given the importance commonly given to technological factors, the assumption is that the residual represents a measure of technological innovation.[31] However, the residual should surely also include all kinds of other things that result in productivity gains: institutional innovations, improvements in education and training, and perhaps also the impact of changes in culture or social norms.[32]

The problem for economists is that they lack a good theory for dealing with this grab-bag of disparate and ultimately non-economic factors. To a large extent this is a consequence of the limits of any theory. The activities of entrepreneurs are unpredictable by definition and are hence necessarily difficult to theorise about. Much the same can be said about technology. Technological change is itself a species of social change that both affects and is affected by all kinds of other changes.[33] If technological change ultimately is what drives economic change then the economists have to present a viable explanation of it. This, however, they have so far been unable to do.[34] Again this is hardly surprising. Technological change is intimately related to a long range of cultural, social and political factors but none of these economists are particularly well equipped to study.[35]

Consider the case of China. There is a long and famous list of Chinese inventions which all were made well in advance of similar inventions in Europe.[36] Yet the mere existence of this technology never allowed China to develop in the European fashion. Or consider the Industrial Revolution. It was not the case, as an economist might argue, that the innovations that provided the basis for the factory system were produced as a result of heavy capital investments.[37] On the contrary, there was in principle nothing to the steam engine that a particularly skilled medieval craftsman could not have developed. Or consider the importance of wars. It is a well established fact that wars have technological spin-offs – in the twentieth century everything from atomic power and jet engines to the Internet – but the logic which produces them is military and political and not economic.[38] Not surprisingly the attempts by economists to theorise about such factors are hopelessly simplistic.

The conclusion is consequently that capitalism surely has played an important role in transforming Western societies but also that references to capitalism explain surprisingly little. Long-term growth depends on improvements in productivity but the sources of productivity growth are badly captured by economic theorising. Technological innovation is crucial but economists have no proper explanation of its sources. Ironically there is not all that much that economists can say in the end about the fundamental causes of economic growth. While economic theorising offers important insights, it does not provide the kind of answer we need.

2 The failure and success of East Asia

Let us try a different tack. Instead of looking for a general explanation for economic and social change, what we could do is to study the issue as a historian would. An economic historian for example – at least an economic historian of the traditional mould – would pay scant attention to abstract theories and instead try to explain actual cases of development. Moreover, he or she would typically have few hang-ups about taking non-economic factors into consideration.[1] As an economic historian might conclude, growth does not only depend on the availability and quality of the factors of production but also, for example, on factors like geographic location, on cultural norms or religious beliefs, the absence or presence of natural or epidemiological disasters, a country's luck on the battlefield, and so on.

In order to bring some order to such potentially endless lists of factors a comparison is often helpful. A well-chosen comparison allows us to observe the variation in some factors while keeping other factors constant. In this way it is possible to understand something about the relative importance of one explanatory variable as opposed to another. If, for example, two parts of the world at one stage seem to have attained a similar level of development but if one of them suddenly changes in a radical manner, it is possible to look for the causes of that change in the factors that differentiate the two. Hence the attraction of comparing developments in Europe with those in East Asia.

That the two parts of the world were strikingly similar was obvious already to the first European visitors to the East.[2] As Jesuit missionaries and Dutch merchants agreed, China and Japan were at least as rich and powerful as ever Europe itself. East Asia was full of sophisticated religions, technologies and arts; people were 'white and cultured,' and lived orderly lives in societies with highly developed institutions.[3] And although Francis Bacon was quick to take credit on behalf of his contemporaries for the invention of the printing press, gunpowder, and the compass, all three were of course Chinese inventions, long in use by the time the first Europeans arrived.

Europe's admiration for East Asia remained well into the latter part of the eighteenth century. Then, however, the assessments suddenly changed and travellers returned with far more negative accounts. What they now had discovered was the poverty of China, the antiquated traditionalism of Japan, and the despotic regimes maintained by all East Asian rulers. By the nineteenth century most European societies were already undergoing profound changes and the promise of ceaseless progress is what gave its inhabitants a new sense of self-confidence. Europe had made a leap into an exciting world of economic prosperity and unprecedented technical mastery of nature; new hopes were connected to individualism, liberalism and democracy. In none of these respects had East Asia managed to follow. Looking at their own part of the world, the Europeans saw change everywhere; looking at the East they saw nothing but stagnation. While Europe was modern, China and Japan had failed to modernise.

Compare the latter part of the twentieth century where a strange, inverted, echo of this discussion suddenly could be heard. Again the topic concerned modernisation and discrepancies between East Asia and Europe, but now the issue was not the failure of the East but instead its astonishing successes. Although it today is easy to forget, the economic situation in 1945 of countries such as Japan, Korea, and Taiwan was not radically different from that of other poor countries in, say, West Africa.[4] As it appeared to international experts at the time, East Asia too would be in continuous need of outside support, not least if it was to be safe from the scourge of communism. In the end of course the Western experts were proven spectacularly wrong. Before long the 'tiger economies' of East Asia were growing at 10 per cent per year and their exports were growing by 20 per cent. Uniquely in the developing world, the countries of East Asia were modernising both successfully and extraordinarily quickly. Although it may have taken many observers by surprise this unprecedented catch-up represents, historically speaking, only a return to the traditional pattern.[5] From the perspective of the twenty-first century, it was the nineteenth and the first part of the twentieth centuries that constituted the anomalies. This was the relatively short period during which developments in East Asia and Europe temporarily slipped out of synch. But after a hiatus of about 200 years, the two are now once again back on parallel tracks. East Asia and Europe are once again each other's twins.

This parallelism allows for two potentially promising comparisons. By looking at the differences between the two parts of the world, we can hope to understand why it was that Europe rather than East Asia was first to modernise. By looking at the similarities between the two, we can hope to understand why it was that East Asia, uniquely among all poor parts of the world, was able to catch up.

Explanations for the failure

To a contemporary observer such as John Stuart Mill the reasons for the backwardness of China were quite obvious.[6] Although the Chinese once had achieved many great things, they had grown conservative over the years and lost their sense of individualism. In the West, people think for themselves, Mill explained, and they never hesitate to embark on new enterprises. In China, by contrast, 'the despotism of custom is everywhere the standing hindrance to human advancement.'[7] The minds of the Chinese are, like the feet of their women, maimed by compression. The best hope for the East was instead that the West – through its colonies, its commerce and its church – would destroy the ancient social structures and rebuild them according to European principles. '[I]f they are ever to be further improved,' as Mill argued, 'it must be by foreigners.'

Karl Marx, for his part, reached strikingly similar conclusions.[8] As he saw it, China was a feudal society ruled by a despotic emperor and a conservative bureaucratic elite. China was subject to an 'Asiatic mode of production' which followed entirely different rules from the capitalist economies of the West. As a result the country would never experience capitalism, and hence never Communism, unless helped along by Europe. With equal self-assurance, the German sociologist Max Weber declared that China was badly suited for capitalist development since Confucianism, in contrast to European-style Protestantism, lacked an existential tension between an earthly and a transcendental realm.[9] Similarly, the technological determinism of Karl Wittfogel purported to show that countries such as China, where agriculture supposedly was dependent on large-scale irrigation works, necessarily would give rise to large, inefficient, bureaucracies.[10]

Japan, meanwhile, was treated with a greater degree of admiration but in the end no less condescendingly. At the turn of the twentieth century European collectors discovered the rarefied æsthetics of Japanese arts, and woodblock prints and Japanese ceramics soon lent sophistication to well-to-do European homes. With Gilbert and Sullivan's *Mikado*, 1885, and Giacomo Puccini's *Madame Butterfly*, 1904, playing to packed opera houses, the craze for things Japanese reached a peak.[11] Japan corresponded to everyone's dream of the exotic East, and the sexual imagery behind the exoticism was compelling. Japanese culture was regarded as fundamentally feminine and just as Asian women it was there to be admired, and dominated, by Western males.

Today all such verdicts are profoundly embarrassing in their condescension and racial triumphalism, and even conclusions that supposedly are based on scientific evidence are often highly bogus. There is something deeply unfair about the way the comparisons have been set up.[12] There is no reason after all why China and Japan should correspond to a set European pattern of development, and to fault them for not doing so is ridiculous. This is not to deny, however, that there is legitimate puzzle regarding how to explain the respective historical trajectories of the two parts of the world. Here a comparison is still surely legitimate. Rather than denigrating the historical experiences of China and Japan, what we need to figure out is what it is that made Europe different. Denying ourselves the right to make such a comparison is at least as foolish as presenting the European pattern as inevitable or universal.

There are today at least four different explanations for these diverging paths, not counting assorted sub-explanations.[13] The first explanation points to factors which are best described as environmental. According to this view, Europe was always far less exposed to natural disasters, earthquakes, contagious diseases, and to inclemancies of the climate, and this is what explains its superior economic performance.[14] Geographical factors could also be included here: the importance of the Mediterranean and the Baltic as conduits of commerce or the great diversity of environmental conditions that existed across Europe which helped to encourage trade. In none of these respects, the argument goes, was East Asia equally blessed.

Another set of factors is demographic.[15] China and Japan have always had a far greater population than Europe, and while this testifies to the productivity of East Asian rice-paddies, it also serves as an inevitable drag on economic growth. Economic improvements in East Asia were always translated into higher birth rates and thus into stagnant, or even declining, incomes per capita. In Europe peasants were able avoid this trap since people married later, had fewer children, and experimented more successfully with various forms of birth control.

A third set of factors is political.[16] For much if not for all of their history, China and Japan were united behind one ruler who in his person combined both secular and religious authority. In Europe by contrast, power was always divided. In the Middle Ages there was a division between the Church and the Empire, and from about the sixteenth century an intense competition ensued between independent kings who all sought to defend the sovereignty of their realms. The need to prepare for war in order to guarantee security spurred technical innovations and forced each country to assure that businessmen and manufacturers could operate under favourable conditions. Only in this way could money be raised to pay for soldiers and guns. In China and Japan military security was far less of an issue and neither country engaged in the kind of military competition which provided incentives for technological or social change.

A fourth set of factors concerns the quite different roles which the two parts of the world have played in the international political economy.[17] Although Europe and China strongly may have resembled each other as comparatively late as in the year 1750, the Europeans were obviously the ones with the global ambitions. They had been 'discovering' the rest of the world for many hundreds of years already and gradually subjecting the societies they found to trade and to their colonial designs. The Chinese had been engaged in similar discoveries throughout South and Southeast Asia, and in the fifteenth century they travelled as far as to the eastern coast of Africa.[18] By the fifteenth century, however, all such explorations had ceased. This difference in international position became crucial once East Asia and Europe in the eighteenth century both started running out of precious resources.[19] In both parts of the world growing populations put pressure on food and on energy supplies, but only the Europeans were able to deal with these problems through overseas expansion.[20] What made the Europeans unique was thus not their inherent ingenuity nor their domestic resources but rather the rapaciousness of their colonial greed.

Explanations for the success

Turning next to the astonishing success of East Asia in the twentieth century, it is no less of a debated issue. And East Asia's performance becomes all the more puzzling given the disappointing experiences of other parts of the world. For about fifty years by now, domestic elites and international agencies tried their best to develop – to 'modernise' – the underdeveloped and poor parts of the world.[21] As the experts would have it, the geographical distance that separated the 'first' and the 'third' world corresponded to a distance in time. Europe and North America were 'far ahead'; they were 'leading the way'; and everyone else was 'following.' The task of modernisation was consequently to find a way for the stragglers to 'catch up.' The goal was itself variously defined. Economic modernisation was equated with the introduction of markets, financial institutions and industrial production; political modernisation meant representative democracy and a multi-party system; social modernisation implied individualism, emancipation of women and urbanisation; religious modernisation meant secularisation, and administrative modernisation came to be understood as the reliance on formal procedures and on the due process of law.[22]

Unfortunately it was never very clear how to reach some or all of these goals. What aid agencies and international experts typically did was to think of modernisation as a question of a particular technique, institution or branch of industry. 'This,' the experts concluded, 'this is what modernisation requires,' and they would then proceed to implement their particular pet project. However, since the technique, institution or branch of industry often fitted quite badly with existing customs and ways of life, the hoped for modernisation did not take place, or it happened only partially and half-heartedly. And even when the European model was accurately copied, the spirit that animated it often seemed to be lacking, and as a result the transplanted copies came to operate in strange and unpredictable ways.

Only a number of East Asian countries are unambiguous examples to the contrary. Here modernisation did indeed happen and these countries did indeed manage to catch up. However, the disconcerting fact is that East Asia's success happened in blatant disregard of the kinds of policies which a majority of the modernisation theorists had advocated. When the development agencies suggested import substitution, the countries of East Asia embarked on export-led growth; when Western experts advocated democratisation and representative institutions, the countries of East Asia remained stubbornly authoritarian; when cultural and social change was taken as a prerequisite for economic take-off, East Asian societies remained strikingly traditional in a large number of ways. East Asia, in short, modernised in its own fashion; it modernised without ever fully Westernising.

Before long the East Asian success story forced the experts to reconsider their views. Perhaps, some scholars speculated, traditional cultural and religious norms actually encourage rather than retard development. One commonly identified candidate here was Confucianism, which, it was now argued, instils norms regarding deference to superiors, frugality and hard work, all values crucial for economic growth.[23] In addition, East Asian societies were often said to be uniquely cohesive. Culturally they are all more or less homogenous, and as a result people are ready to make sacrifices in the name of common goals. This means, for example, that corporations are able to operate in quite different ways than in Europe and North America. Relations in the workplace are more personalised, more consensual, and people subject themselves more readily to collective decision-making. As a result the workforce is more dedicated and fewer days are lost in industrial disputes.

Other explanations focused instead on the role of the East Asian state.[24] Throughout the region, the state has taken an active role in relation to the economy. In Japan, bureaucrats at MITI, the Ministry of International Trade and Industry, exercised a controlling influence over the direction of private enterprises; providing financing, foreign exchange, patents and coordinating research.[25] In Korea, the entirely financial system was state owned, and in Taiwan all basic industries were nationalised after the Guomindang takeover in 1949.[26] In all three societies, the aim was to use state power in order to channel resources away from stagnant sectors of the economy and into sectors of growth.

A third explanation concerns instead the international context of the East Asian miracles. It is obvious, for example, that all countries in the region have benefited greatly from support from the United States.[27] The US lent money, gave grants, and provided military security. Above all, the US guaranteed access to a capitalist world market where tariffs and customs duties constantly were being lowered. In the end it was consumers in North America and Europe who constituted the main market for East Asian oil tankers, cars, and all kinds of electronic consumer goods. Without the help of a surging world demand, and a US guaranteed peace, no East Asian miracles would have been possible.

The secret

Historians, including economic historians, are usually quite dismissive of general purpose explanations, we said. As they point out, general theories can usually explain few historical cases, and as such they are when it comes right down to it of little but academic interest. This is not least true of general explanations of economic growth. In practice there will always be a wealth of factors that intervene between the model and the world and confound the theoretically grounded expectations. The *ceteris*, in short, is never quite *paribus*. At most we can hope to draw some general conclusions from a comparison of successful, as opposed to failed, cases of economic development.

However, from the point of view of an economist – or any other social scientist for that matter – historical knowledge of this kind will never be particularly convincing. The explanations that economic historians provide resemble long shopping lists: they are full of assorted items, some necessary and important, others obviously superfluous or even eccentric and self-indulgent. What a social scientist is likely to want is not just a list but an account of the exact contribution of each item on it. Exactly how important, in other words, was the demographic difference between East Asia and Europe? What role did Confucianism or Protestantism really play? Granted that states and inter-state competition matters, how much does it actually matter and under what circumstances? Unfortunately historians can rarely answer such questions with any proper degree of precision.

In this book an alternative venue will be explored, an explanation which cuts across the explanations provided both by social scientists and by historians. The problem with most existing theories of change, the argument will be, is that they proceed by identifying an agent, or agents, which are seen as responsible for bringing change about. Change, in other words, is defined as an action for which someone or something is to be held responsible. Hence the economists' attempts to account for growth by breaking it down into various factors of production plus an, embarrassingly large, residual. Hence also the inconclusive debates concerning of what exactly this residual may consist.

This was also the intellectual *cul-de-sac* in which the modernisation theorists found themselves trapped. They equated modernisation with a particular technique, institution or branch of industry in the mistaken belief that these were the engines that would help jump-start the development process. But these programmes failed since the theorists never had more than a superficial and incomplete understanding of what modernisation requires. Modernisation is not a product of any particular technique, institution or branch of industry. In fact, a modern society cannot easily be characterised as one thing rather than another; there is no particular something that a modern society necessarily is and something else that it definitely is not. People in Europe and North America tried to remake the world in their own image but they failed since they never knew their own image. Similarly, people in the rest of the world failed to catch up with them since they never really understood what chimera it was they were supposed to be chasing.

The truth of the matter is that social change – including economic growth – takes place for all kinds of different reasons. It is wrong to imagine that change is the result of a long chain of causes and effects which always begins with the same kinds of factors. There is no smoking gun and no *primum mobile*, not capitalism and not technology.[28] To merely point to an agent or another is never going to be enough since this begs the question of the origin of that particular agent. If we take capitalism to be the origin of all change, we will find that capitalism has its own causes; if we point to technology, we will find that technology too needs to be explained, and so on.

This was ultimately the reason why the modernisation projects failed. Modernising elites and foreign experts were unable to capture the essence of modern society for the simple reason that there is no such essence. Poor, non-European, countries were advised to follow the latest European achievements, but this only reinforced their status of backwardness the day when, inevitably, the latest European achievements were replaced by even later ones. Instead of a showcase of the future, the developing world became a historical museum where yesteryear's European modernity was put on pathetic display. The result is as embarrassing to the model as it is to the epigone.

Instead of a predetermined content, modern society has only a form, a form constituted by continuous changes. Modern societies, at least since Francis Bacon's time, are societies that always are becoming different from themselves. What modernisation requires can never be defined beforehand for the simple reason that we never know where the development of history will take us. Whenever modernity is equated with a particular something – the modernisation theorists' techniques, institutions or branches of industry, for example – this something is only the latest manifestation of modernity, never its essence. Since modern societies constantly change, they have no essences and every characterisation of them will for that reason soon become hopelessly out of date.[29] Modern societies are never themselves, always other.

Given this situation, we might as well give up on the attempt to look for causes. Modern society, change and economic growth have no easily identifiable cause as causes usually are understood. The suggestion of this book – to be developed further in the next chapter – is instead that an explanation should proceed by identifying what could be referred to as the 'enabling conditions,' or the 'permissive environment,' in which change is most likely to take place. Rather than looking for causal agents, the task should be to identify the kinds of situations under which causal agents of whatever kind are likely to become operative. Social transformations can happen for a large variety of different reasons – and which cause that is singled out by an observer is to a large extent a coincidence – but this is not true of the conditions that allow social transformations to take place. There is essentially only one kind of environment that is fully conducive to change, and this environment can be described with a relatively high degree of precision.

3 The self-transforming machine

Let us begin by considering the notion of change in some more detail. As a matter of philosophical speculation, the question of the nature of change has been discussed at least since the pre-Socratics.[1] For Heraclitus, for example, change was the permanent state of the world, and for that reason 'you can never step into the same river twice.' Others, like Parminides, firmly denied the possibility of change. Aristotle's contribution to this debate was to introduce the notion of potentiality. Some things are actual, he taught, whereas others are merely potential. Change takes place when something potential is transformed into something actual; when something that could be, but is not, is turned into something that is. For example: a seed is actually a seed, but potentially a tree; a girl is actually a girl, but potentially a woman; a statue of Hermes exists potentially in a chunk of marble. In all cases, change is what turns the one into the other. The world in which we live is the actual world but when previously unrealised potentials are explored and acted on, the actual world changes. Change, in short, is the actualisation of the potential.

The aim of this chapter is to use this Aristotelian insight in order to provide a description of the kind of social environment which is likely to be most conducive to social change. This is the social setting which provides the best possibility for constant and relentless transformations to take place. This is the setting, in other words, which we would identify as that of a modern society.

The logic of change

Although Aristotle's metaphysics has been thoroughly discredited by modern science, his notion of potentiality still underlies many scientific discussions of change. Consider, for example, changes that take place as a result of biological evolution. A specie changes, an evolutionary biologist might say, when the potentiality that exists in its genes is actualised in new members of the specie.[2] An analogous framework can be applied to cases of social change. Just as in biological evolution, social change is a matter of translating potentiality into actuality. In society this happens to the extent that people have ideas for new projects, to the extent that these ideas are realised, and to the extent that the new projects survive, prove popular, and are emulated by others. Everything else equal, the more potentiality that is discovered, the more of it that is actualised, and the more accepting the social environment is of the new, the quicker the pace of change. To the extent that this process of discovery and actualisation takes place continuously, change too will be continuous.

Looking at this process in more detail, it is possible to think of social change as taking place in three analytically separable steps. The first step is that of reflection. This is where the potentialities that exist in the world first are discovered and explored. To be a human being is constantly to reflect on the world and to try to envision alternatives to it; we day-dream and philosophise, we write or paint, work for think-tanks or research institutions.[3] It is through such activities that the difference between the actual and the potential is discovered. Suddenly we realise how much better, or at least different, our lives would be if only this, that, or the other feature of it were altered.

The second step is that of entrepreneurship. This is where reflection ends and action begins. It is the entrepreneur who actualises the potential that reflection has discovered; it is he or she or it who brings new things into the world. While entrepreneurs and entrepreneurship usually are associated with economic activities, there is no reason why the term should be this narrowly confined. Entrepreneurship takes place also in fields such as politics, culture and religion. Here too there are plenty of people who embark on new projects and on more or less well-conceived attempts to change the world.

For change to happen, however, reflection and entrepreneurship are not sufficient in themselves. The reason is that both activities are bound to produce conflict. Reflection is a critical activity and as such it is potentially subversive. The activities of entrepreneurs are equally sources of conflict. Since resources are limited, it is necessarily the case that not all but only some projects can be realised. As a result there will always be a competition over who gets what. For change to be possible, a way must be found of dealing with such clashes. Nothing accomplished by reflection and entrepreneurship will last, that is, unless society is tolerant of pluralism – the co-existence of different, perhaps contradictory, projects, entities, beliefs and ways of life.

When taken together, these three steps – reflection, entrepreneurship and pluralism – is what makes social change possible. Reflection allows us to discover the potential which exists in the actual; entrepreneurship allows us to act on our discoveries and to put them into practice; pluralism ensures that a multitude of different solutions survive once they come into being. Everything else equal, the more the world is reflected on, the more potentiality will be discovered; the more potentiality that is discovered, the more alternative courses of action will be embarked upon; the more alternative actions that are embarked upon, the quicker the pace of social change.[4]

While all societies are reflective, entrepreneurial and tolerant to some extent, some are more so than others. Reflection can be encouraged or restricted by political or religious authorities, but even where it is perfectly allowed, it may be more or less difficult to engage in. Reflection requires time and leisure, and while time and leisure are scarce in any society, they are scarcer in some societies than in others. Entrepreneurship too can be more or less encouraged and is more or less possible. Entrepreneurs need resources – information, money, access to markets – but societies differ in their ability to provide these things. The same is true for pluralism. While some societies are reasonably tolerant of the simultaneous co-existence of radically different kinds of things, many are more sceptical or even outright hostile.

This small set of ideas provides the beginnings of a model which allows us to understand the differences between modern and pre- or un-modern societies. Modern societies, the argument goes, are far more efficient in translating potentialities into actualities. In modern societies people are actively encouraged to imagine alternatives to the existing order; here it is easier to put new ideas into action; and society has worked out a way of dealing with the coexistence of many incompatible things.

Institutionalised change

Yet the argument needs one more component before it is complete. So far change has been discussed as though it was a matter of choice, as though modern society was the result of individuals suddenly making change possible. This picture is false. On the contrary, social change is usually extra-ordinarily difficult to bring about. Change undermines traditions and long-standing habits and poses threats to established structures of privilege and power. Change breaks our connection with the people who came before us and with those who will come after us and it isolates and alienates us from our families and our societies.[5] Given its destructive nature it is not surprising that social changes often are resisted, and those with most of a stake in the maintenance of the *status quo* are usually the ones best placed to block them. If nothing else, sheer inertia assures that most features of social life remain more or less as they always have been. Given these formidable obstacles, individuals are basically powerless to bring about changes, even when acting together with others. If it only were down to individuals, that is, modern society would not be possible.

Considering these and other obstacles like them, it is remarkable that change has become such a prominent feature of contemporary society. Unless we are very young indeed, the world really is very different today from what it was like when we were born, and we can expect it to become quite different again by the time of our deaths. The question is what it is that drives these processes. How can something which is so difficult to accomplish become such an intrinsic feature of social life?

The answer is that change in the end has little or nothing to do with the qualities of individuals or with their actions and inactions. In fact, on the level of individuals, modern societies are in no important ways different from pre-modern societies. Contemporary Britain, United States or Japan are *not* modern because they contain individuals who are uniquely reflective, entrepreneurial or tolerant. On the contrary, reflective, entrepreneurial and tolerant individuals have always existed. If all it took were extra-ordinary human beings, a modern society would have been produced a long time ago, in classical Greece or in Song dynasty China, if not before.[6] What makes modern societies different are instead the institutions they contain. Institutions are far more powerful than individuals acting alone or together with others. Institutions can swiftly and effortlessly do what none of us can accomplish, and transformations which individuals are powerless to bring about are easily brought about by institutional means. A modern society is a society in which change happens automatically and effortlessly because it is institutionalised.

The power of institutions rests above all in their ability to dispose people to act in certain ways.[7] Institutions consist of rules prescribing how people should behave, and not behave, in given situations. Some of these rules are formal but many are informal and not even explicitly defined. In either case, the rules provide incentives for action; if we follow the rules we are rewarded, if we break the rules we are punished. Sometimes the incentives are monetary but often they are social. We act in a certain fashion not since it will make us better off but since it brings us recognition and approval by our peers. By determining rewards and punishments, institutions constrain and mould our behaviour.

Reacting to these incentives, people come to behave in predictable, meaningful, ways. Before long rule-following becomes second nature and our reactions become instinctual and automatic. Our actions are institutionalised, as it were. This is also why the contributions which institutions make to social life tend to be under-appreciated. Institutions are similar to pieces of furniture: ready to be used, but rarely to be questioned or even noticed. Taking a certain social furniture for granted, people just do whatever it makes sense to do in a given situation without thinking too much or too deeply about it. In this way institutions come quite imperceptibly to take care of things behind our backs. Churches deal with god and parliaments deal with politics, giving the rest of us the time to concentrate on more important matters.[8]

A crucial role of institutions is to co-ordinate the activities in which individuals engage. Institutions provide procedures for how interaction is to take place, languages and jargons in which people can communicate, and standards and protocols with which various contributions can be judged. Institutions are also important for creating individual and collective identities. Institutions provide rituals with which people can identify and through which they can be identified. In addition, there are procedures for how social esteem is to be awarded and structures that encourage people to exert themselves and compete with each other.

Another important function of institutions concerns the division of labour.[9] Often institutions provide procedures which make it possible for people to specialise on ever more minute and better defined tasks. We can concentrate on what we know best, safe in the knowledge that others are concentrating on the tasks they know best. The contribution of the institution is to bring these people together and to provide them with opportunities to exchange the products of their single-minded efforts. In this way the institution vastly magnifies the power of each individual contribution thereby multiplying the combined output. As a result, the institution taken as a whole soon becomes far more efficient than any of its constituent parts.

Institutions also allow for the automation of individual tasks.[10] By breaking activities down into ever smaller units, each task becomes increasingly easy to perform. In the end each person only knows, or does, one thing, and this thing is constantly repeated. This is the reason why modern society has nothing to do with the achievements of extra-ordinary individuals. Modern societies are highly sophisticated and complex but the sophistication and complexity are almost exclusively located at the level of institutions. As far as individuals are concerned, the tasks they perform have instead steadily become less complex and less sophisticated.[11] In general, when less complexity and sophistication are demanded, less is supplied. Thanks to the sophisticated institutions they contain, modern societies can be operated by dummies, and strikingly often they are.

This is not to say, of course, that all institutions necessarily produce change. On the contrary, many institutions are highly conservative and backward rather than forward-looking. Historically speaking, institutions that impede change are far more common than those that promote it. It is only in societies that we call modern that institutions explicitly operate to bring changes about. Only here are individuals given the kind of institutional support they need for continuous transformations to be possible.

What makes modern societies modern is the fact that institutions are in charge of the three activities that make change possible. Change which in previous societies was down to individuals and good luck is in modern societies pursued by institutional means. In a modern society there are institutionalised ways of discovering the potentiality which exists in the actual, institutionalised ways of acting on this potential, and institutionalised ways of accommodating the new once it is actualised. Since the three prerequisites of change are institutionalised, change itself is institutionalised.

What ultimately matters is not how these institutions operate by themselves, however, but rather how they operate together. When properly designed and calibrated, the three sets of institutions lock on to each other and work together much like the cog-wheels in a machine. The institutions of modern society constitute a piece of social machinery that constantly churns out new and unexpected products. As a result, change is not *ad hoc*, but automatic; not occasional, but permanent; change just happens without people thinking or worrying much about it and without anyone consciously trying to bring it about.[12] And, most disconcertingly of all, although the modern machine is man-made, we are neither its designers nor its masters and for that reason change cannot be predicted, stopped or even properly controlled. Modern society is a kind of self-transforming machine from whose constantly changing output we both benefit and suffer.

The origin of institutions

If modern society is a product of a certain institutional environment, everything comes to depend on how this environment was created in the first place. The problem here is that the history of most institutions simply loses itself in time. There is, for example, no proper way of determining the origin of institutions like marriage, money or religion, and even a comparatively recent institution such as the state has a disputed provenance.[13] As it turns out, surprisingly few institutions are consciously created, and even in the cases where they are, the motives of the creators are often obscure. Somehow institutions are just there, and there is where they always seem to have been. Differently put, institutions do not seem to have causes, if we by a cause mean that they were created at a particular time and for a particular reason.

In fact, even if an original founder and an original intention magically could be unearthed, it would tell us preciously little about why the institution still is in place.[14] Once an institution is established it quickly escapes the control of its makers. An institution that was created for one reason often survives for an entirely different – perhaps even a contradictory – reason. Parliaments were, for example, created in the Middle Ages as a way for the king to control the people but before long they instead became ways for the people to control the king. Much the same can be said about an institution such as the United Nations which was created by the Unites States as a way to exercise influence over poor countries but which for a while in the 1970s – if ultimately unsuccessfully – became an instrument through which poor countries sought to control the Unites States.

An alternative is to explain the existence of the institution in terms of the functions it serves. According to this view, functions can legitimately be identified as causes.[15] The existence of marriage could, for example, be explained as a result of the social needs it fulfils or a religious ritual could be explained as a result of religious needs. Capitalism, an economic historian might consequently say, has certain 'functional requirements' that institutions are created in order to serve.[16] These functional requirements explain why the institution exists. This, however, is blatantly *not* the story of most institutions. While institutions often remain more or less unchanged for centuries, their functions tend to vary considerably over time. In fact, there are many institutions – consider the British monarchy – which remain in place although they no longer serve any clearly identifiable purpose. Just like the appendix, or nipples in males, the queen is still around mainly since she has not yet been abolished.[17]

The relationship between institutions and functions is rather the inverse of what functionalist explanations require. The institution comes first and the needs develop only later. Far from being functionally required, institutions, once in place, create the needs they then go on to satisfy.[18] It is thus the existence of marriage that creates social needs rather than the other way around, and the existence of rituals that creates religious needs. Similarly, since the queen is there, various functions are invented to keep her busy. The functions are consequences of the existence of the institution, but consequences cannot be the causes of that of which they are the consequences.

Instead most institutions must be understood as the eventual outcome of a large number of historical coincidence. Institutions evolve in a spontaneous, undirected and cumulative fashion. When people continuously do things over extended periods of time, rules and patterns spontaneously develop that organise these activities. Marriage, money and the state were not planned, instead they slowly emerged as the unintended consequences of one person reacting to the actions of another. Once created they maintain themselves by sheer momentum, not because they are ideally suited to perform any particular task. It follows that institutions are best explained in terms of the path through which they developed; that is, through the history of their evolution. If this is the case, the question of why a modern society came to be established can only be answered in the form of a story of how it happened; a story of how the institutions responsible for self-reflection, entrepreneurship and pluralism came to be established, how they developed and changed.

This book

Time to briefly recapitulate. What more than anything has characterised societies in Europe and North America over the last couple of centuries is their ability to constantly transform themselves. Some time after the year 1500 these societies became 'modern' and began changing in a continuous and relentless fashion. The question which this books seeks to answer is why. Why was it that some European societies suddenly became very different from their predecessors and very different also from societies elsewhere in the world? Why was it, for example, that China and Japan, which in the seventeenth century still could rival the power and wealth of Europe, in the nineteenth century came to be seen as hopelessly behind the times?

To an economist these are questions concerning the sources of economic growth. What happened in Europe, he or she will explain, was that growth rates suddenly picked up and changes in the economy, in turn, brought about changes everywhere else in society. Probing a bit further, this explanation points to the importance of technological innovation. More than anything it is Europe's ability to constantly invent new things that has set it off on a path of continuous economic growth. Not denying the importance of capitalism, or technology, we pointed out that these explanations are insufficient as they stand. Capitalism and technology certainly have a large number of far-reaching effects but they also have a number of equally far-reaching causes. Since there are no smoking guns or single culprits, the quest for the *primum mobile* of social change is likely to remain unsuccessful. Modernity for that reason has no cause.

At this juncture we made a suggestion. Instead of looking for whatever it is that directly causes social changes to take place, an investigation should focus on what it is that makes social change possible. What we are interested in are not causal factors but rather what perhaps could be called the 'enabling conditions' or 'permissive environment' of social change. How such conditions and environments developed is a historical rather than a theoretical question; they came about for a large variety of contingent reasons that only a historical account can do justice. And while such a historical investigation may sound like a less ambitious enterprise than the search for straightforward causes, it is also one far more likely to meet with success.

The hypothesis presented in this chapter is that change is most likely to take place in an environment where reflection, entrepreneurship and pluralism are highly institutionalised. Reflection, entrepreneurship and pluralism are ways of making sure that the potentialities that exist in social life are converted into actualities. Everything else equal, the more such conversions that take place, the quicker the pace of change, and in a society where such conversions are highly institutionalised, change will take place continuously and automatically. A modern society, we said, is a society where change is institutionalised.

The chapters that follow provide an investigation of this hypothesis. The aim is first of all to understand the role played by reflection, entrepreneurship and pluralism in the development of Europe, and to look for institutions that help people reflect, act, and sort out their differences. Once we have a better understanding of how Europe developed in these regards – including an understanding of the very considerable differences that exist between the historical trajectories of various European countries – we can turn to East Asia. The question here is to what extent, if any, social change in China and Japan can be understood with the help of this abstract model. How reflective, entrepreneurial and pluralistic were East Asian societies and to what extent and in what ways were reflection, entrepreneurship and pluralism institutionalised?

Part II
Reflection

4 The discovery of distance

Consider first the notion of reflection. Derived from the Latin *reflectere*, to reflect is, etymologically speaking, 'to bend or fold back'; it is the action of 'returning,' 'restoring,' or 'diverting' an object.[1] In this sense the word has been used since classical times but in the seventeenth century the meaning became more specific as the term was adopted by the new science of optics.[2] Here reflection came to apply to the way in which rays of light bounce off obstacles, change course, and go off in new and different directions. A 'reflector' is, for example, a telescope that uses a concave mirror to collect light.

The seventeenth century was also when the first metaphorical use of the word appeared.[3] To reflect in a metaphorical sense is to 'go back in thought,' to 'consult with oneself'; it is to throw out an idea and let the mind try to retrieve it. Thus understood, reflection is an aspect of thinking, but to say that someone 'reflects on a matter' gives a particular emphasis to the technical aspects of the process of cognition. To reflect is not just to think but it is to put in motion what perhaps could be called the 'optics' of cognition. Just as reflections of light, reflections of the mind require a certain set-up: you need distance, a focus, and an appropriate point of view.

Distance is no doubt the most basic requirement for a process of reflection to take place. It is only once you take a few steps back that you are able to see what something actually looks like. Distance is also required if we are to be able to reflect on ourselves. Somehow we need a way of seeing ourselves as others see us; from the outside and as objects among others in the world. Lacking such distance we will not become aware of ourselves as social beings and we will not develop a proper conception of who we are.[4]

Societies too differ in their ability to reflect on themselves. Some societies are more reflective than others. Everything else equal, modern societies are far more reflective than pre- or non-modern societies. But this is not because the inhabitants of modern societies somehow are more intelligent or imaginative than the inhabitants of other societies. In fact, the reflective capability of a society has next to nothing to do with the characteristics of individual human beings. The difference is instead entirely a matter of technology and social organisation. People in modern societies are more reflective since they have access to particular technologies and to particular institutions. How these technologies and institutions came to be established are the topics of the next two chapters. First, however, and in this chapter, consider some of the differences between reflection as it took place in medieval societies and as it takes place in the modern world.

The fishbowl world of the Middle Ages

The received view of the Middle Ages is of a society where creative thoughts were repressed and everyone was forced to conform with the official teachings of an all-powerful Church. Accordingly little by means of reflection was possible; radical ideas were suppressed, especially if there was a risk that the criticism would escape the small coteries of dissenters and have real social effects. And while this received view of the Middle Ages is a caricature, it is easy to see how it arose. To be too persistent in one's questioning – to be too curious regarding the state of the world or the heavens – was regarded by the Church as a sign of *vanitas* and hence as a sin.[5] St Augustine, for one, condemned the 'unhealthy curiosity' of men who

> are led to investigate the secrets of nature, which are irrelevant to our lives, although such knowledge is of no value to them and they wish to gain it merely for the sake of knowing.[6]

Obedience to God meant that man should refuse to go where his questions might take him. Some things were revealed, some other things were hidden; the latter were for man to praise, the former for God alone to know. You ate from the tree of knowledge only at your peril.

Instead the answers to most people's questions were taken off the Church-administered rack of well-worn Christian dogma. Ordinary people's everyday questions were dealt with by parish priests while more intellectually challenging attacks were addressed by theologians and philosophers. The things that man needed to know about life, death and eternity could easily be looked up in a small collection of authorised texts, mainly passages from the Bible and snippets of writings by pre-Christian authors. Once this material had been edited, annotated, and glossed by generations of scholars, the result was a body of knowledge which not only was surprisingly complete but also suspiciously coherent. The world has never been as well and as completely understood as in the thirteenth century. The official canon, and the Gothic cathedral which was scholastic philosophy, provided a total explanation of everything, everywhere.

And yet, the received wisdom exaggerates the differences between the modern outlook and the medieval. In fact, to perpetuate this exaggeration was always a conscious strategy of the 'moderns,' designed to put their predecessors in a bad light and to further their own careers. For a fairer assessment consider first of all what a great achievement medieval theology itself represented. The whole body of Christian dogma, from creation myths to apocalyptic visions, was nothing if not a glorious attempt to reflect on the human condition. By expressing these myths and externalising them in the forms of a body of set texts, the Church allowed people to see themselves *sub species æternitas*, as it were, from the point of view of eternity. The fact that the texts were standardised and read across Europe also meant that people everywhere were able to contribute to the same reflective enterprise.

And even if it is true that Christian doctrine stifled as well as encouraged reflection, it is important to remember that the ideological hegemony of the Church never was complete. In all conceptual systems there are bound to be inconsistencies and when these are worked out quite different conclusions can usually be drawn even by people who fully accept the authority of the same dogma.[7] As a result no conceptual system will ever be fully coherent. This was certainly true of the teachings of the medieval Church which in practice were quite an unstable mixture of Hebrew traditions and classical Greek influences. Instead of staying loyal to the simple faith of the mid-Eastern shepherds who founded it, Christianity soon incorporated the sophisticated Greek tradition of philosophising. The price to be paid for philosophical sophistication, however, was continuous philosophical debate. Throughout the Middle Ages, endless intellectual quarrels raged on a number of abstruse issues; that is, people were forced to reflect on the foundations of their own faith.[8]

But reflection could also take far less high-brow forms. Consider, for example, the carnival.[9] Although medieval society was hierarchically organised, and ordinary men and women had few opportunities to change their lot, the carnival was an occasion when this rigid social order temporarily was suspended. The carnival was a *monde à l'envers*, a topsy-turvy world, where normal status hierarchies were inverted and different social rules applied. At the feast of fools, for example, the feudal lord was dethroned and the village idiot made king; in the *parodia sacra*, monks said the mass backwards and in pig Latin; at inductions at medieval universities, students mixed obscenities with parodies of the Bible and legal texts.[10] The carnival was a time of laughter, and as such it contrasted sharply with the official seriousness of medieval culture.[11] A text, a rule or a god that once had been thoroughly made fun of would never again be seen in quite the same light.[12]

Alternative social arrangements were explored also in the distinctly calmer setting of the medieval monastery. The monastery provided an institutionalised setting where nuns and monks could come closer to god, but also a place where they could get away from society. This half-way house between heaven and earth provided them with plenty of opportunities for reflection. Not surprisingly, monasteries were the leading intellectual centres of the age and medieval monastics were notorious visionaries.[13] During a prayer, a monk would perhaps see a blinding light and temporarily take leave of his senses or a nun would be transported away to another world during her sleep. When they returned, they told stories of miracles and other amazing events; they had talked to God or to the dead. Often they had messages with them from the other side: admonitions to sinners to repent but occasionally also demands for more general ecclesiastical or social reform.

For the Church the problem was how to relate to such extravagant claims.[14] If the visionary seemed sane and the demands acceptable, a new religious order could perhaps be established with the blessings, and within the official para-meters, of the Church. But if the visionaries seemed crazy, or the demands too radical, no such compromises were possible. In this situation the visionary would sometimes make an appeal directly to the people, and in this way a number of millenarian sects were born.[15] Once they found themselves in opposi-tion to established society, the message would soon turn increasingly radical. Many sects abolished the priesthood or the sacraments of the Church, and in some of them earthly possessions, and even women, were held in common.

Scholastic philosophy, carnivalesque antics, and the ecstasy of monastics, were all simple but powerful ways of reflecting on the world. They were means of establishing external points of view from which the existing social order could be better observed. And yet there were always limits to how much that could be seen from these alternative perspectives. The basic problem was above all a lack of distance. The medieval conceptual system, no matter how dynamic in its own terms, was in the end next to perfectly closed and self-referential; every part of it pointed to and supported every other part.[16] The European Middle Ages was an inside without an outside, a fishbowl world where nothing was unknown or unexplained.[17] Reflection was always restricted since there were no external points of view from which the system as a whole could be observed.[18]

As a result there were also definite limits to the kinds of criticism that could be formulated. Thus, although theological debates often were heated, the reli-gious language itself could not be questioned or replaced. Similarly, while the world could be turned upside-down, it would not be taken apart and reassem-bled in some fundamentally different fashion. And for the same reason, the political programme of even the most radical millenarian movement was sur-prisingly unimaginative.[19]

Modern self-reflection began with the sudden and unexpected discovery of alternative worlds located outside of the medieval fishbowl. Three such break-throughs were particularly important – the discovery by Humanist scholars of the heritage of classical Greece and Rome; the discovery by Spanish, Portuguese and Italian explorers of the Americas and other continents across the seas; and the discovery by astrologers-turned-astronomers of a universe which not only had the sun at its centre but which also was infinite in size. As a result of all three breakthroughs, enormous distances opened up together with a wealth of new perspectives. Placing themselves in classical Athens, in the Americas, or at a randomly given point in limitless space, the discoverers were suddenly in a position to view Europe, its habits and inhabitants, in entirely different ways.

The view from Antiquity

Take first the discoveries of the Humanists.[20] Admittedly, the heritage of clas-sical Greece and Rome never quite disappeared during the Middle Ages. The works of the medieval Church fathers incorporated occasional references to classical texts and quotes culled from Plato, Aristotle, Cicero and Ovid were used in textbooks at medieval universities. In addition, many ancient manuscripts existed in individual copies in monasteries scattered across Europe. Yet since the official canon did not include them, they were not read. The poet Francesco Petrarca and his friend Giovanni Boccaccio were among the first to collect these ancient manuscripts in a systematic fashion, but they were soon followed by others and by the end of the fourteenth century the search for old books had turned into a widely shared obsession. As one book after another was recovered, the body of classical works expanded rapidly.

What the Humanists discovered in these texts was a world that was well known to them yet at the same time also curiously unfamiliar. On the one hand, what the classical authors described was Europe itself and its inhabitants. On the other hand, these were Europeans who obeyed alternative gods, had alternative traditions and social norms and were subject to alternative cultural standards. What the Humanists had encountered were their *alter egos*, their other selves located in a different time and place.[21]

It did not take long however before the Humanists began engaging their classical counterparts in conversation. Petrarca wrote letters to Cicero, introducing himself as his son and disciple, and Niccolò Machiavelli, out of favour with the Florentine government and desperate for company, turned to the classics for consolation.[22] 'On the coming of evening,' as he described the scene, 'I turn to my house and enter my study.' Here, 'I enter the ancient courts of ancient men,'

> I am not ashamed to speak with them and to ask them the reasons for their actions; and they in their kindness answer me; and for four hours of time I do not feel boredom, I forget every trouble, I do not dread poverty, I am not frightened by death; entirely I give myself over to them.[23]

As a result of these and many similar conversations, the Humanists came to acquire an alternative view of themselves. They learnt new ways of expressing themselves in poetry, drama and in letters; they discovered how to describe natural sceneries and the history of their native cities; they received advice on military matters, on politics and oratory, on painting, medicine, law, and even on animal husbandry.[24] The Christian religion too had to be reconsidered when seen from this alternative point of view. Some Humanists were highly impressed by the civic religion of the ancients while others started studying the Cabbala and magical Egyptian cults.[25] And even the vast majority of scholars who stayed with classical Christianity often developed a faith much stronger and more immediate than anything taught by the official Church.[26]

The greatest transformation was not, however, to be found in individual doctrines or beliefs but rather in the medieval notion of the canon understood as a coherent body of eternal truths. As a result of their studies, the Humanists came to see the ancients less as representatives of a consistent tradition and more as individual human beings, each one with qualities and quirks which were distinctly their own. Moreover, when putting the ancient texts side by side, it was easy to spot variations in style, contradictions between arguments, and even a historical progression in the use of vocabulary and grammar. The idea of a canon broke down when it became obvious that its various parts were written by different people, at different times, and with different purposes in mind.[27] As the Humanists came to realise, statements had to be interpreted within their own historical contexts before they could make sense.

Once they stopped looking for coherence and instead began looking for contradictions, the Humanists found them everywhere. Anachronistic expressions made it possible to reject some texts, or parts of texts, as later additions or even as outright forgeries. It was, for example, through such textual criticism that Reginald Pecock and Lorenzo Valla, both writing in the fifteenth century, managed to show that the Donation of Constantine – the legal basis for the temporal power of the pope – was nothing but a rather clumsy ninth-century forgery.[28] Naturally this information was gratefully seized upon by religious reformers in subsequent centuries.

More generally speaking, it was obvious that the position of human beings changed to the extent that the position of traditional authorities was questioned. From the sixteenth century onward, man was no longer subjected to all-embracing, all-explaining, dogma since such a dogma no longer existed. The canon no longer spoke in a single voice but instead in many competing voices. Faced with such diversity, people were increasingly forced, best as they could, to make up their own minds. With traditional authorities undermined, people were desperate for new authorities to whom they could subject themselves.

The view from Utopia

Next consider the impact of the European discovery of the Americas and other continents across the seas. The first sustained inter-continental exchange began during the *Pax mongolica* of the thirteenth century when the empire of Genghis Khan made it safe for Europeans to travel as far as to China.[29] After the fall of the Mongol empire in 1368, however, over-land travel suddenly became impossible, and as the Arabs monopolised trade with the Orient, imported luxury goods became prohibitively expensive. This shift in relative prices provided an incentive to look for alternative trade routes to the East, and Portugal was the country that took the lead. Little by little Portuguese ships worked their way southward along Africa's western coast, and in 1488 Bartolomeo Dias returned with news of a way to the Indies around the Cape of Good Hope.[30] In 1492 the Genovese map-maker and sea-captain, Cristoforo Colombo instead tried his luck in a westward direction. Returning to Europe after three months in the 'West Indies,' he promised a ship full of gold to any investor brave enough to sponsor his next voyage.[31]

In contrast to the men and women of Antiquity which they had come across in their readings, the people the Europeans encountered in the Americas were not, at least not initially, considered to be anything like themselves. They were not long lost *alter egos* with whom they felt like striking up conversations. On the contrary, according to the Florentine explorer Amerigo Vespucci, the Indians were naked and lived 'as Epicureans' in communal houses; they had never heard of Jesus Christ, were neither Moors nor Jews, and appeared to be completely without both law and religion.[32] Yet these initial assessments gradually changed. Once they had spent a bit more time in the Americas, the Indians started to display more familiar traits. Some Spaniards compared them to the Greeks and the Romans since they too were pagan, or to Arabs since they were brutal, or to Adam before the Fall since he too had been innocent and gullible.[33] There were even those, such as Bartolomé de Las Casas, bishop of Chiapas, who went so far as to recognise himself in the Indian other. In fact, when he compared the peaceful lifestyle of the native Americans with the atrocities committed by the Europeans, it was clear to Las Casas who he would rather be. 'Who are we,' he asked in bewilderment, 'who can commit such heinous crimes in the name of our God?'

> The reader may ask himself if this is not cruelty and injustice of a kind so terrible that it beggars the imagination, and whether these poor people would not fare far better if they were entrusted to the devils of Hell than they do at the hands of the devils of the New World who masquerade as Christians.[34]

As far as the Spanish Crown was concerned, the Indians posed above all an administrative problem. The question was what to do with them but also how Spanish rule over the new continent could be legitimised in the eyes of the world. Characteristically these issues were discussed in the legalistic terms valid within medieval scholasticism.[35] As everyone seemed to agree, the Spaniards had a *ius predicandi*, a right to preach, and a *ius peregrinandi*, a right to travel, in the new continent, but the question was whether they were entitled to anything more. With what right, above all, could Spain make war on the Indians, occupy their land and lay claim to its riches?[36]

In order to consider such questions in more depth, an inquest was opened up in Valladolid in 1550 with Bartolomé de Las Casas defending the Indians and the scholastic philosopher Gines de Sepulveda making the case for the conquistadors.[37] Hearing testimonies and philosophical expositions in favour of both sides, relations between Europe and the rest of the world were subject to unprecedented scrutiny. The tribunal forced the judges to reflect not only on the Indians but also on themselves and their received opinions. For example: before they could decide who owned the wealth of the Americas, they had to come up with a better definition of ownership; before they could determine whether the Indians indeed were human, they had to draw a sharper distinction between human beings and animals.[38] And even if there was no doubt that Spain was civilised and the Indians uncivilised, the question remained which rights and duties civilised and uncivilised nations legitimately could lay claim to.

Although the eventual outcome of the disputation at Valladolid may have been less than fully satisfactory from the Indians' point of view, the arguments made in their favour, once stated, were there to be invoked and built on by others. One outcome of this reflective activity was the new discipline of international law, first formulated by Francisco de Vitoria at the University of Salamanca but soon developed by a number of other authors – Domingo de Soto, Francisco Suarez and Alberico Gentili among them – and influential across Spain and in Europe in general.[39] International law codified the conditions under which wars legitimately could be fought and stipulated which rights that belonged by nature to individuals and to states. In subsequent centuries the idea of natural law, and natural rights, was to have far-reaching, and often subversive, implications for the established political order.[40]

A similar impact was achieved through the stories told by the intercontinental travellers themselves. All over Europe tales from and about the New World were eagerly received by an avid readership. As the publishers soon discovered, however, since even the true stories were perfectly incredible, it hardly mattered whether poetic licence occasionally came to replace actual first-hand accounts. In fact, the authors often travelled far better, and definitively more safely, in their minds than on board ships and across mountains. In this way, in the early sixteenth century, a new genre of imaginary traveller's tales was invented which soon became at least as popular as the real thing.

The first example of the new genre may have been the account which Raphael Hythlodæus gave in 1516 of the previously unknown island of Utopia. As his author, Thomas More, tells us, Hythlodæus had been a passenger on Vespucci's ship but his stories of Utopia 'made us feel that Vespucci had seen absolutely nothing!'[41] Although More's main aim may have been to entertain his readers, he also had a critical purpose. Utopia as he described it was a mirror which allowed the Europeans to reflect on themselves more clearly.[42] Thus, as Hythlodæus pointed out, the enclosure movement in England had made it possible for idle men to become rich while the hardworking poor were driven off the land and turned into thieves. In Utopia, by contrast, all men were equal, life was communal, and property was shared.[43] Utopians worked only six hours a day and they enjoyed a healthy mix of physical and mental activities; they were happy even though they knew nothing of the Christian God.

While the novelty of the Americas eventually wore off, the idea of the alternative world as a mirror remained an indispensable intellectual tool. The imaginary traveller's tale afforded its author plenty of opportunities to show the familiar in an unexpected and ridiculous light. It was also, at least in theory, a safe way to express social criticism since anything after all can be said about worlds that do not exist. Putting the genre to good use François Rabelais let his Pantagruel travel to Utopia in Hythlodæus' footsteps, and in the process make fun of both fat prelates and scholastic philosophers.[44] Even more well travelled was Lemuel Gulliver who came to see human beings as they never before had been seen.[45] 'What if we, like the Struldbruggs, lived for ever?' Jonathan Swift asked, and 'what if the world were run by horses and we were lowly yahoos?' In an elegant inversion of the genre, Baron de Montesquieu had a Persian prince report on the curious goings-ons at the French court in his *Lettres Persanes* from 1721.[46] 'Isn't it strange how the French cut their hair off, but then wear wigs?' 'Why is life in the king's court at the same time so elegant and so gross?'

In a slightly more serious vein, the idea of alternative worlds could be relied on to score philosophical points. Consider, for example, the way in which Niccolò Machiavelli compared himself with his compatriots, the famous sea captains. I have 'set off in search of new seas and unknown lands,' he boasted in the preface to the *Discourses*, 1513, and 'I have decided to enter upon a new way, as yet untrodden by anyone else.'[47] Similar trips were undertaken by philosophers such as Thomas Hobbes and John Locke who told stories about what came to be known as 'the state of nature,' an original condition in which they imagined human beings to have lived before the emergence of the state. By comparing this potential world to the actual, they hoped to come up with principles on which legitimate political authority could be based. Although the state of nature was a hypothetical condition, its features were unmistakably those of the Americas. '[I]n the beginning,' as Locke put it, 'all the world was America.'[48]

The view from infinite space

Consider, finally, the impact of the new cosmology. In 1543 Nicolaus Copernicus published his *De revolutionibus orbium cœlestium* in which he placed the sun rather than the earth in the centre of the universe.[49] From that time onward a small group of astronomers began to throw doubts on the Aristotelian vision of the universe embraced by the Church. Meticulous observations made by the Danish astronomer Tycho Brahe in the 1580s and 1590s lent support to Copernicus' version. Building on Brahe's results, Johannes Kepler at the imperial observatory in Prague cast the new theory in a scientific and mathematical form. And in January 1610, when the Paduan instrument-maker Galileo Galilei turned his telescope towards the sky, what he saw was the 'most beautiful and delightful sight.'[50] There were stars never previously observed by human eyes, and there were many more of them than anyone ever could have imagined.[51] Although these empirical observations in themselves failed to conclusively settle the matter, the balance of probabilities had shifted, and with the publication of Isaac Newton's *Principia mathematica* in 1687 the new vision of the universe received a comprehensive, and what seemed to be a conclusive, explanation.[52] As it turned out, the earth was not stationary after all, and it was not at the centre of the universe, but instead simply one of millions upon millions of heavenly bodies whirling around in an endless void.

As contemporary Europeans soon came to realise life in the modern, infinite, universe was quite different from life in the fishbowl world of the Middle Ages.[53] One difference concerned the position of man in relation to god and the cosmos. While medieval man had been sinful and insignificant, he was nevertheless the centrepiece of God's creation, and as such the constant object of divine attention. When observed from an arbitrary point in limitless space, however, man was not only insignificant but also hopelessly peripheral. There was no longer a centre that man could occupy and it was far from clear whether God paid him any particular mind. In fact, it was not even clear whether there was a God. Although ever more sophisticated telescopes made it possible to discover ever more stars, no one had so far come across any evidence of a divine presence.

This failure had a number of profound implications. Perhaps, as some philosophers began speculating, man had been abandoned in an endless, godless, void?[54] But if that was the case, what was the point of our lives and our deaths? How should we live and why? Pondering such troubling questions, the French seventeenth-century philosopher Blaise Pascal was suddenly overcome by existential fear:

> When I consider the *brief* span of my life absorbed into the eternity which comes before and after ... the small space I occupy and which I see swallowed up in the infinite immensity of spaces of which I know nothing and which know nothing of me, I take fright and am amazed to see myself here rather than there; there is no reason for me to be here rather than there, now rather than then. Who put me here? By whose commands and act were this time and place allotted to me?[55]

Although not everyone was convinced by the new science, its conclusions were in the end quite impossible to ignore. And while Christianity continued to attract followers, mankind never quite regained its simple faith in Providence. We are all still suffering from some version of Pascal's existential homelessness.

But the new cosmology also had profound consequences in a number of seemingly unrelated fields.[56] A general implication was that authority became more easy to question. After all, if the position of the ultimate authority – God – had been undermined there was no reason to accept the claims of lesser authorities – princes, say, clergymen, or even fathers.[57] '[The] new Philosophy calls all in doubt,' the English poet John Donne wrote in 1611, a year after Galilei's initial discoveries:

> 'Tis all in pieces, all coherence gone;
> All just supply, and all Relation:
> Prince, Subject, Father, Son, are things forgot,
> For every man alone thinks he hath got
> To be a Phoenix, and that then can be
> None of that kind, of which he is, but he.[58]

As the new science had demonstrated, not even the authority of man's own senses could be considered reliable. The most basic of observations had turned out to be wrong: the sun, after all, does not move around the earth as our naïve sense impressions would have it. The lesson of the new cosmology was consequently not that empirical observations had triumphed over dogmatic beliefs. On the contrary, observations and dogma were in agreement and both were wrong. What finally settled the case in favour of the new cosmology was instead a more comprehensive theory that allowed for more powerful explanations to be constructed. What triumphed, that is, was not man's ability to observe as much as man's ability to reason. It was thanks to our rationality that the laws that governed the universe had begun to be revealed.

The impact of the new science was thus quite contradictory. On the one hand, it made man insignificant and peripheral; on the other hand, it made man infinitely more powerful. The urge to know the secrets of the universe – previously labelled as *hubris* and *vanitas* by the Church – was now the first requirement on the job description of every practising scientist. Although that Pascalian homelessness never went away, and few of the traditional authorities regained their former stature, human beings increasingly learnt to cope on their own. In place of the discredited authorities of the past, man put the authority of his own reason.[59] From this time onward, science rather than god attended to the needs of man.

This empowerment of man, in turn, had far-reaching political implications. If nature was governed by laws and by reason, it was not unreasonable to conclude that society could be governed in the same fashion. From the eighteenth century onward, philosophers and scientists set out to look for such laws, and political debates became a matter of how society best could be rearranged so as to become ever more rational.[60] As Immanuel Kant famously argued, reason can be the arbiter in matters of morality even in the absence of a god; and as G. W. F. Hegel and Karl Marx agreed, reason is active in history, inevitably taking us, step by dialectical step, closer to the best of all possible worlds. Or, as a number of latter day social engineers have insisted, society can be organised in such a way that human happiness and prosperity are maximised.

5　The face in the mirror

The discovery of worlds outside of the medieval fishbowl created enormous distances and alternative perspectives from which the Europeans could observe themselves. Although the reflective capability of medieval society never should be underestimated, the change was nevertheless profound. When looking at the world from these new points of view, a distinctly modern outlook gradually came to emerge. And naturally, the people most directly associated with these breakthroughs soon came to be regarded as heroic figures and as icons of the modern age. As generations of schoolbook writers have informed their impressionable readers, it was the discoveries of men like Petrarca, Columbus and Copernicus that created the modern outlook. But for their seminal contributions, we would still be living in the dark ages.

This version of history, however, is a *post hoc* rationalisation which completely distorts the facts. When viewed up close, none of the alleged heroes turns out to be heroic or even particularly unique. The more we read of Petrarca's own writings, the more of a traditional Christian he becomes; the more we learn about Copernicus, the more he turns into a brooding Renaissance alchemist; and Columbus is of course the very archetype of a lucky fool, arriving at the wrong place for the wrong reasons.[1] There is no doubt that all three discoveries easily could have been achieved earlier and by others.

The fact is of course that all three discoveries were achieved earlier and by others. Compare, for example, what usually is referred to as *the* Renaissance with what could be called the 'pre-renaissances' – the 'Carolingian Renaissance,' or the 'Renaissance of the twelfth century.'[2] Already at the time of Charlemagne, Benedictine monks were busy editing classical texts in a way which strongly remind us of the Humanists' painstaking labours, and already in the twelfth century there was a revival of long-lost Latin learning. Or compare Columbus with the Vikings. As archaeological evidence from Newfoundland shows, America was not discovered in the late fifteenth century by Italians, but instead in the late tenth century by Scandinavians.[3] Or consider Nicholas Oresme, a teacher at the University of Paris in the fourteenth century whose ideas on cosmology in many ways predated those of Copernicus.[4] The more we read about such 'precursors,' the more impressed we are likely to become and the more blurred the distinction will appear between a modern and a pre-modern outlook.

On the level of individual achievements there is indeed little difference between the one set of accomplishments and the other. The Humanists were not really all that different from the Carolingian monks, and Columbus and Copernicus were not all that different from Oresme and the Vikings. The real difference between the two sets of achievements is instead social and techno-logical. In the Middle Ages, there was no way of continuing the explorations that new discoveries made possible and for this reason alone whatever was accomplished perished with the individuals responsible. Before long the Car-olingian empire fell apart, the Viking colony in North America succumbed to attacks by Indians and disease, and Oresme's cosmological speculations were ignored by his successors.

When the same breakthroughs happened a few hundred years later, however, everything was different. Or rather, two things were different. First the Euro-peans had access to new and far more sophisticated technological means through which their reflections could be pursued. Second, and crucially, institu-tions were in place through which the reflective activities of individuals could be magnified and far better co-ordinated. Technologies and institutions perpet-uated the initial achievements, made them permanent and easy to build on by others. The new technologies is the topic of this chapter and the new institu-tions is the topic of the next chapter.

Technologies of reflection

Consider again the problem of reflection. Reflection requires distance, we said, but distance is difficult to achieve, especially if the object of our reflection is our own person or the society in which we live. Since we never can leave ourselves, we can never see ourselves from the outside, and while we physically can remove ourselves from our societies, this in itself does not provide a better point of view as long as we do not also shed our society's preconceptions. In order to get a better view of ourselves, we must find a way of extending ourselves, of making ourselves into objects available for observation. And while this may seem quite impossible to do, technical solutions often provide ingenious answers. Perhaps it is possible to talk about different 'technologies of reflection.'

One simple such technology is language. Language abstracts from and organ-ises reality and provides a distance between the thing present and its re-presentation in our minds. Moreover language allows us to express ourselves and in this way to turn our thoughts into objects in the world to which others, or we ourselves, can relate. Here, as always, the creation of distance allows new per-spectives to open up. Re-reading an old diary, for example, or over-hearing a conversation behind our backs, we are suddenly able to see ourselves from the point of view of others. This may be a profoundly alienating experience but it is often also an enlightening one. In fact it is enlightening precisely because it is alienating.

Since technologies of reflection vary widely in their effects, the presence or absence of a particular technology will make a huge difference to the reflective capability of society. For purely technical reasons some societies are more reflective than others. Compare, for example, the advantages of writing over purely verbal communication.[5] If a cultural heritage can be kept on paper instead of only in people's minds much more of it can be recorded and the material can be preserved more easily and added to by each successive generation. A written tradition will for this reason always be richer than a spoken tradition, at least in quantitative terms. The written tradition is also easier to reflect on than the merely verbal and individuals can relate to it in a more independent manner. As long as you can read there is no reason to sit listening, attentively, at the feet of the village elders; you can break with the long-established customs of your society without jeopardising their existence.

Given the impact of technology, it is possible to compare societies and to rank them according to their reflective potential. Everything else equal, the more and the better technologies, the more reflective a society. Note, however, that this is *not* a comment on the quality of the thought produced. While thought is best judged in terms of its content or its results, reflection is best judged in terms of technical criteria. In order to think well, that is, you should arrive at correct, interesting, or morally praiseworthy results, but in order to reflect well all you really need is access to a certain technological gadgetry. Although thought hardly can be said to have made much progress from Socrates or Confucius until today, reflection decidedly has.

The best evidence for this thesis are two technologies, the Venetian mirror and the printing press, which in the fifteenth century revolutionised the ability of the Europeans to reflect on themselves. Today, hi-tech means of communication – radio, television, computers, the Internet – have continued that revolution and new technological breakthroughs are no doubt just around the corner. None of these inventions has made people in modern societies smarter than men and women in other times and other places, but for technical reasons they have made it easier for us to reflect on ourselves. In order to better understand the role of technologies of reflection, consider briefly the impact of those two early-modern inventions: the Venetian mirror and the printing press.

The Venetian mirror

A mirror is no doubt the most obvious example of a technology of reflection. Since human beings never can see their own faces, and since they have a highly distorted view of much of their own bodies, it is only with the help of a mirror that they ever get a chance to take a good look at themselves.[6] An image in a mirror is an external object to which people can relate as they would to any other object in the world. We are here but also there – inside ourselves, but also on the wall in front of us – and the distance between the two is what makes reflection possible. In the mirror we can see and reflect on ourselves without leaving ourselves.

Mirrors made from polished stone or metal existed already in Mesopotamia and ancient Egypt but they were rare, of low quality, and reserved for religious purposes or for members of the elite.[7] In the Middle Ages there were round mirrors made of glass but they were expensive and due to their small size and convex form they provided only a partial view. Ordinary people could perhaps catch their reflection in the still water of a lake, but such glimpses were infrequent, and besides it is both inconvenient and unsatisfactory to look at oneself from a horizontal position. As a result, strange as it may sound, before the modern era most people had little or no idea of what they really looked like.

All of this changed with the invention of the modern mirror. Venetian mirrors – a flat sheet of glass covered with silver – were much cheaper than pre-modern mirrors and of vastly superior quality. From the workshops in Murato, outside of Venice, the new production technique spread quickly across Europe, and before long mirrors came into use not only among the rich but among most social classes. Looking into these glasses, the men and women of the Renaissance obtained for the first time a cheap, accurate, and vertical representation of themselves.[8]

Since people now were able to see themselves for the first time, it is not surprising that they became conscious of themselves in a new fashion. People began to worry about their appearance since they now were able to regularly inspect and control it. Faces could be checked for baggy eyes or running make-up and corrective counter-measures could speedily be applied. There was no reason not always to look one's best. Although there is no doubt that our contemporary preoccupation with self-image and self-presentation have many diverse causes, the invention of the mirror was its precondition.

The new self-consciousness had a number of far-reaching cultural consequences. Consider, for example, the autobiography, a literary genre which admittedly is of medieval origin but which came to flourish only once mirrors became readily available across Europe.[9] Or take the *Fürstenspieghel*, the 'mirror of princes,' another medieval literary genre that received a boost once mirrors became common. In these books of political advice, the aim of the author was to hold up a metaphorical mirror to the ruler in which he could see himself and the conditions obtaining in his kingdom.[10] By looking into the *Spiegel*, the *Fürst* was able to reflect on the requirements of statecraft. The most famous such book was Machiavelli's *The Prince*, 1513, but Erasmus of Rotterdam, Julius Lipsius, and many other authors contributed to the same genre.

The availability of mirrors also had broader cultural implications. Consider, for example, portrait painting.[11] In the Middle Ages, no proper portraits were painted but human beings were instead depicted as representatives of given types. A picture could, for example, show two hundred saints who all displayed the same, rather blank, expression.[12] With the advent of the mirror such stereotypes became unacceptable. People knew what they looked like and they often took considerable pride in their individual features. The artists responded with a new realism of representation and attention to detail. Soon every person who owned a mirror wanted a picture, and not only members of the elite were portrayed but ordinary individuals as well.

The printing press

The fifteenth-century invention that truly revolutionised reflection, however, was the printing press.[13] Paper was imported from the Arabs in the twelfth century and by the end of the thirteenth century the Italians began making their own; wood-block printing started around 1380 and the technique was steadily improved. Once Johann Gutenberg had printed his bibles in Mainz in the 1440s, the new technology was quickly disseminated across Europe and already after a couple of decades most European towns had their own presses. An enormous amount of books were published in a short period of time: already before the year 1500 some 30,000 editions and a total number of 20 million volumes.[14] Since the price of a printed book was radically lower than that of a hand-copied manuscript, the reading audience broadened and the number of books a person could afford increased dramatically. While a private book collector in the year 1300 had many books if he had 200, a private library in the year 1500 could contain several thousands of volumes.[15] Literacy spread together with the cheap books, and books were more in demand since people increasingly were able to read.

While hand-copied books had given reflective powers to the small elite who had access to them, the printing press helped empower far larger groups. And as more, better, and cheaper books began circulating across Europe, so did the ideas they contained. Printed books revolutionised reflection by creating a tension between the text and the context provided by the lives of its readers. That which is out of context is often comic, sometimes tragic, and occasionally it is simultaneously both. For an example of the comic consider the constant jokes made in the early modern period about scullery maids and man-servants who forgot their duties while engrossed in the reading of cheap romances.[16] For an example of the tragic, consider the readers who committed suicide in solidarity with the hero of Johann Wolfgang von Goethe's *The Sorrows of Young Werther* from 1774. For an example of the tragicomic, consider the life of the protagonist of Miguel de Cervantes' *Don Quixote*, from 1605, who spent too much time emulating the lives of the characters of ancient chivalry books.[17]

Sometimes, however, the tension was resolved in the opposite direction. That is, instead of rejecting the text as out-of-context, the context was changed to correspond to the letter of the text. The best example of such a readjustment is the Reformation. In the Middle Ages, Bible reading had actively been discouraged by the Church since it wanted to protect its monopoly on the correct interpretation of the word of god. Yet such prohibitions made little practical difference at a time when books were rare and most people were unable to read. In the Middle Ages, access to god was always mediated through the priests and the sacraments safe-guarded by the Church. The advent of printing changed this spiritual arrangement. Martin Luther's translations of the Bible into German and his *Small Catechism*, 1529, were among the first best-sellers of the modern age.[18] All that Martin Luther and the other reformers asked people to do was to read the Bible and to compare its teachings with the teachings of the established Church. The discrepancies that were encountered were such that the authority of the Church establishment necessarily was undermined. According to the Lutheran dispensation, salvation was mediated not by priests and sacraments but instead through faith in the printed word.

As soon as they realised the subversive implications of the new technology, the Church authorities began censoring texts and restricting access to printed material. In 1559, the Catholic Church put together a list of banned authors, the *Index librorum auctorum et librorum prohibitorum*, which over the course of the years came to read as a compendium of European civilisation and thought.[19] The *Index* comprised Catholic, Protestant, Jewish and Muslim heresies but also authors as diverse as Erasmus of Rotterdam, Niccolò Machiavelli, Voltaire, Emanuel Swedenborg, Immanuel Kant, and in the twentieth century, Henri Bergson and Jean-Paul Sartre. The *Index* went through 300 editions and was abolished only in 1966.

But not only the Church felt threatened by the power of the printed word. Texts could also come into tension with the demands of political authorities. The seventeenth century in particular was a time of intense political pamphleteering both on the Continent where the Thirty Years War was pitting Protestants against Catholics and in England where the Puritans gathered their forces against the Stuart monarchy. In order to restrict access to subversive material – in order to limit reflection and protect public peace – the state too relied on censorship. Even classical authors were occasionally singled out as targets. As Thomas Hobbes explained in *Leviathan*, 1651:

> by reading of these Greek, and Latine Authors, men from their childhood have gotten a habit (under a false show of Liberty,) of favouring tumults, and of licentious controlling the actions of their Soveraigns; and again of controlling those controllers, with the effusion of so much blood; as I think I may truly say, there was never any thing so deerly bought, as these Western parts have bought the learning of the Greek and Latine tongues.[20]

Public opinion

People who communicate with the help of the same medium often form communities, and the kind of community that is formed will vary depending on the technology employed.[21] Literate societies tend for example to be far larger than illiterate societies since the existence of writing makes it possible to communicate with many more people than with those few who can be reached by a person's voice. The advent of printing vastly magnified this advantage. Through print people communicated far more efficiently, more widely and more often, and as a result much larger and more tightly knit communities could be formed. Communities became virtual; that is, they no longer depended on the physical proximity of their members. People felt close not only to those few others they met in person but also to those they had been acquainted with only indirectly as readers of the same texts.

Consider, for example, the new intellectual communities that were created.[22] A person who can read can think and people who read together, even at a distance, are in a sense thinking together, they are pondering the same problems and contributing to the same on-going debates. Although the first generations of Humanist scholars relied heavily on letter-writing – many of them wrote more letters than most people today write emails – print technology vastly improved the opportunities for scholarly discussions. As a result intellectual movements could form more quickly and have greater impact. But much the same applies to communities of scientists. From the sixteenth century onwards, news of scientific discoveries was more widely disseminated and as a result experiments could be repeated more often and confirmations or refutations of research results more accurately reported. In this way, the printing press allowed a new form of collective intelligence to emerge, a considered judgement which belonged not to any particular individual but to the scientific community taken as a whole.

Another example are national communities. Once texts began to be printed in the vernacular they brought together all those who understood the same language while those who did not effectively were excluded.[23] Before long these communities of language specific readers came to constitute a collective 'we' radically set off from the 'they' made up of people reading in a different language. As a consequence people came to see themselves as belonging together even though they often had little more in common than a particular vernacular. The label most commonly used for these communities of readers is a 'nation.'

The newspaper was particularly important in this respect.[24] Newspapers are cheap, widely disseminated, and published on a daily basis. The first papers, appearing in the seventeenth century, were simply printed sheets with information about commercial opportunities or reports on major events such as wars. Gradually, however, the occasional pamphlets expanded their coverage and developed a more permanent readership. This was particularly the case in England and Holland.[25] Once pre-publication censorship was abolished in England in 1695, newspaper sales increased dramatically. The first daily paper, the *Daily Courant*, appeared in 1702 and a number of other papers soon followed. The annual sale of newspapers in England reached 7.3 million in 1750 and 50 years later it had more than doubled. Most readers belonged to the 'middling classes': manufacturers, merchants, professionals, shopkeepers, farmers and small free-holders. In Paris the staunchly pro-government *Gazette de France* was first published in 1631 and until the Revolution it was the only newspaper which was officially permitted.[26] In Scandinavia and parts of Germany the press developed in a more independent manner, although the audiences were small.[27] The oldest newspaper still being published is *Post- och Inrikes Tidningar* which began appearing in Sweden in 1650.

For their readers the newspapers served a dual function. While they reflected the affairs of a particular community, they also allowed a particular community to reflect on its affairs. In these respects newspapers were exactly analogous to mirrors, and this mirroring function was often obvious already from the paper's name. Among many similar titles, there appeared publications such as the *Mirror of the Times*, London, 1796; *The Columbian Mirror and Alexandria Gazette*, Alexandria, Virginia, 1792; *Political Mirror*, Staunton, Virginia, 1800; *Daily Mirror*, London, 1903, and *Der Spiegel*, Hamburg, 1947. Reflection was also the obvious task of *The Spectator*, London, 1709, *The Observer*, London, 1791, and the *Christian Science Monitor*, Boston, 1908. And the same can be said for newspapers who in their name preferred to emphasise the reflective function of the voice – *The Echo*, Edinburgh, 1729; *L'Écho de Paris*, Paris, 1884, or *L'Écho de la bourse*, Brussels, 1881.

Looking into these mirrors – or hearing these echoes – the readers were able to learn many new things. Here they obtained news and financial information, learned who had been born, married or died, and picked up useful tips on anything from the affairs of the heart to the pickling of herring.[28] From the middle of the eighteenth century onward all major events – revolutions, wars, discoveries and inventions – were quickly and extensively reported in the pages of the press. From the end of the eighteenth century, parliamentary debates were extensively reviewed in British newspapers and the proceedings of revolutionary bodies in their French counterparts.[29] And from the middle of the nineteenth century, regular bulletins reached European readers from the most exotic of locations: Japan, the darkest heart of Africa, the battlefields of the American civil war.

Relying on these widely shared reports, people began reflecting far more efficiently together. In the press a range of different views were expressed but also subject to scrutiny, critique and restatement. This was the forum where political agitators, *Schriftstellern* and philosophers propagated their ideas, attacked the authorities or each other. Participating in these public debates, as readers if not as contributors, people gradually acquired the ability to reason coherently about common affairs; they developed views which were increasingly well informed and responsible. The eventual result of such exchanges was the notion of an *opinion publique*, a 'public opinion,' defined not as an aggregate of individual opinions but instead as a verdict reached only after an extensive period of collective deliberation.[30]

Originally the word 'opinion' had designated a point of view which was subjective and uncertain; opinion was the flickering light of 'mere opinion' as opposed to the brightly shining light of irrefutable reason.[31] Yet understood as a verdict reached as a result of collective deliberations, the opinion of the public came in the eighteenth century to be regarded as a formidable force. In France the *opinion publique* was the tribunal before which all writers, artists and philosophers had to present themselves before they could make a name for themselves in society.[32] In England, by contrast, public opinion was concerned above all with political matters and the tribunal in question passed its verdicts primarily on the actions of statesmen and politicians. Much the same came to be true in other parts of Europe. At least from the end of the eighteenth century onward politicians would ignore public opinion only at their peril.[33] As the editor of the German paper, *Deutsche Nation*, put it in 1785:

the invention of the newspaper is incontestably one of the great beneficial acts of the European nations. By that invention, an enormous step has been taken towards Enlightenment. The general spirit of participation in all public matters, which the English call *public spirit*, has thereby been transmitted from nation to nation.[34]

6 Institutions that reflect

It would be a mistake, we said, to give named individuals – Petrarca, Columbus, Copernicus or anyone else – the credit for the new perspectives that suddenly opened up in Europe around the year 1500. Although individuals make history, they never make it in the manner of their own choosing and, above all, without access to technologies of reflection even the most imaginative person will have little impact. Yet technology in and of itself is never enough. In order to make a difference, the technology must first be put to efficient use and this can only be done if it is embedded in a social organisation of some kind. The technology must be institutionalised, as it were.

It was institutions in the end rather than individuals or technical gadgetry that made reflection into an automatic, sustained and self-perpetuating, activity. Institutions picked up on the discoveries of classical scholars, geographical explorers and natural scientists and routinised and formalised them. Institutions provided the means of gathering, combining and comparing perspectives; they supplied procedures to follow and ways of coordinating individual contributions. Institutions made it possible for people of different backgrounds to meet to exchange information and points of view; institutions supplied the infrastructure, the material, the funding, the archives, the laboratories, the jargon, and the ways of judging contributions. And perhaps most importantly, institutions allowed for vast increases in the intellectual division of labour.[1] Just as modern factories, reflective institutions allowed tasks to be ever more narrowly defined and performed by ever more skilled people. As a result the production of knowledge and new ideas expanded rapidly although no individual had a grasp of more than an infinitesimal portion of the process in which they were involved.

Although there are many different institutions which engaged in reflective activities in the early modern era, three were particularly important: universities, scientific academies, and parliaments.[2] While universities and parliaments are of medieval origin, they came to play quite different roles in the sixteenth century, and academies are pure seventeenth-century inventions. The aim of this chapter is to briefly discuss the reflective activities of all three.

Universities

In classical Greece and Rome there were plenty of outstanding teachers but few organised ways of perpetuating their achievements. There were loosely organised 'schools' associated with particular teachers – Plato's *Akademeia* comes to mind – but there were no faculties, fixed curricula or academic degrees.[3] As a result the schools were always only as good as the teachers teaching there. Not surprisingly, when the Roman empire fell into a state of disrepair, so did the tradition of classical learning. In the post-Roman period some monasteries and occasional cathedral schools established themselves as centres of education, and while they provided a few rudimentary routines for intellectual pursuits, the standards were thoroughly basic.

The situation improved in the twelfth century when some of the cathedral schools began to become more famous than their teachers. Turning to the authorities of the towns in which they were located, the schools asked for privileges similar to those of medieval guilds.[4] The word *universitas* originally referring to any type of corporation or brotherhood, the 'universities' established themselves as guilds of masters and apprentices specialising in the delivery of services of higher education. Once the first two universities were founded in Paris and Bologna, similar institutions soon sprung up across the Continent: in Padua, Vercelli, Rome, Naples, Orléans, Angers, Toulouse, Montpellier, Valladolid, Salamanca, Lisbon, Cambridge and Oxford. By the year 1500, there were 63 European universities in all.

The short-comings and successes of the medieval university are well illustrated by the subjects they taught and the pedagogy they employed. At the University of Bologna, and in Italy generally, law and medicine were the most important disciplines but north of the Alps the emphasis was firmly on theology.[5] Here the vast majority of university teachers were members of the clergy, educating young men to join their ranks. The traditional liberal arts included the *trivium* of grammar, rhetoric and dialectic, and the *quadrivium* of musical theory, astronomy, arithmetic and geometry. There was little place, however, for physical experiments or historical and philological analyses; in fact, there was little place for empirical investigations of any kind.

As far as the pedagogy was concerned there were similar limitations. Regardless of the subject matter concerned, the education started with the *auctoritates*, the authoritative texts and the authoritative commentaries made on them. In the *lectura* this material was read and expounded on by the teachers while the students took notes, and in the *disputatio* the same texts were used to derive questions which were debated according to the well-established rules of Aristotelian logic.[6] The aim of a university education was above all to allow students to draw correct conclusions from premises which not only remained unquestioned, but which were true by definition and hence unquestionable.

And yet, to compare medieval universities to their latter day counterparts is to ignore their considerable achievements. Above all medieval universities were responsible for a number of institutional innovations. As the intellectual home of Scholasticism they developed mechanisms through which the logical implications of the Christian faith could be worked out. Hence the creation of settings such as the disputation, the lecture and the academic seminar, where arguments could be evaluated and systematically compared. In addition, and just like other medieval guilds, the universities spent much effort on self-regulation. There were fixed curricula, set texts and standardised degrees which for the first time made higher education into a uniform and continuous activity. Like other guilds the universities were successful in wrestling privileges away from the authorities. The idea of 'academic freedom' gave them the right to teach whatever they wanted and the institution of tenure provided professors with protection from political pressure.[7] This academic apparatus, put in place for theological and bureaucratic reasons, provided an institutional legacy which later was to be expanded on by others and with other purposes in mind.

The university began to change once the state in the course of the fifteenth century established itself as more important than the town. The state was headed by a prince, adorned by courtiers, and staffed by the rudiments of a state bureaucracy. In contrast to the lawyers and theologians educated by medieval universities these men were *hommes d'état*, they were statesmen and bureaucrats. As such it was their task to speak on behalf of the state both in relation to the state's own subjects and in relation to the representatives of other states. In both roles they were called upon to make decisions on the best course of action for the prince to follow. These were duties for which a traditional, Scholastic, education provided insufficient preparation. Practical, everyday, problems of statecraft cannot, after all, be settled with the help of logical syllogisms.

What the *hommes d'état* required was instead a good judgement and above all the ability to express themselves well and to persuade the audiences they were addressing. To these ends a knowledge of classical civilisations came to be seen as essential.[8] As the Humanist scholars were quick to point out, the Greeks and Romans had been statesmen too, and often brilliant orators, and by studying the examples set by their lives contemporary statesmen had much to learn.[9] Scornful of the limited training provided by medieval universities, the Humanists' ideal was the *uomo universale*, the complete human being well versed in all the sciences and the arts.[10] Only such complete individuals, they argued, would be ready to deal with whatever life in politics would throw at them.

Despite the urgency of these new demands the universities were slow to change. At first the new curriculum was employed mainly by individual humanists working as tutors to princes or by school masters teaching young noblemen how to become more successful courtiers. It was only with the rapid expansion of the state in the course of the seventeenth century that the demand for people with a Humanist education came to outstrip supply.[11] Reluctantly the medieval universities began to change and in many places new, explicitly humanist, universities were established. The university in Wittenberg, with renowned teachers such as Philip Melanchton, was a celebrated example which attracted students from all over northern Europe.[12]

In addition to introducing new subjects, the Humanists replaced the logic-chopping of the medieval pedagogy with a thorough training in rhetoric.[13] The aim of the *rhetor*, they explained, is not to deduce true conclusions from irrefutable premises but instead to persuade whichever audience he was addressing. And while logical proofs may play a role in this respect they are not sufficient. Consider, for example, the difference between the skills taught in the medieval *disputatio* and in the *pro et contra* debates organised at the new universities. The aim of the *disputatio* was above all to reach the truth but in the *pro et contra* debate the point was instead to consider all the arguments for and against a given position.[14] In staged confrontations one student would be asked to argue a case *pro* while another would be asked to argue a case *contra*. Such intellectual play-acting – the ability to simultaneously see an issue from a number of alternative points of view – soon became a standardised feature of every educated person's education.

Despite such innovations in procedure the important contribution of the university over the course of the centuries has not been as a source of innovation but rather as an agent of cultural transmission.[15] Although none of the great intellectual movements of the last 500 years can be said to have originated in the university, they all sooner or later came to influence the university curriculum. The Reformation and Counter-Reformation, the Scientific Revolution and the Enlightenment, the Industrial and the Computer Revolutions, have all had an impact on society first of all by having an impact on the university. It was when passing through the university in their most formative years that young people learnt about the latest intellectual developments.[16]

Since the seventeenth century universities have changed in profound ways and often in response to new demands raised by the state. In the nineteenth century for example medieval French universities received strong competition from professional schools designed to train a new administrative elite. Simultaneously in Germany, universities became vehicles for the creation of a pan-Germanic *Kultur* and were thus heavily implicated in the effort at state building.[17] In the United States many universities received large land grants and established themselves as independent centres of intellectual activity, a novelty in this rural republic.

In the twentieth century, however, the university has been less a servant of the state than of the economy. Since companies need people with technical expertise and scientific knowledge universities have become institutions of professional training and research. New types of educational institutions have also appeared: business schools, law schools, polytechnics and agricultural colleges. Since the demands of the economy are far more extensive than ever the demands of the church or the state, the student body has expanded dramatically. Today universities are educating not just an elite, but large swathes of the population.

Despite these and other changes a good education still means more or less what it meant to the Humanists of the sixteenth century. The point is not only to acquire a few marketable skills but above all to develop a good sense of judgement and an ability to express oneself persuasively in writing and in speech.

The search for truth still means less than one's ability to consider alternatives to it and the ability to reflect is still taught according to basically the same procedures as 500 years ago. The *pro et contra* format continues to characterise university seminars, essays, presentations and debates, and the ideal of the *uomo universale* is alive, at least in the – admittedly diminishing number of – universities that still provide a liberal arts education.

Scientific academies

In contrast to the university, the scientific academy is not a medieval institution. Its respectable origins are instead located in the scientific revolution of the seventeenth century, but its true origins are to be found in the Renaissance and its revival of magic.[18] The first academies began as informal gatherings of people interested in alchemy and related esoteric arts.[19] One famous such group met in Florence under the chairmanship of Lorenzo de' Medici, another group was formed in England by the necromancer John Dee, and at the splendid court of Emperor Rudolph II in Prague astrologers like Tycho Brahe and Johannes Kepler mingled with magicians, theurgists and clock-makers. In the sixteenth century every court with self-respect had its own informal academy of magi.

These *ad hoc* associations received a definite institutional form only once the state began to take a more sustained interest in them. This happened first in Italy. In Naples, a scientific academy, the Academia Secretorum Naturæ, was established in 1560; in Rome the Accademia dei Lincei appeared in 1603, and in Florence the Accademia del Cimento received its charter in 1657. In the course of the seventeenth century this institutionalisation gained momentum also north of the Alps. In the late 1620s in Paris the physician Theophraste Renaudot founded the Bureau d'Addresse, a weekly seminar for scholars interested in experimental science and the mechanical arts.[20] In London in 1660 a group of like-minded men – including Christopher Wren, Robert Boyle and John Wilkins – founded a 'a College for the Promoting of Physico-Mathematicall Experimentall Learning.' Two years later it was incorporated as the Royal Society of London for the Advancement of Natural Knowledge. In France the Académie des Sciences was established in Paris in 1666, and similar societies were formed in the Dutch Republic, throughout Germany, in Scandinavia, and in the overseas territories of North America.

What the members of these academies had in common was above all that they were practical men, and as such they were sceptical both of Humanists and medieval Scholastics.[21] As the academicians saw it both groups concerned themselves far too much with words and not enough with the world. Words are necessarily imprecise, they pointed out, their relationship to reality is ambiguous, and above all words are fundamentally divisive. Making a conscious effort to stay away from the religious wars that raged across Europe at the time it was founded, the charter of the Royal Society urged its members 'not to meddle with Divinity, Metaphysics, Moralls, Politics, Grammar, Rhetoric or Logic,' but instead to focus squarely on 'the useful and the material.'[22]

This practical bent is no doubt what motivated political authorities to back the academies financially and to give them a royal blessing. As the kings quickly realised, the new science had the potential of bringing both fame and riches to their realms. Geographers and geologists supported by the academies would, for example, conduct surveys of each country and enumerate whatever mineral and other resources they could find and mechanical engineers reported on advances made in the military sciences. Even botanists had a role to play. The Swedish Academy of Science, for example, under the chairmanship of the botanist Carl Linnæus, took it as its patriotic duty to sponsor research into how to grow potatoes, saffron, tea, and soybeans on Swedish soil and thereby to reduce the dependence on foreign imports.[23] Of these experiments only potatoes – used for aquavit production – proved to be truly successful.

As a setting for reflection the uniqueness of the scientific academy rested, and still rests, in its mode of organisation. No one made this point more forcefully than Francis Bacon, the seventeenth-century philosopher and statesman. Bacon made two separate but equally seminal suggestions. The first was that science must follow a method.[24] For science to make progress it is not enough, he argued, to look haphazardly at individual phenomena; instead you have to gather all cases, both similar and dissimilar, and compare them in a systematic fashion. If you want to know more you can conduct experiments by isolating certain elements and by studying how they react with each other. In this way, and this way only, is it possible to construct scientific laws, and the construction of laws is a precondition for the accumulation of knowledge.

Bacon's second suggestion concerned the physical organisation of scientific pursuits. In the imaginary society described in *The New Atlantis*, 1624, Bacon took the reader to a place called Solomon's House, a scientific academy, where research activities were as perfectly organised as ever life in More's Utopia.[25] Among the many experiments conducted here there were investigations into fermentation, refrigeration, hydration and maturation; there were flying machines and boats for going under water; some researchers studied the prolongation and restitution of life while others looked into the transformation of bodies into other bodies. While several previous writers had discussed scientific activities none had done so as comprehensively as Bacon and with his attention to detail.

As Bacon realised what he had devised was a kind of machine with the help of which the secrets of the universe gradually could be revealed.[26] In his academy he had a blue-print for its physical organisation and in his scientific method he had a programme for how the machine was to be operated. Following Bacon's guidelines scientific investigations came to be divided into ever smaller and better defined tasks.[27] Specialisation allowed each researcher to become ever more knowledgeable about their chosen topics but at the same time their efforts were also united in a new way. Researchers specialised on their chosen topics but only in order to co-operate more efficiently; the discoveries of individuals only made sense as part of a collective scientific effort.

Scientific research was soon automated along Baconian lines.[28] In fact much of the work of the Royal Society was directly inspired by his suggestions. Two years after receiving its charter, the Society constituted itself into permanent committees divided by eight fields of study: astronomy, optics, anatomy, chemistry, surgery, history of trades, a committee for correspondence together with a committee for the general purpose of collecting 'all phenomena of nature hitherto observed.'[29] With these committees as their hubs scientific networks were created through which research could be both further extended and better coordinated.

Across Europe most scientific academies came to operate in a more or less similar fashion. They financed exhibitions, expeditions and excavations; they kept in contact with foreign and domestic correspondents, organised public lectures and debates; they gathered specimens and artefacts in their museums and books in their libraries. Discoveries were published in reports – the first scholarly journals – which were widely disseminated and consulted by academicians across Europe. In 1665 the *Journal des Sçavants* began appearing in Paris and, in the same year the *Philosophical Transactions* started publishing in London. By means of such publications the academies came to have an influence far beyond the circles of their own members.[30]

As most people saw it the academies were ivory towers and the people who dwelled there were unapproachable eccentrics who took an inexplicable interest in the minute, the obscure and the disgusting.[31] As such they were easily made fun of. Yet the strange jargon and habits are best understood as devices designed to protect the academics from the outside world and the outside world from the academics. Reflection requires distance, we said, and ivory towers are institutional settings where distance can be achieved. The monastic habits and the unworldly attitude were ways of gaining a better perspective on the world. Further protection from outside influences was provided by the way academics were rewarded through prestige rather than through money. While some scientists certainly became rich and achieved high positions in society, what they all secretly yearned for were rewards which made little sense to anyone else. In academia there were rankings of academic positions, research institutes, publishing houses and journals. Prestige was, and is, given to those who work and publish with the best and to those whose results are most commonly cited.

Parliaments

Parliaments are another arena where reflection has been institutionalised. The parliament is where the people as a whole – or at least its representatives – get together in order to make decisions on matters of common concern. Ideally the parliament should mirror the composition of the people and its interests; there should be representatives of different social groups, political ideologies, cultural outlooks and religious and sexual inclinations. Yet the representatives should not only reflect the interests of the people but also reflect on the interests thus represented. Parliaments should re-present the wishes of the voters – make them 'present once again' – and consider them from as many perspectives as possible. The job of parliamentarians, in short, is not only to make decisions, but also to reflect on the decisions they make.

Arguably this deliberative function is at least as important as ever the task of electing a government or passing legislation. Derived from the Latin *fabulare*, 'to talk,' parliaments are 'talking shops' by definition. 'I know not,' as John Stuart Mill pointed out in 1861, 'how a representative assembly can more usefully employ itself than in talk.'

> A place where every interest and shade of opinion in the country can have its cause even passionately pleaded, in the face of the government and of all other interests and opinions, can compel them to listen, and either comply, or state clearly why they do not, is in itself, if it answered no other purpose, one of the most important political institutions that can exist anywhere, and one of the foremost benefits of free government.[32]

Or as Walter Bagehot, editor of *The Economist*, pointed out in 1867, the diversity of the opinions expressed in parliament 'makes us hear what otherwise we should not.'[33]

Parliaments just as universities have their origins in the Middle Ages.[34] While medieval kings often had forceful personalities, they rarely had enough power to impose their will on the people nominally subject to them. For one thing kings were chronically short of information. Since communications were rudimentary at best, it was always difficult to know what was going on in remote parts of a country or even in the next town. In addition the lack of an administrative machinery and a standing army made it difficult to raise taxes, and since tax revenues were low bureaucracies and armies were difficult to pay for. As a way to deal with these problems the kings asked representatives of the people to come to their courts to provide them with both information and tax revenue.[35] The result was a parliament understood, simultaneously, as a forum where views were exchanged and financial commitments negotiated.

Understood as a setting for reflection, however, medieval parliaments left much to be desired. Parliaments met only infrequently – perhaps once every few years – the sessions lasted only a couple of days, and the debates were clearly stage-managed by the kings. Yet the mere fact that a forum was established where public deliberations could take place was itself significant. As long as the parliaments met the kings had to give reasons for their actions and inactions and persuade rather than simply to force people to follow them.[36] Although medieval parliaments had nothing to do with the modern conception of democracy, they established the first outline of what later would come to be referred to as a 'public sphere.'

With the rise of the state as a sovereign political entity the parliament's role as an information gathering device gradually became less important and some kings were also able to raise revenue without asking the representatives of the people for help.[37] In rich and centrally located countries such as France, Spain and Austria, where the rulers acquired their own sources of income, the parliaments lost dramatically in importance or were entirely abolished. In poorer and more peripheral countries – England, Sweden, Poland and Hungary – the kings never gained this measure of independence and the parliaments remained in place. In fact since constantly escalating wars required constantly increasing revenues, the kings here became more rather than less dependent on their subjects. What emerged was thus a division of the political map of Europe between so called 'absolutist' regimes and those of *monarchia mixta*, or 'mixed government.'[38] In this latter set of countries, parliaments, initially established by the king to control the people, increasingly became a way for the people to control the king.

And yet, according to the most commonly held theory of representation, the point was never simply to reflect the wishes of the people but also to reflect on the wishes which the people expressed. The Members of Parliament were there to deliberate on the choices before them rather than slavishly to follow the popular will. Only in this way would it be possible to make sure that the decisions reached were the best ones, corresponding to the enlightened long-term interests of the people at large. 'Your representative owes you, not his industry only, but his judgement,' as Edmund Burke warned the voters of Bristol in 1774, 'and he betrays, instead of serving you, if he sacrifices it to your opinion.'[39]

Yet the relationship between representation and deliberation was never straightforward. The two principles are most easily combined in cases where the franchise itself is broadened. The better the parliament reflects the views of the people, the more, and the more diverse, material will go into the deliberative process and the better the decisions are likely to be as a result. Medieval and early modern parliaments failed abysmally in this respect and in the nineteenth-century parliaments were still seriously unrepresentative. As Walter Bagehot pointed out, land owners were over-represented among MPs and industrialists were under-represented. As a result the British parliament 'gives too little weight to the growing districts of the country and too much to the stationary.'[40] John Stuart Mill made the same point in support of female suffrage.[41] To exclude women from parliament is not only undemocratic, he argued, but it is also to make society as a whole less reflective than it otherwise would be.

There are, however, also situations in which the demands of representation and deliberation contradict each other. As we all know good discussions are often difficult to sustain if there are too many, and too many different, people involved. The more intimate the context, and the better we know the other participants, the more likely we are to consider an issue carefully and on its merits. Before the introduction of universal suffrage in the early twentieth century parliaments came close to this intimate ideal. Parliaments were gentlemen's clubs filled with the members of an upper-class who all knew and trusted each other. As a result MPs were less inclined to exaggerate the rhetoric and more ready to honestly contemplate each case.[42] Thus, although the restricted membership seriously reduced the range of perspectives available, nineteenth-century parliaments reflected very well within those exceedingly narrow limits.

To broaden the franchise was to admit more points of view but also to make honest exchanges of views more difficult.[43] Much the same can be said regarding attempts to make parliaments 'more accountable' by giving media access to the proceedings. Already when the British Houses of Parliament were opened up to journalists after 1771 it became obvious that the speakers began 'playing to the galleries' rather than debating with their colleagues.[44] And much the same complaints have been heard in recent years when TV cameras have been let into various parliamentary chambers. While increased public scrutiny may make the representatives more accountable it may also make it more difficult for them to change their minds or to appear as something less than fully partisan. For the sake of the quality of the deliberative process, it could be argued, representatives must be shielded from the people they represent, at least to some extent.

This is one reason why plenary debates seem to have lost in importance in recent years and why debates held in committee rooms have gained.[45] Committees are in the end where the actual parliamentary work takes place; committees are smaller, more intimate, settings and as such better places to reflect. In addition, the committee structure allows Members of Parliament to specialise in particular subject areas and a committee membership provides them with the opportunity to develop their own expertise. The committees usually have the right to call witnesses, to conduct research, and to commission reports by outside experts. Moreover, by interacting with committees, interest groups and lobbying organisations have a way of influencing these deliberations.

For an example of the trade-off between deliberation and representation consider the constitution of the United States.[46] When the founding fathers were drafting the constitution in 1787, they were able to consider the way in which various state legislatures had operated during the ten years that had passed since independence. As they agreed these experiences left much to be desired.[47] Controlled by majorities who behaved selfishly and short-sightedly, a number of states had embarked on foolish projects: outlawing banks, for example, or causing inflation by printing too much money. As James Madison put it in the *Federalist Papers*, 1788,

> the mild voice of reason, pleading the cause of an enlarged and permanent interest, is but too often drowned, before public bodies as well as individuals, by the clamors of an impatient avidity for immediate and immoderate gain.[48]

The question was how such short-sighted immoderation could be avoided in the federal constitution and 'the mild voice of reason' given a chance to be heard. The answer, everyone agreed, was to design the institutions in such a way that public reflection would be both protected and encouraged.[49] As an example consider the terms of the representative mandate.[50] If representatives were instructed by their constituents to vote in a particular fashion there would be no room for independent deliberation. The same was true if the representatives could be recalled during an on-going session, given new instructions, or dismissed by the electorate. The length of the mandate also mattered. As the founding fathers argued, the longer the politicians spend in office the less frequent will be the pressures of re-election and the freer they will be to make their own decisions. This was also why the electoral districts were made fairly large.[51] Since a large district is likely to contain many different kinds of people its representative is likely to be freer from the pressure of any particular interest group.

What the framers of the American constitution explicitly designed are features that have evolved more or less spontaneously in other Western political systems. Reflection in the end is what most parliamentary procedures are about. There are set ways of conducting debates and procedures for making sure that everyone has a chance to speak and a chance to be heard; there are rules for how new legislation should be proposed and voted on. Representatives often have immunity from prosecution in order to protect them from pressure from the executive. To the extent that this reflective machinery operates smoothly the personal qualities of individual MPs are not particularly important. Everything else equal, it may be preferable to have highly intelligent and dedicated representatives, yet an efficient institution can cope even with MPs who are stupid and self-serving. All the reflective capacity is built into the institution and less is required of individual MPs.

Part III

Entrepreneurship

7 Origins of the entrepreneurial outlook

But reflection alone is never going to be enough. Change requires a changer, a someone who acts in order to alter the way things are. This someone could be called an entrepreneur. Today entrepreneurship is usually associated with economic activities, and entrepreneurs are typically defined as anyone who owns or directs a company. But there is no good reason why a definition of the term should be this narrowly constrained. Entrepreneur, from the French *entreprendre*, 'to embark upon,' 'to set out on,' 'to undertake,' is simply anybody who embarks on or undertakes activities not embarked on or undertaken by others. Or in the vocabulary introduced above, an entrepreneur is somebody who acts on the potentialities that reflection has revealed; somebody who brings things into the world which previously did not exist. Thus understood, entrepreneurship is not limited to the field of economics but can be found in any walk of life.

Surprisingly enough, neo-classical economics – economics as taught by contemporary textbooks – has next to nothing to say about entrepreneurs and what they do.[1] As so often is the case in the sciences, this silence is theoretically induced. A common assumption of neo-classical theorising is that economic actors have perfect information, that they know everything that all other economic actors know.[2] Given this assumption, supply will always smoothly adjust to demand, producers will always receive their expected returns, and the utility of consumers will be maximised. Under such conditions of universal and automatic satisfaction of desires there is simply nothing for entrepreneurs to do.

In the world outside of the neo-classical model, however, few of these assumptions apply. On the contrary, information is often of poor quality and is usually highly unevenly distributed.[3] And such asymmetries are precisely what entrepreneurs rely on in order to make a living. Their job is to look for price and quality differences between markets and to buy in places where things are cheap and sell in places where things are expensive. But in addition entrepreneurs also create new demand; they sell new products, in new ways, and to new customers. Defined in this fashion, the entrepreneurial function is something quite different from the managerial function required of most owners of businesses.[4] While managers are content to make money from ever-decreasing profit margins in ever more mature markets, entrepreneurs are bent on improving markets or on creating new markets where previously none existed.

Thus understood, entrepreneurship is not restricted to the economic field but can also comprise for example political, cultural or religious activities. A political, cultural or religious entrepreneur is someone who takes policies, artistic expressions or beliefs from one social setting and introduces them into another social setting. To the extent that such transpositions are successful, policies, expressions, and beliefs will become more widely distributed. In addition, however, the entrepreneur is also someone who comes up with policies, expressions or beliefs which people previously did not know existed and which they perhaps did not even know they craved.

Regardless of the field in which they operate, entrepreneurs are today commonly regarded as individuals of unique insights and abilities. Entrepreneurs are seen as the creative agents of change, and in a society where change is worshipped the entrepreneur becomes a hero. Yet such hero-worship is quite misplaced. Far from being all-powerful, there is next to nothing that individuals can do by themselves. This is true also of entrepreneurs of a truly world-historical stature. They too – or they in particular – always require the support of others in order to carry out their plans. Entrepreneurs need vehicles for their activities that amplify their powers; they need ways of making people work together for common goals. More than anything, entrepreneurs need the support of institutions. They need institutions that provide them with resources and with an independent capacity to act, and they need institutions that reduce insecurity and lower the risks of engaging in new enterprises.

The question is consequently how it came to be that modern individuals began thinking of themselves as personally responsible for social change. There is a history of entrepreneurship that can be retraced and retold. And as we will see, this history is intimately connected to the development of a particular definition of what it means to be a human being. Human beings are not naturally entrepreneurial, in other words; it is not the case, as market enthusiasts like to believe, that entrepreneurship will thrive as long as all external obstacles – government regulation – are removed. Rather, the entrepreneur is a distinct social type and as such the product of a distinct social and cultural outlook. The question to be addressed in this chapter is how this social type first was created. In the next chapter the modern conception of the entrepreneur will be discussed in more detail, and in the subsequent chapter we will look at how institutions helped make entrepreneurship into an automatic and self-perpetuating activity.

Medieval obstacles

Let us once again use the Middle Ages as a foil for our discussion. As should be obvious from a visit to any Gothic cathedral or from reading books about the Crusades, the Middle Ages had plenty of extraordinarily resourceful entrepreneurs. In addition there were many less spectacular projects – applications of the waterwheel and the windmill, the opening up of mines or the invention of crop rotation techniques – which had revolutionary long-term consequences although they cannot be connected to named individuals.[5] And yet it seems that people in the Middle Ages became entrepreneurs for rather different reasons than today; that they had other conceptions of what it was they could accomplish and other kinds of resources available to them.

For example: people in the Middle Ages never seem to have thought of themselves as able to radically break with tradition. Consider the role of a medieval artist. Medieval works of art were all considered as parts of a canon, from the Latin *kanon*, denoting the wooden pipes of a hydraulic machine. Through the canon, accepted interpretations, models and techniques were transmitted – 'pumped' as it were – from one generation to the next. As in all hydraulic machines, it was important to minimise loss and leakage; the heritage of the past could only be preserved if it was faithfully conveyed. Hence the obvious repetitiveness of the statues, icons and altarpieces.[6] As all artists knew, it was the common heritage that was to be presented and not any particular individual's view of it. For this reason, it mattered little that a certain work was executed by one artist rather than by another.[7] While the artists concerned no doubt were proud of their craftsmanship, there was no reason to sign the work once it was completed. A signature could easily have been interpreted as a sign of *vanitas*, the empty ambition of someone bent on punching a hole in the canonical machinery.

This relative lack of individual assertiveness was reflected also in the way people thought about social life.[8] The vast majority of people occupied one or another of the few recognised positions that existed in medieval society. Basically everyone was either a member of the clergy, a peasant, a craftsman, a merchant or a knight. The lives of these characters were quite different to be sure but within each type there was little variation. The truth about a person was determined from the outside as it were, by social convention, by a rigidly hierarchical feudal order, and ultimately by god himself. In the Middle Ages, people were subjects to the extent that they subjected themselves to these authorities.

This conception of the person is well illustrated by medieval literary genres such as the epic, the fairy tale and the saga.[9] Here the protagonists – like modern-day cartoon characters – were all equipped with the same easily recognisable features. There was no character development through the course of the narrative and the protagonists rarely stopped to reflect on themselves and their actions. Even biographies such as those told about the saints provide highly conventional stories about how a life of sin and sloth was converted, through the grace of God, into a life of piety and faith.[10] In the Middle Ages there was nothing unique about a person and for that reason individuals had little by means of individuality.[11] The fact that each person was a particular someone no doubt mattered enormously to him or to her but it had little social significance.

Given this outlook there were definite limits to what most people could do to improve their lot. Like the characters in a fairy tale, the best they could hope for was to find a treasure or to be married off to a handsome prince. Barring such unlikely changes in fortune they were bound to die in the same social position into which they had been born. In addition, the collective action required for entrepreneurial projects to be successful was exceedingly difficult to organise. Since people were poor and illiterate, and often lacked effective means of communicating with each other, it was difficult to get them to unite behind common goals. This was particularly the case for projects that went against the interests of the elites. To alter the established order of things was to invite chaos, and anyone who tried was regarded as a troublemaker and dealt with as such. The social ideal was the contemplative life, the *vita contemplativa*, of the monastic.

There were also a number of more specific hurdles to overcome. As tales of the fabulous wealth of particular individuals make clear, the hoarding of money was not an unknown activity in the Middle Ages. And yet there were not all that many opportunities to make money and greed was, officially at least, condemned as a sin. In general what mattered for most people was not profit maximisation but instead the ability to provide for themselves and their dependants.[12] For society as a whole what mattered most was fairness. Since there was little by means of economic growth – at least little economic growth perceptible to the naked eye – economics was thought of as a zero-sum game where one person's gain necessarily meant another person's loss. Hence the easily drawn analogy between profit-makers and thieves. Since the economic pie was of a given size, you could increase your slice only at someone else's expense.

This outlook explains such medieval oddities as the doctrine of the just price and the prohibition on usury. According to the idea of the *justum pretium*, prices should be dictated by moral considerations rather than by the interplay of supply and demand.[13] Just prices were customary prices universally agreed on, and to charge more than this was to take advantage of arbitrary shortages for personal gain. To lend money against interest was also to benefit from someone else's predicament and was as such condemned in the strongest possible terms by the Church.[14] In practice there were always numerous ways around such prohibitions – and the Church itself was often the first to spot them – yet even when the obstacles were avoided they served to increase the cost of capital and to promote corruption and fraud.[15] In the Middle Ages money had no temporal dimension and as a result long-term investments were difficult to justify.

With the emergence of towns from the eleventh century onward, new centres of economic activity were created yet this did not automatically translate into a new spirit of entrepreneurship. The medieval economy, also in the town, continued to be heavily regulated. Craftsmen and merchants had to belong to guilds before they could practise their trades, and guilds controlled working hours, prices and wages, as well as the number of workers and tools that could be employed in each workshop.[16] The effect of these regulations was to restrict entry into each trade and thereby to reduce competition. Although the negative economic impact of the guilds has been exaggerated, they did little to spot changes in consumer demand. The guilds reduced risks and protected their members but they also penalised anyone ready to embark on new enterprises.

To later advocates of free markets such as Adam Smith, the guilds were the very symbol of the anti-entrepreneurial ethos of the age.[17]

Marginal activities

The best counter-examples to this picture of relative stagnation are provided by people who were active on the margins of European society. In general terms this is easy to explain. It has long been noticed that entrepreneurs often occupy a marginal position in relation to the mainstream of the society in which they live.[18] Often they have one foot in another culture, another set of conventions or another social class, and this in the end is how they get their new ideas. In the Middle Ages a number of particular advantages were added to these general ones. On the margins of European society the influence of the Church was usually more diluted and the guilds were weaker or non-existent. This was also where the best business opportunities presented themselves. By acting as middlemen between the centre of Europe and its periphery, new groups of entrepreneurs emerged who both accomplished great feats and made plenty of money.

To be more precise, it may be possible to talk about both a social and a geographical margin to European society. On the social margin were people who for one reason or another failed to fit into the structure of the medieval order. These landless farmhands, members of the urban proletariat, or the minor sons of impoverished nobility were more easily recruited for collective enterprises. One example were the weavers and dyers working in the cloth factories of Flanders and northern France who were the first to join the new millenarian sects that sprung up from the twelfth century onward.[19] Another example were the superfluous members of the elite who joined the great religious reform movements started by Saints Francis and Dominic. A third example were the urban poor who in large numbers joined the Crusades.[20]

The social margin was also occupied for example by the Jews.[21] Jews were not full citizens anywhere in Europe but neither were they full aliens, and while they never enjoyed the protection of the Church they also did not have to follow its prohibitions. This ambiguous position opened up a host of opportunities. Jews mediated between people separated by wars, creeds, allegiances and levels of culture. They also engaged in activities regarded as dishonourable by mainstream society; they were tanners, tax collectors, doctors and money lenders. While the section of the Old Testament that outlawed usury applied equally between Jews, it did allow loans from Jews to Gentiles.[22]

But there was also a geographical margin to European society where the continent shaded over into non-European lands. One such region was the Baltic Sea, occupied first by Vikings and later by Hanseatic merchants.[23] Another region was the Mediterranean, divided between the Catalonians in the west and Italian merchant republics in the east. While the Vikings were raiders, they were also traders, and the Hanse connected merchant communities around the Baltic with those in Russia, Germany and the north Atlantic.[24] Meanwhile the

Venetians made good money trading with the Arabs and yet further beyond. Some of these peripheral entrepreneurs, such as Leif Erikson or Marco Polo, ventured very far indeed in search of profits and adventures.

The geographical margins were also places with a thriving entrepreneurship of a more political nature. One such place was Scandinavia at the time of the Vikings, another was Spain at the time of the Reconquista. Both were settings where few of the normal rules applied; uncertain frontiers and harsh conditions encouraged an entrepreneurial spirit which in retrospect seems both rugged and surprisingly modern.[25] People like El Cid – who captured Valencia from the Moors in 1094 – or Gisli – the Icelandic outlaw who single-handedly killed eight of the 15 men who had come to capture him – accepted few limitations on their freedom of action. Like modern day entrepreneurs, they knew both what they wanted and how to get it.

Yet even these self-confident individualists seem to have been motivated by rather different goals than their contemporary counterparts. On average, entrepreneurs on the European margins may have been less preoccupied with the glory of God and more interested in profits, but they also had a strong sense of acting within the framework of obligations determined by their communities. People like El Cid or Gisli were heroes and heroes were always avenging the death of their fathers, defending the good name of their masters or rescuing damsels in distress. Heroes, that is, always acted in defence of their honour and the honour of their families.[26] The idea of honour is a distinctly pre-modern notion and it can only make sense in a society where a solid structure of loyalties connects people to each other.[27] The aim of the hero was to fulfil his obligations within this structure. His ultimate hope was to live the kind of life that would be remembered, and recounted, in epics and sagas told by future generations.[28] When measured by this standard, the entrepreneurial projects embarked on by El Cid and Gisli were not only spectacularly successful but also not quite as modern as they at first may appear to be.

The world as a stage

Jumping a few centuries, it is instructive to compare the medieval outlook to the attitude of the inhabitants of the fifteenth century city-republics of northern Italy. If we are to believe the Swiss historian Jacob Burckhardt, these Renaissance Italians were the first modern individuals. In the Middle Ages, Burckhardt argued, human consciousness had been obscured by 'faith, illusion and childish prepossessions,' and man had understood himself 'only as a member of a race, people, party, family, or corporation.'[29] This all changed in the Renaissance when man for the first time became conscious of himself as a unique someone who could be defined independently of the groups to which he ostensibly belonged.

Naturally one would expect people defined in this manner to be far more entrepreneurial than their medieval counterparts. This is also the impression one gets from reading the historical record. In the Renaissance no one seems to have had much time for the established canons and fewer still seem to have worked exclusively for the glory of God. Instead the constant preoccupation was how to break with tradition and to increase the glory of one's own name. And while this sounds like perfectly contemporary obsessions, Renaissance individualism was above all an aristocratic ideal reserved for a small elite. Most people at the time did not think of themselves in these terms and they did not act for these reasons. Fame, in the Renaissance as well as today, is a scarce commodity since not everyone, but only unique individuals, can become truly famous.

The metaphor describing the world as 'a stage' illustrates perfectly this outlook. The men and women of the Renaissance always talked about themselves as actors on a stage performing their roles before society, the world or before god himself. The task of each person thus understood was to provide as convincing a performance as ever possible and in this way to establish his or her reputation. Hence the ostentatious lifestyles and clothes which characterise the age and the extravagant self-promotion of many Renaissance individuals. Compare for example the autobiography of the Florentine sculptor Benvenuti Cellini with the autobiographies of the medieval saints.[30] Where the saints all basically told the same story, effectively effacing themselves through their narratives, Cellini went out of his way, through obvious lies and the proudest of boasts, to establish himself as a unique individual worthy of the widest possible attention.

Yet such mythomania reveals a deep sense of insecurity. The individualism of Renaissance individuals is strangely precarious. There was a violence in the obsessive quest for status and a childish over-sensitivity to anything that could be interpreted as insults.[31] What these individuals were in private – 'off stage' as it were – is impossible to say just as the role played by an actor holds no key to his or her private life. In the end Renaissance individuals were nothing more and nothing less than whatever their public reputations said they were. For this reason, just as in the Middle Ages, the authority to determine the truth about a person remained external to him or her. In the Renaissance people were subjects to the extent that they were subject to the ever-changing verdicts of these notoriously fickle audiences.

At the same time the theatre metaphor provided the basis of a new spirit of entrepreneurship. As all actors, the men and women of the Renaissance were aware of the need to capture and hold the attention of the audiences they were addressing. In order to establish one's fame it was important always to have new and ever more dazzling things up one's sleeve. As all actors, that is, the actors on the Renaissance stage were forced to act. In this way, under influence of the stage metaphor, the medieval monastic ideal of a *vita contemplativa* became less attractive and the classically inspired ideal of a *vita activa*, the active life of the statesman or the merchant, gained in prominence.[32]

Consider first the case of economic entrepreneurs. The Renaissance was a time of a great revival of trade – a 'commercial revolution' – associated most obviously with the discoveries of new markets overseas but also with a boom in intra-European trade. Essentially this is the story of how people in the centre of the continent came to emulate the success which people on the fringes already had attained in the late Middle Ages. Thus the profitable journeys which Italian, Spanish and Portuguese sea-captains were the first to embark on were increasingly undertaken by English, Dutch and French ships. Similarly the legal and financial methods of the Venetians were copied by Genovans and Florentines, and with Italian bankers they spread across the continent. The result was the emergence of cities like Antwerp and London as hubs of international commerce. By the middle of the sixteenth century the main trade routes no longer went across the Mediterranean but instead across the Atlantic, and Holland had taken the place of the Hanseatic League in the lucrative Baltic trade.[33]

And yet what mattered even to the most insatiable merchant adventurer was not money as much as fame. Or rather, true to the thespian spirit of the age, fame was the entrepreneurial coin in which the real profits were counted. Hence money-making did not serve the purpose of satisfying private desires as much as the purpose of public self-promotion. Money was not quietly stowed away but instead ostentatiously flaunted and consumption was pointless unless it was conspicuous. As soon as money was made it was translated into impressive palaces, fancy clothes, sumptuous feasts and artwork for the churches.[34] And even low-ranking explorers made sure to bring home exotic objects – everything from colourful birds to narwhal tusks, conch shells and stuffed zebras – which could be displayed in menageries and *Wunderkammern*.[35] The occasional case of *vanitas* encountered in the Middle Ages had by the seventeenth century become the lifestyle of an entire social class.

The theatrical metaphor motivated also political entrepreneurs. As the *Fürstenspiegel* literature reminded their aristocratic readers, stagecraft and statecraft were simply two aspects of the same exercise of authority.[36] The power that really mattered was the power that a political actor held over his or her audience. Hence the constant staging of masques, ritual tournaments, progresses and *intermezzi* where the rulers themselves often took an active part. And the princes who treated the stage as their world would before long treat the world as their stage. Political action in the early modern era was more than anything a matter of establishing oneself as a legitimate actor and making sure that this status was safely maintained. Hence the obsession with matters of precedence and with the minutiae of diplomatic protocol.[37] At an international conference a serious incident was provoked if a carriage of a lower ranking country passed through a gate before the carriage of a higher ranking country, and a ruler that consistently was slighted by others could even resort to full-blown war.

The star demon

The most elaborately significant symbol of the Renaissance, and the most powerful motivation for the activities engaged in by entrepreneurs, was gold. Gold was first of all a measure of the wealth of the state. According to the bullionist doctrine which defined the financial considerations of the era, a rich state was one which hoarded as much hard metal as possible.[38] Consequently the search for gold became a prime motivation of the geographical explorations and of the subsequent colonialisation of the world. Africa was a first target, but later all the rapacious greed was focused on the search for El Dorado in the Americas. The list of atrocities committed by the conquistadors in the name of gold is notorious but the largest number of people died in a silver mine: Potosí, discovered in Peru in 1545, where slave labour and maltreatment caused the deaths of hundreds of thousands of people.

The search for gold was not only an obsession of states, however, but also of individuals. Gold equalled wealth and power for the person who had it, found it, stole it or made it. Not surprisingly individuals such as the Spanish conquistadors were prepared to risk life and limb to get their hands on the stuff, and reading the personal accounts of Columbus, Bernal Díaz or Hernán Cortés, every page discusses its quality and how much of it that could be obtained in one place after another.[39] Just as for states, gold provided a straightforward measure of success in life. As Las Casas pointed out in 1542:

> The reason the Christians have murdered on such a vast scale and killed anyone and everyone in their way is purely and simply greed. They have set out to line their pockets with gold and to amass private fortunes as quickly as possible so that they can assume a status quite at odds with that into which they were born.[40]

But gold was also a symbol of power and this connection is particularly clear in case of the alchemists. In the Renaissance there was a revival of the medieval art of alchemy, but what motivated its practitioners was not the search for riches above all but rather a desire to gain control over the forces of nature. What the gold one made might buy was as nothing compared to what the ability to make gold said about its maker. Surely a person who could make gold was capable of anything; a gold-maker was magus, a magician, and a magus was simultaneously a manipulator and a creator who partook of a divine substance. In some respects the alchemist even rivalled god himself; he was, in the words of the fifteenth-century Florentine philosopher Giovanni Pico della Mirandola, a 'star demon.'[41] As Pico's Florentine colleague Marsilio Ficino put it:

> Who could deny that man possesses as it were almost the same genius as the Author of the heavens? And who could deny that man could somehow also make the heavens, could he only obtain the instruments and the heavenly material?[42]

These star demons were the first modern entrepreneurs fully conscious of their world-creating powers. The alchemists were not imitating, but creating; they were not passively awaiting their preordained fates but instead actively engaging with the world and changing it in accordance with their wishes.[43] This, as Pico explained, provided man with an entirely new sense of self-confidence.[44]

Among these entrepreneurs were many statesmen whose aim was either to gain power for themselves or to look for a more secure hold on the power they already had. Often, such as in the case of the Italian condottieri, they were armed only with the most dubious of credentials. By dabbling in all sorts of black arts, however, they too hoped to turn themselves into magi who could manipulate the world according to their wishes. There was an alchemy of state-craft, conveyed by select teachers through oral transmission, which was reputed to contain all the secrets, the *arcana imperii*, which a successful prince needed to know. Machiavelli's name was often associated with this hidden tradition, espe-cially as long as his works only existed in hand-copied manuscripts.[45] As many of their opponents were convinced, entrepreneurial statesmen like Henry VIII of England or Gustav I of Sweden, who ruthlessly desecrated the holiest of values, were active practitioners of this satanic doctrine.

Compare the myth of Doctor Faustus which became wildly popular in the seventeenth and eighteenth centuries. Faustus, possibly born Jörg Faust in Germany about 1480, was a conjurer who travelled around various market towns displaying his tricks.[46] He made claims for his art which sounded at least as extravagant as those of Pico or Ficino, but without their philosophical sophistication. Faust, it was reported, said 'in the presence of many that the mir-acles of Christ the Saviour were not so wonderful, that he himself could do all the things that Christ had done, as often and whenever he wished.'[47] According to the mythology that grew up around him – in England above all popularised by Christopher Marlow in 1616 – Faust had done a deal with Mephistopheles himself whereby he would be given unlimited creative powers during his life-time in return for giving his soul to the devil after his death. In subsequent cen-turies this became the central myth of the European entrepreneur, the man who possessed the powers of god but who had derived them from a pact with the devil.[48]

Martin Luther seems to have been the first to draw an explicit connection between Faust and the devil.[49] The Faustus character appears twice in Luther's *Table Talk* and on both occasions he is identified as an associate of Luther's supreme enemy. While learned scholars had little time for low-class conjurers of this ilk, to Luther, Faust's powers were only too real. The Devil – the 'emperor from Hell' – was active everywhere in the world, he was armed and dangerous, and Luther, spent much of his time being tempted by, cursing or throwing inkwells at him.[50] And when Luther realised that even the pope and the Church had been taken over by these satanic forces, he was quick to react. While Luther never would have dared to defy the authorities in his own name, it was an obligation to fight the devil in the name of god. Against the entrepreneurship inspired by the prince of darkness he pitted the counter-entrepreneurship inspired by the prince of light. In this way the devil eventually succeeded in breaking up the Church.

8   The age of the demiurge

The outcome of all this mythologising was the modern conception of the entrepreneur. In contemporary society where change is ever-present, the entrepreneur is the hero. The entrepreneur is the maker of rules and the breaker of rules; it is he or she or it who destroys the old and creates the new thereby making the future possible.[1] As we have seen, in previous times such extraordinary qualities were more often associated with gods or demiurges than with human beings. Today, however, divine forces are no longer actively intervening into the world and human beings are left to their own devices. Today society is understood as an artefact that human beings have made and which they for that reason are uniquely qualified to change.[2] Considering ourselves independent of the social, cultural and natural contexts that determine us, we take ourselves to be free to settle our own fates. No longer acted upon, human beings become actors who can change the world in accordance with their own wishes. Abandoned by the gods, we are now our own star demons and our own demiurges.

Yet all such talk of heroism and entrepreneurial dare-devilry is of course only so much hyperbole. In practice entrepreneurs are never as powerful as they think they are. When acting alone there is next to nothing that even the most entrepreneurial among us can do to have an impact on the world. The question is thus how to account for this discrepancy between the belief in our omnipotence and the reality of our next-to complete impotence. The mystery is how we can be so oblivious to the truth about ourselves. The answer, in short, is that individuals can sustain the entrepreneurial illusion since they have access to social resources of various kinds. First of all they have numerous informal ways of collaborating with others, thus making sure that the skills and industry of one person are added to those of another. Second, there is a plethora of institutions that provide the entrepreneurs with all the resources they require. What these institutions are and how they operate are the topics of the next chapter. First, however, the modern notion of entrepreneurship will be described in some more detail.

Robinsonian entrepreneurs

A good way to learn more about contemporary entrepreneurs is to read any of the many novels that have been written about them.[3] The very emergence of the novel as a literary genre is itself an indication that a shift that has taken place in how human beings think of themselves. The novel is a genre written for and about modern individuals. Compared to medieval genres such as the epic or the saga, novels are not about heroes, cartoon characters or typecasts, but instead about ordinary men and women. As ordinary people they have ordinary names and think and do ordinary things; they live in actual places and are born and die in historical time. The protagonists of the novel are in charge of their destinies not just fulfilling their predetermined fates, and they act in their interests rather than out of social obligation.

Compared to the literary genres of the Renaissance there is nothing theatrical about the characters of a novel. We identify with them not because they are larger-than-life but on the contrary because they are exactly life-sized. If they are actors they are performing not on the 'stage of the world,' but instead above all on a stage constituted by their own consciousness. As readers we are privy to their inner-most thoughts – they are indecisive, of mixed emotions, torn between conflicting goals – and they change and develop in response to their experiences. In all these respects, the protagonists of the novel resemble the readers for whom they were created.

Daniel Defoe's *The Life and Adventures of Robinson Crusoe* from 1719 is a good example of the new genre, in fact it is sometimes considered as the first novel in the English language. As every reader of Defoe's book knows, Robinson left his family in the north of England to look for adventures and riches in foreign lands. He made a good start on a plantation in Brazil but soon his quest for higher profits took him on a voyage to Africa to buy slaves. A storm and a shipwreck later he landed on the island which was to be his home for the following 28 years. Completely alone and initially without water, food or shelter, Robinson should have faced real danger, yet as it turned out both his physical and social needs were surprisingly easy to satisfy. He found plentiful supplies on the wrecked ship and for company he had his animals and his Bible. As he discovered,

> [t]his made my life better than sociable for when I began to regret the want of conversation, I would ask my self whether thus conversing mutually with my own thoughts, and, as I hope I may say, with even God Himself by ejaculations, was not better than the utmost enjoyment of humane society in the world.[4]

Robinson's self-sufficiency is only the most extreme form of what has become the social ideal of the modern age. Like Robinson we are supposed to live withdrawn from the world and to manage without the support of others.[5] Today we are no longer subject to the all-too-predictable rules of the medieval world, nor to the all-too-unpredictable verdicts of fickle Renaissance audiences. Not determined by others, human beings are for the first time free to determine themselves.[6] Man is a subject only since he is subject to his own judgement and his own independent will. Well, thus far the rhetoric.

This conception of the individual has obvious implications for the work of entrepreneurs.[7] Defined as the masters of their own fates there is suddenly nothing we cannot do; no longer determined by our environments we are free to follow our own inclinations. And Robinson Crusoe is of course the relevant role model. As Defoe makes clear, Robinson saw his insular predicament not as a threat but rather as a challenge. As soon as the initial drama of the shipwreck was over, the book turns into a long catalogue of the various entrepreneurial projects he embarks on. Robinson built a home, storage rooms and a summer cottage; he planted corn and rice, caught and domesticated goats, dried grapes and baked bread.

Where Defoe obtained the inspiration for his creation is no mystery. At the turn of the eighteenth century England was going through a period of intense entrepreneurial activity.[8] This was when the great overseas trading companies, the Bank of England, and a long-range of joint-stock companies were founded, and when many more or less hair-brained schemes sought financial backing at the London stock market.[9] Defoe himself was one of these entrepreneurs, and at various times he had made a living as a hosier, a merchant trading with Portugal and Spain, and as a tile manufacturer.[10] At the time entrepreneurs were known as 'projectors,' and as Defoe pointed out, he was himself living in 'the Projecting Age.'[11] Not all projectors were necessarily such pleasant characters.

> A mere projector, then, is a contemptible thing, driven by his own desperate fortune to such a strait that he must be delivered by a miracle or starve; and when he has beat his brains for some such miracle in vain, he finds no remedy but to paint up some bauble or other, as players make puppets talk big, to show like a strange thing, and then cry it up for a new invention; gets a patent for it, divides it into shares, and they must be sold. Ways as means are not wanting to swell the new whim to a vast magnitude.[12]

But there were also, Defoe makes clear, projectors of a far more appealing disposition:

> the honest projector is he who, having by fair and plain principles of sense, honesty, and ingenuity brought any contrivance to a suitable perfection, makes out what he pretends to, picks nobody's pocket, puts his project into execution, and contents himself with the real produce as the profits of his invention.[13]

Defoe himself never struck it rich on any of his projects. His business acumen never rivalled his ability to turn a phrase. Exploiting his comparative advantages he instead wrote profusely – altogether some 500 works – and most of the titles are not novels at all but rather tracts on political and economic matters. In one of the pamphlets, *An Essay upon Projects*, 1697, Defoe praised the work of his fellow projectors and suggested various ways in which their activities could be better promoted.

What motivated these projectors was by now quite clear. What the projectors wanted above all was money, and by Defoe's time money-making was a respected activity which required no additional justification.[14] The search for profits had also been the initial inspiration for Robinson Crusoe's travels. Once alone on his island, however, money suddenly comes to mean nothing and it is instead the quest for dignity that occupies most of his time. By recreating the trappings of civilisation he turned the alien, tropical, environment into a setting fit for an Englishman; through ceaseless activity he ensured that he controlled nature rather than nature controlling him. For these purposes it was actually very fortunate that he was alone. As Defoe points out, Robinson was not only legislator and judge but also king in his own kingdom; '[t]here were no rivals, I had no competitor, none to dispute sovereignty or command with me.'[15] This was the perfect political community in that it allowed its single inhabitant the complete freedom to organise life entirely in accordance with his own wishes.[16] Just like the alternative world once visited by More's Hythlodæus, Crusoe's island is a utopia.

Robinson was not the last person to stand up for these values. Rather all modern political entrepreneurship has taken place under the same banners. For the last 250 years, politics has more than anything been a matter of defending the dignity and sovereignty of modern individuals. As political pamphleteers constantly have reiterated, it is dignity that is undermined by the lack of political rights, by dehumanising working conditions or by inequalities between races and genders. And it is sovereignty that is denied whenever democratic institutions are suspended or whenever a country is occupied by foreigners. The most successful political entrepreneurs – from the French Revolutionaries to Mahatma Gandhi and Nelson Mandela – have all rallied people in support of such causes.

The question is only how dignity and sovereignty can be upheld outside of the utopian location of a Robinsonian island. The ideal of dignity requires a political system where every person can exercise sovereign over him or herself, yet there are obvious problems how to organise this in a setting where people are forced to live together with others. This is the central puzzle of all modern political theory. Reading Defoe, Jean-Jacques Rousseau suggested one set of solutions to the problem; reading Rousseau's reading of Defoe, Immanuel Kant suggested another solution, and assorted philosophers have discussed the same problem ever since.[17] What is required, but so devilishly difficult to organise, is a Robinsonism suited for a social setting.

Problems of collective action

But as we said, the story of Robinson is a modern myth and so are the stories told about modern entrepreneurs. As individuals we are never as autonomous as we think we are and as entrepreneurs we are never as powerful. The fact that Robinson Crusoe is a fictional character is not a coincidence after all. In the end only a fictional character – someone who does not exist – can fully live up to the conceptions that people in modern society are supposed to have of themselves.[18]

What successful entrepreneurship requires is not an individual but instead a collective effort. It is only by joining forces together with others that we actually can accomplish what we set out to do. Yet in modern society collective efforts have become exceedingly difficult to organise. The reason is that Robinsonian individuals are supposed to think only of their own interests and to care little for the collective interests of the groups to which they ostensibly belong.[19] In fact, Robinsonians are unlikely to volunteer their contributions even in cases where they stand to gain from the outcome which the collective action would produce. As long as everybody is in a position to enjoy the results regardless of their efforts, they will always be better off free-riding on the contributions of others. When everyone reasons in this manner, collective actions will not take place.

But this is itself a puzzling conclusion. We may indeed wonder why it is that the myth of the modern entrepreneur has become ever more pervasive in contemporary society while the collective actions which alone could lend credibility to this myth have become ever more difficult to organise. Perversely, the demiurge seems to be emasculated by his own hubris. And yet it is obvious that collective action problems can be and continuously are being solved. Look at the way in which an average entrepreneur spends his or her average working day. Most of it is taken up by tasks such as the managing of staff, the negotiating of contracts or the persuading of political or religious supporters. That is, much of what entrepreneurs actually do is to prepare the ground for and to organise collective actions. Similarly, looking at contemporary society what we see are not all-powerful and self-sufficient individuals but instead a plethora of organisations, associations, clubs, fraternities, federations, unions and movements of all kinds.

In practice collective action problems are solved in either of three ways: through legal contracts, through side payments or through the establishment of trust.[20] Legal contracts allow you to force others to cooperate with you or to suffer the legal consequences; side payments allow you to bundle the public good of cooperation with a private good which only can be consumed by those who chose to act collectively; trust makes it possible to convince others that you will help them if only they first help you. Of these three trust is probably, historically speaking, the most important mechanism, and yet, as we know, trust is often exceedingly difficult to establish. This is the case in all societies but the problems are exacerbated in a situation where most social interaction takes place between self-sufficient strangers who never know when they next will meet. As Edmund Burke complained in 1770:

> Where men are not acquainted with each other's principles nor experienced in each other's talents, . . . no personal confidence, no friendship, no common interest, subsisting among them; it is evidently impossible that they can act a publick part with uniformity, perseverance, or efficacy.[21]

Somehow the trust which fails to materialise by itself must be artificially created. A way to do this is to force people to interact with one another on a continuous basis. Having met once or twice, the idea is to make them expect another meeting and to consider cooperative strategies which can benefit them all in the long run. In this way a network of social relations will be superimposed on the barebones logic of the rational interaction. The more knowledge the potential co-operators have of each other, the easier it is to decide whether to collaborate or not.

The most obvious setting in which this problem is solved is the family. Since family members live together and interact on a daily basis, they will, whether they like it or not, come to know one another very well indeed. Exit from the family is impossible during childhood but even after that it is often surprisingly difficult to fully achieve. Since family members interact repeatedly over time, they have an incentive to behave fairly towards each other, and since they interact closely, it is easy to detect and punish free-riders.[22] As a result transaction costs are considerably lower within the family than in relation with strangers, making the family into a powerful entrepreneurial unit.

Not surprisingly the first businesses were usually family-run.[23] The fledging banking industry of the Renaissance is the most striking example. At a time when credit was dear or simply unavailable, and when there was little by means of legal protection against highway robbers – or for that matter against the arbitrary actions of feudal lords – family members were often the only people who could be relied on. The first Italian banks were all owned and operated by families rather than by individuals: the Scoti of Piacenza, the Salimbene, Buonsignori and Gallerani of Sienna, the Frescobaldi, Pucci, Peruzzi, Bardi and Medici of Florence.[24] But family enterprises have continued to be important into our own era.[25] As the aspiring entrepreneurs of the Industrial Revolution quickly realised, children and wives provide a good source of free labour, and the hope of seeing the business flourish usually made family members acquiesce in the most blatant forms of exploitation.

Already by the end of the sixteenth century, however, much business in continental Europe took place on the basis of commissions.[26] A business based on commissioned agents is in many ways preferable to a business based on family members since agents allow far more flexibility in adjusting to changes in market conditions and make it possible to form much larger organisational units. The only problem is how trust can be created. A thriving business requires loyalty, scrupulousness and respect for instructions. In the early modern era such values were often easiest to uphold among members of the same ethnic community. Hence the thriving businesses made up entirely of Sephardic Jews, of Italian 'Lombards' or Armenians.[27] But religious organisations such as the Knights Templars could fill the same purpose. Exploiting trans-European connections originally formed in the Crusades in the twelfth century, this secret brotherhood served as bankers among others to the king of England.[28]

The first public corporations, the join-stock companies, founded in the seventeenth century brought people together on the basis of shared economic self-interest rather than family connections or bonds of ethnicity or religion. The Dutch VOC, the Verenigde Oostindische Compagnie, started in 1598 is perhaps the most celebrated example.[29] This corporate setting is the world described by Defoe and the place where we would expect to find his Robinsonian projectors. And yet it is striking how also these more impersonal business ventures tried their best to mimic the trust-inducing practices of family firms and brotherhoods. From the Latin *corpus*, meaning 'body,' a corporation was a body of which investors and employees were the constituent parts; or, changing the metaphor, it was a 'company,' from the Latin *cumpanis*, denoting 'someone with whom one shares bread.'[30] In either case, however, it was the responsibility of the enterprise to organise feasts throughout the year and to provide its stakeholders with everything from emergency loans to help with weddings and funeral expenses. The first employees were often considered as 'brothers' and their wives as 'sisters,' and the company never hesitated to regulate their personal conduct also outside of the workplace.[31] Often clerical staff would live with the merchants for whom they worked, eat at their table and join in the family prayers.

The alternative strategies for inducing cooperative behaviour among self-regarding individualists – legal contracts and side payments – are more fully compatible with Robinsonian ideals. Parties to a contract, or people who cooperate only in order to reap private benefits, need far less by means of social glue to keep them together. Since Defoe's time both mechanisms have become more important as the fiction of the self-sufficient individual has come to be more widely believed. As a result there is less emphasis on trust-inducing activities today than there was in the early modern era.[32] And yet it is clear that personal relationships still matter enormously to the success of our projects, and that also contemporary projectors spend much of their days 'networking' and 'team-building.' Relying only on contracts and on lawyers to keep our collective actions going is often prohibitively cumbersome and expensive.

The new consumerism

The illusive nature of the self-sufficiency of Robinsonian individuals is never better illustrated than through the new consumerism that appeared in the course of the eighteenth century. The more individuals came to think of themselves as self-sufficient and free, the more they turned themselves into slaves of fashion.[33] They increasingly began buying things not because they actually needed them but because others already had them and because it was the fashionable thing to do. Above we saw how Renaissance elites obsessively sought to impress each other and their social inferiors by surrounding themselves with extraordinary objects of all kinds. By the eighteenth century such ostentation had been universalised, democratised, and turned into a requirement for anyone aspiring to social status.

It is surprising how little time economists spend on questions of consumption; while they have much to say about the origins of supply, they have next to nothing to say about the origins of demand.[34] The discussions of the sources of economic growth is a case in point. As economists all firmly believe, economic growth must be explained in terms of supply-side factors. The origins of the Industrial Revolution is a case in point.[35] Factory-based industrial production took off, they will say, above all as a result of a series of remarkable technological inventions of which steam engines and spinning machines are the most celebrated. Making labour more productive and goods far cheaper, the inventions opened up new opportunities for entrepreneurs. This, according to the economists, is how modern economic growth began, and markets have expanded ever since.

There are, however, some historical facts that go against such an economistic interpretation. For one thing, consumption seems to have risen well before most, or even all, of the celebrated technological inventions were made. This at least was the case in England, Holland and northern France.[36] Here there were well-developed markets in prestige items for the elite already in the sixteenth century and for ordinary people there were burgeoning mass markets in everything from knitted stockings, felt hats and cooking pots to glass bottles and pewter ware.[37] By the early eighteenth century large swathes of the middle class, and even many farmers and labourers, began emulating the consumption habits of the elite, and by the end of the century everyone seemed to have followed the same fashions. Before long consumption had become, contemporary moralists complained, 'an epidemical madness' and a 'universal contagion.'[38]

The problem for economic theorising is that since this rise in demand took off well before the inventions associated with Industrial Revolution the inventions cannot explain the rise in demand. Instead, as many cultural historians have argued, the causal relationship should be turned on its head.[39] The Industrial Revolution was demand rather than supply-driven. It was demand not supply which expanded the markets, triggered technological inventions and produced economic growth. Reading contemporary sources there is certainly plenty of views in support of this interpretation. 'Fashion,' as the English projector Richard Barbon pointed out in his *A Discourse on Trade*, 1690, 'occasions the Expence of Cloaths before the Old ones are worn out.'[40] Or, in the doggerel of Bernard de Mandeville's *Fable of the Bees*, 1714:

> Luxury employ'd a Million of the Poor
> And odious Price a Million More.
> Envy it self, and Vanity
> Were Ministers of Industry;
> Their darling Folly, Fickleness
> In Diet, Furniture and Dress.
> That strange ridic'lous Vice, was made
> The Very Wheel, that turn'd the Trade ///
> Thus Vice nursed Ingenuity,
> Which join'd with Time, and Industry
> Had carry'd Life's Conveniences,

> Its real Pleasures, Comforts, Ease,
> To such a Height, the very Poor
> Lived better than the Rich before.[41]

At the time, Mandeville's shameless apologia for self-indulgence was widely regarded as scandalous but later in the century his views had become firmly established as commonsensical.[42] In 1776 Adam Smith stated categorically that '[c]onsumption is the sole end and purpose of all production; and the interest of the producer ought to be attended to, only so far as it may be necessary for promoting that of the consumer.'[43] This maxim, Smith concluded, 'is so perfectly self-evident, that it would be absurd to attempt to prove it.'

There are, however, problems also with this account. Above all it fails to explain where the new demand originally originated. It is not clear why people suddenly started asking for these fashionable items and it is not clear how they found the money to pay for them. In fact, looking at incomes for the period concerned it seems real wages may have been lower in the early eighteenth century than they had been in the fifteenth century, and although incomes subsequently improved somewhat the recovery was cut short after 1750 by rampant inflation.[44] And the intermediate 50 per cent of the population – that 'middling sort' which was supposed to constitute the vanguard of the consumer revolution – seems to have been particularly badly hurt. Combining these conflicting facts, the result is puzzling: there was indeed a consumer boom but it is unclear where the increased purchasing power came from.[45]

The answer is that although individual per capita incomes hardly improved in the course of the eighteenth century, household incomes decidedly did.[46] This happened above all as families mobilised a number of previously under- or non-utilised resources. And just as the cultural historians have argued, this happened well before the Industrial Revolution itself and above all in western and northern Europe. Here an 'industrious revolution' preceded the industrial.[47] People started working far harder – longer hours in a day and many more days in a year – and they also brought new land under cultivation.[48] As a result English farmers could harvest up to four times as much grain as their medieval predecessors had done with roughly the same input of capital and technology. Women and children too increasingly began working for a wage. The flourishing *Verlagsverein* or 'putting-out system', whereby farming families completed assorted piece-work for itinerant entrepreneurs, made sure that all family members always had something to do and stayed productively employed.[49]

As a result of this new-found industriousness, the supply of labour increased dramatically and the aggregate income of families rose. The question is only what the families intended to do with the money. Before the modern era, as we pointed out above, the predominant rule of the household had been to make sure that everyone's needs were adequately met.[50] The aim was to assure a certain target income but once this income was reached there was no reason to go on working. Thus if wages went up, the target could be reached sooner and as a result people would work fewer hours than before. Although this may seem strange and irrational to us, the opposite is the case. It is perfectly rational to stop working when one has enough and quite perverse to go on working beyond this point.[51] We are the ones whose behaviour is in need of an explanation.

Somewhere along the line something strange seems to have happened to our schedule of preferences. For economic markets to go on expanding indefinitely, demands must be limitless; enough can no longer be enough. In medieval society intemperance of this kind had been universally condemned, but in the course of the seventeenth century the same attitude came to characterise the archetype of a new human being. Man, as Thomas Hobbes explained, has a 'perpetuall and restlesse desire' which 'ceaseth onely in Death.'[52] Obviously, if desires are insatiable, there are endless opportunities for markets to expand and endless opportunities for entrepreneurs to make money. The 'spur to Trade, or rather to Industry and Ingenuity,' wrote the English Puritan Dudley North in his *Discourses upon Trade*, 1691, 'is the exorbitant Appetites of Men, which they will take pains to gratifie, and so be disposed to work, when nothing else will incline them to it.'[53]

For this new archetype to become firmly established, a shift was required in the definition of human needs. The needs officially acknowledged in the pre-modern era were above all physical ones.[54] Yet there are necessarily limits to physical needs since human beings only require so much food, drink, shelter and rest. From the latter part of the seventeenth century, however, the needs that really mattered were social ones. The consumption through which social needs are satisfied is a way of identifying ourselves to others and comparing ourselves with them. What matters is not how much we consume, but rather how much we consume in relation to others.[55] As long as others have more and better items than we have, we are unlikely to ever be completely satisfied. For this reason social needs know no bounds.

What we find is consequently that the history of the development of consumption runs in close parallel with the history of the concept of the person as it developed from the Renaissance onward. The aggressive self-promotion of Renaissance elites corresponded perfectly to the aggressive nature of their demand for goods and services. Consumption was more than anything a vehicle of self-promotion, a way to increase one's fame. Hence the sumptuous feasts and the outlandish clothes, the palatial lodgings and the ravenous taste for *curiositas* and *mirabilia*.[56] Looking for a way to satisfy this demand, new worlds of opportunity opened up for entrepreneurs. This was when a proper intra-European market in assorted luxury items came to be established, but the most exciting opportunities were all extra-European: in overseas trade with India, East Asia and the Americas. If it had not been for this insatiable desire for the exotic, it is difficult to see what would have tempted the Europeans to embark on these long and perilous journeys.

In the eighteenth century demand continued to be aggressively self-promotional among the members of the elite. Hence the physical appearance of the aristocracy which was more be-laced, be-powdered and be-feathered than ever previously.[57] Yet the dominant trend was for elite tastes to become universalised and thereby simultaneously standardised and lowered. By now everyone was touched by the forces of fashion and entrepreneurs could for that reason cater to a mass market in fashionable goods.[58] The self-confident members of the middling classes used fashion less as a way to stand out from the crowd than as a way to associate themselves with it. More than anything fashion was a marker of membership and hence a guarantee of one's dignity as a human being. In order to be recognised as a legitimate part of society, you simply had to consume certain things. As Adam Smith put it in 1776:

> A linen shirt, for example, is, strictly speaking, not a necessary of life. . . . But in the present times, through the greater part of Europe, a creditable day-labourer would be ashamed to appear in publick without a linen shirt, the want of which would be supposed to denote that disgraceful degree of poverty, which, it is presumed, no body can well fall into without extreme bad conduct. Custom, in the same manner, has rendered leather shoes a necessary of life in England. The poorest creditable person of either sex would be ashamed to appear in publick without them.[59]

9 Institutions that get things done

What we have witnessed is a remarkable sociological make-over. First human beings were Robinsonified, individualised and denuded of their social obligations. Next they were told that they could reach out to others and form new social ties if they only found a way of building trust and learnt how to consume. Suddenly everybody was scrambling to obtain membership in sects, parties, clubs and associations and to get hold of the latest fashion. In this way the Robinsonians maintained the illusion of their freedom even as they made themselves ever more dependent; no longer bound by religious dogmas or feudal customs, they were now free to conform out of their own volition. For entrepreneurs this presented both challenges and opportunities. Although the new individualism constantly threatened to undermine their ability to organise collective actions, the new conformism provided wonderful opportunities for selling new things, lifestyles, programmes and truths.

And yet none of this actually explains the persistent myth of the all-powerful entrepreneur. New opportunities are not enough unless people have a reasonable chance of taking advantage of them, and as we have argued, individuals alone are quite powerless in this respect. What the Robinsonian entrepreneurs needed, what boosted their power and made the modern myth about them into an account which seemed even halfway credible, was the frantic activity of a large number of different institutions. People in modern society are entrepreneurial above all since there are institutions that allow them to think of themselves that way. The aim of this chapter is to discuss the operations of some of these.

Property rights

Consider first the institutionalisation of property rights.[1] Property rights matter to entrepreneurs since they make it possible to distinguish what belongs to one person from what belongs to another. If a resource is held in common, or if it belongs to no one in particular, there is a temptation to overexploit it, to over-graze, over-fish or over-fell. But if you legally can keep people out, you can preserve the property for your own exclusive use now and in the future. In addition to a right of possession, however, you must have a right to dispose of the

property as you yourself see fit. Such alienability is a precondition for the formation of markets since it allows what one owns to be exchanged. For entrepreneurs – and not just for economic entrepreneurs – markets make a crucial
difference. Without markets things will be distributed by nature, by luck or by
hallowed tradition, and there is no way for people to get their hands on the
resources they need in order to carry out their plans. Markets turns dead objects
into productive assets which you can invest in, sell or mortgage.[2]

Medieval conceptions of property were quite different from those of modern
society.[3] Much of the land was controlled by the feudal manors and as such not
readily alienable and never bought and sold. Instead land was understood as an
inheritance, it was one's origin and one's home, and owned not by individuals
as much as by the succeeding generations of the same family.[4] Other land was
held in common by all villagers and used as pasture for animals, for hunting, or
for the gathering of firewood and berries. Labour was primarily regarded as a
service; it was something you gave to the lord in exchange for protection and
the right to till the soil. As such labour had no price and people were not free to
move between the manors. In short, there were no proper markets in factors of
production, no prices and no exchange. For that reason, medieval entrepreneurs
had to rely on the assets they were born with or whatever they could steal,
borrow or obtain as gifts.

The feudal economy changed as a result of the creation of the first towns in
the eleventh and twelfth centuries.[5] Towns were commercial centres and as
such ruled by their own legal system, the *lex mercatorum* or 'law merchants,'
which in practice came to recognise both private property and alienability.[6]
International commerce too – or rather inter-town commerce – was governed
by the same decentralised legal system and there were commercial courts where
disputes between merchants were resolved, apparently with great efficiency.[7] As
for the manorial system it was fatally undermined by the great plague of the
fourteenth century which made labour into a scarce resource and made land
comparatively more abundant. As a result the serfs obtained the power to rene-
gotiate their feudal obligations and the lords increasingly found that they had to
pay people if they were to stay on the land. Labour could increasingly be
obtained at a price, and in Tudor England over a half or even two-thirds of all
households received some part of their income in the form of wages.[8] 'A mans
Labour also is a commodity,' as Hobbes unceremoniously put it, 'exchangeable
for benefit.'[9] Once monetised and commodified in this fashion, markets began
taking off across Europe, although the process was highly uneven and not really
completed until well into the nineteenth century.

The spread of markets had a corrosive effect on the structure of medieval
society. Although traditional hierarchies persisted, the bonds between superiors
and inferiors became less personal and people could increasingly choose which
superior to subject themselves to.[10] If the lord tried to impose his will, the serf
could simply escape to another manor or take refuge in a town; *Stadtluft*, as
the saying went, *macht frei*. Similarly, while a lord who demanded a certain
quantity of honey or poultry could determine the activities of a peasant in some

considerable detail, the moment the request was converted into money the peasant was free to engage in whatever money-making activities he fancied. Although markets in this way made society more impersonal and more abstract, these were the exact qualities that served to empower the entrepreneurs. For the first time they could hire people and buy the things they needed – including political patronage and religious blessings – for their projects to succeed.

Eventually the law was expanded to incorporate these new facts. In Germany, from the latter part of the fifteenth century onward, the legal system came to include an increasing number of statutes from Roman law, and the Romans had been surprisingly modern in their conception of property.[11] In Holland in the early seventeenth century, Hugo Grotius among others pointed out that property rights were required for man to exercise his prerogative to use the natural world.[12] Rights were apportioned like seats in a theatre, he argued, they must be claimed by physical occupancy. In England, the customary law was retained but it was fundamentally reworked in order to establish private property on a firmer basis. As John Locke insisted, people have a property right in whatever it is they mixed their labour with, and according to Hobbes, the most fundamental property right is the right each person has to his or her own body.[13] From this, Hobbes believed, followed the right of self-defence but also the right to extend one's being into property.

Property rights must not only be established, however, but they must also be made secure. Although property rights exist, they are not necessarily respected. For entrepreneurs this is potentially fatal since they have no guarantees that their investments are safe, and in the absence of such safeguards they have no reason to embark on their projects. Entrepreneurs need assurances that *pacta sunt servanda* and that disputes regarding contracts are speedily and equitably resolved. 'Commerce and manufactures can seldom flourish,' as Adam Smith pointed out in 1776,

> in any state which does not enjoy a regular administration of justice, in which the people do not feel themselves secure in the possession of their property, in which the faith of contracts is not supported by law, and in which the authority of the state is not supposed to be regularly employed in enforcing the payment of debts from all those who are able to pay.[14]

This was where the medieval *lex mercatorum* had fallen down. Its decentralised decision-making may have been efficient in settling commercial disputes but only as long as the class of merchants was relatively small and united by a common sense of fellowship. And already in the Middle Ages the law merchant had been quite powerless when it came to disputes between merchants and kings. If the king defaulted on a loan, there was little legal recourse.

As far as the legal protection of property rights was concerned, the emergence of the state as a sovereign actor presented new opportunities and new problems. Potentially property rights were now far better policed than ever before. By claiming a monopoly on the legitimate use of violence, the state could throw people in jail if they failed to follow its rules. On the other hand, the fact that different states established quite different sets of rules put up new obstacles to international commerce.[15] Potentially even more damaging was the fact that the sovereign state had unprecedented ways of ignoring property rights, by for example taxing people punitively or defaulting on its loans.[16] Although the financial position of the king temporarily could be improved through such unilateral actions, they had disastrous long-term effects. The uncertainty of the situation created an unfavourable business climate which was detrimental to entrepreneurship. To attract new financiers the king had to offer higher interest rates and this raised interest rates in society as a whole.

What was needed were credible guarantees that the king would behave responsibly and that property rights were secure.[17] To this effect a constitution was crucial since it laid down the rules according to which power was to be exercised and limited the king's freedom of action. Examples of such constitutional provision include the *Regeringsform* promulgated in Sweden in 1634 and the English Act of Habeas Corpus, 1679, and the Bill of Rights, 1689.[18] But absolutist states were no less constitutional, in fact often they were more so. As Baron de Montesquieu pointed out, while democracies required their citizens to be virtuous, monarchies required good laws in order to be well governed.[19] Hence the idea of the *Rechtsstaat*. From the eighteenth century onward countries such as Prussia or Austria were not ruled by arbitrary rulers, but instead only on the basis of codified laws. Under the law all subjects were equal, or as the introduction to the Prussian *Allgemeines Landrecht*, 1794, put it: 'the state's laws bind all its subjects, without regard to status, rank, or family.' In Prussia it was even possible to prosecute the king himself.[20] The paradox is that by constraining the power of executive action, the king became more rather than less powerful. It became easier to raise revenue since kings were easier to trust and to control.

Dealing with risk

Yet even if these problems are successfully solved, entrepreneurs may still be facing obstacles. Even if property rights are securely established and entrepreneurs have access to markets, they may decide that a project on balance is not worth undertaking. The problem here is often risk. Although modern entrepreneurs usually describe themselves as risk-takers and as gamblers, this is always just so much hyperbole. What they really want is not risk but instead certainty and predictability; they want to be 'incentivised' by a 'favourable business climate.'[21] Thus if risks are high and the environment uncertain, entrepreneurs will demand a premium for undertaking their activities, and if the risks are too high the projects may never happen at all. Hence, for a society to become truly entrepreneurial, risk must somehow be lowered or at least controlled.

Compare pre-modern times when the sheer inscrutability of life was something people simply learnt to live with.[22] Much of the time everything that happened seemed either as entirely predetermined or as completely accidental;

human beings were ruled either by an unknowable god or by a capricious Lady Fortuna. In modern societies by contrast, people are ruled above all by probabilities. Neither completely determined nor completely accidental, there are odds attached to everything that takes place. Learning how to calculate these odds is a key to successful entrepreneurship. If we understand the risks involved and learn to measure them, we know the likelihood of success; we also know what compensation we require and on what terms we can invite people as investors. Hardly surprisingly, such risks are far easier for institutions to calculate than they are for individuals.

The emergence of the idea of probability can be dated with some considerable degree of precision.[23] It was only in the middle of the seventeenth century that people began calculating probabilities in mathematical terms, and northern France, Holland and England was where it happened. 'Pascal's wager' is perhaps the most famous expression of this new way of approaching the world.[24] As Pascal had argued, it makes rational sense to believe in god since any sacrifice that such a belief may impose on us today will be more than adequately compensated for by the uncertain but infinite prospect of salvation in the after-life. Or as the Dutch mathematician Christiaan Huygens argued in his *De rationciniis in ludo aleæ*, 1657, risks are best understood in terms of the expectation of future gain with which an investor enters into a contract.

The simplest way of dealing with risks is to pool them. People get together in a common enterprise and share the risks associated with it, or they gather small sums and form a common fund from which they can draw in the eventuality of some disaster.[25] This is the principle behind mutual societies, self-help organisations and all kinds of co-operatives; the medieval guild is an early example of the principle and similar arrangements have always existed in peasant communities. In the eighteenth century the institution was formalised in cities like London and Paris as mutual societies responsible above all for the protection against fire. The number of self-help organisations increased dramatically during the Industrial Revolution.[26] People who were forced to leave the countryside to take up jobs in cities were exposed to unprecedented insecurities and this was particularly the case for migrant workers who arrived in the cities alone.[27] Risks were pooled together with everyone's loneliness and the proceedings of the mutual aid societies were often carried out in pubs. In early nineteenth-century England, risk-pooling of this kind provided perhaps one third of all households with some form of security against sickness.

Risk-pooling is also the original idea behind the joint-stock company. The first public companies emerged in fields where not only the financial needs but also the risks were the greatest.[28] It was for example both expensive and risky to equip ships and to send them off on inter-continental journeys. Perhaps the ship would return only years later and it was rarely clear with what cargo. Despite the potential for high profits, the risks involved in such enterprises made it difficult for entrepreneurs to raise capital. The solution, first institutionalised by the Venetians in the late Middle Ages, was to allow investors to buy parts of a cargo or parts of a ship, but before long the merchant companies themselves became objects of joint investment.[29] From the eighteenth century onward the corporate form spread to other risky and financially demanding sectors of the economy such as canal building, breweries or mining. Risks were further reduced in the nineteenth century through the introduction of limited liability whereby investors would stand to lose no more than they originally had invested in the business. As always, the more the risks were restricted, the more capital was ventured.

A more direct way of dealing with risks, already implied by these solutions, is insurance.[30] Instead of asking all partners to an enterprise to share the risks, they can be sold to a company that specialises in managing them. Shipping was the first field where this institution developed, again because so much money was at stake and because the risks were high. The Genovese operated a system of maritime insurance already in the twelfth century and an ordinance issued in 1435 by the magistrates of Barcelona regulated the sale of similar policies.[31] The earliest Italian law on the subject dates from 1523. At the *Beurs* in Amsterdam insurance rates were publicly posted for a large number of different destinations in Europe and beyond, and in London, Edward Lloyd's coffee-house had their own tariffs.[32] After the great fire of London in 1666, fire insurance became popular with investors and in 1696 the first life insurance policies were sold.[33]

Buying a risk may perhaps itself be considered as a rather risk-filled venture, but this was less and less the case. Modern insurance companies pooled risks just as self-help societies always had done but in addition they also calculated them with unprecedented precision. Risks are necessarily difficult for individuals to assess, and this is particularly the case when it comes to risks associated with events that happen only rarely such as fires, shipwrecks or deaths. As it was discovered in the latter part of the seventeenth century, however, such calculations are easily undertaken by institutions. Institutions can assemble far more statistical data and draw conclusions which, although never true in individual cases, nevertheless are true in the aggregate. While no one knows at what age they will die, insurance companies know exactly at what age a person with a certain income, medical history and lifestyle is most likely to do so. The first such calculations were compiled by the English projector John Graunt in his *Observations on the Bills of Mortality*, 1662, and in 1671 the statesman Johann de Witt used actuary tables to construct the annuity schemes used to raise money for the Dutch state.[34] The most accurate calculations, however, were carried out in Sweden in the course of the eighteenth century, mainly as a result of the excellent statistical records maintained by the official, state-run, church.[35]

While these insurance schemes dealt with natural disasters and cases of *forces majeurs*, there still remained plenty of purely commercial risks that could hamper investments. A way of dealing with these was to buy patents and monopolies. Today patents and monopolies are talked about in quite separate terms. Patents are generally regarded as beneficial to enterprise since they reward inventors and allow entrepreneurs temporary protection while developing their products.[36] Monopolies, on the other hand, are considered as bad for enterprise since they allow companies to ignore market forces. In early modern

Europe, however, patents and monopolies were initially taken as the same thing and both were above all ways for the state to raise money.[37] The attraction for the king was that he by selling monopolies could bypass the parliament and raise revenue quickly to fund for example the participation in a war.

From the point of view of the person buying the patent the attraction was that commercial risks could be reduced.[38] Buying a monopoly he would buy himself the assurance that there were no competitors in a certain market. Although the consequences for consumers no doubt were negative, the existence of monopolies made it possible for entrepreneurs to undertake projects which otherwise would have been difficult to undertake. This was, for example, the case with the high-risk business of overseas trade. All the European East India companies – including the VOC – operated under official charters which guaranteed them a captive domestic market in exotic produce. This, in the end, was how the European commercial empires came to be created. Monopolies, one could say, were market expanding even if they meant that resources were less than perfectly efficiently allocated.[39] In the end, however, they did not escape the biting critique of the proponents of market forces. 'Such exclusive companies,' said Adam Smith,

> are nuisances in every respect; always more or less inconvenient to the countries in which they are established, and destructive to those which have the misfortune to fall under their government.[40]

The idea of the patent faired much better. As we have come to use the term, a patent covers not the production or sale of a commodity but instead to the exclusive use of a certain technology.[41] In this case the trade-off between market creation and efficient resource allocation is firmly resolved in favour of the former. Few complain when inventors get what is regarded as their just desert and society as a whole is assumed to profit by providing entrepreneurs with attractive incentives. In Venice individual inventors were granted such *privilegi* already in the fourteenth century and in 1474 the Senate passed a general law protecting those who had registered 'any new and ingenious device, not previously made within our jurisdiction.'[42] Later this protection was extended also to copyrights on printed material. Similar laws were set up in the Dutch Republic and, with the Statute of Monopolies of 1624, in England. In France the connection between patents and monopolies remained closer and inventors often obtained not only exclusive commercial rights but also support in starting a business and perhaps a state pension.[43]

An in many ways easier solution is to let the market deal with the problem. You can deal with risks, that is, not only by selling them to a specialised institution such as an insurance company but also to whoever cares to purchase them. Again it seems unlikely that anyone willingly would gamble in this fashion and yet this clearly depends on the returns a gamble may bring. Whenever there are risks there are profits to be made and the temptation of making a profit will always attract speculators as long as the price is right.[44] While some people are risk-adverse by nature or by professional training, others are more risk-tolerant, even risk-inviting. The trick is to somehow make it possible for the non-gamblers to sell the risks to the gamblers.

A futures market is a solution to this problem.[45] In a futures market the person who wants to avoid risks can buy the right to sell a product in the future at a price decided on in the present. The person who sells this right to buy will then take all the risk and all the potential profits derived from any changes in the price. In contemporary markets futures are bought and sold in the form of so called 'derivatives' which have become financial products of great sophistication and complexity.[46] And yet the idea itself is far older. Already in the 1550s Dutch merchants traded in future deliveries of Baltic grain and North Sea herring, and at the Amsterdam *Beurs* future contracts were concluded for a long range of products including pepper, coffee, tulips, cacao, saltpetre, brandy, whale oil and whale bones.[47] Clearly the people who bought these contracts never had the intention of actually taking possession of the products. All they cared about was the speculative gain derived from changes in the value of the papers themselves.

Financial support

Above we briefly discussed the creation of markets in land and labour, but in addition entrepreneurs also need access to money. Money is required for commercial or industrial ventures but equally for political or religious ones, and in practice fund-raising often takes up more of the entrepreneur's time than the entrepreneurial activities themselves. The question is only where one can get one's hands on the stuff. If we are lucky we may perhaps have the money ourselves, and many entrepreneurial projects have indeed been self-financed.[48] If we do not have it, however, we have a problem, but in modern societies this problem is addressed by financial institutions. We go to the institution and ask them to support our project and if we qualify the money will be given to us. Support is given according to rules and it does not rely on the magnanimity of individuals – this, at least, is the theory.[49] At the same time there are many different kinds of financial institutions and they operate in rather different ways, giving money to different kinds of projects and on rather different terms.

The spread of the money economy from the twelfth century onwards led more or less spontaneously to the creation of the first banks.[50] There were big-time merchants who made exorbitant profits which they needed to recycle; there were money-changers who helped out with foreign payments; there were goldsmiths who took people's metals for safekeeping in return for receipts; and together they developed the various functions of a modern bank: loans, transfers, deposits and credit creation. A particularly important instrument was the bill of exchange, basically a check which allowed entrepreneurs to engage in long-distance trade without any of the risks or hassle of actually paying in specie.[51] Italian bankers were active at the fairs in Champagne and Lyon in the twelfth and thirteenth centuries, and as they spread their off-spring around the

Continent they established branch offices in places like Bruges, Antwerp and Amsterdam. In London the Italians were known as 'Lombards' and Lombard Street was for a long time the centre of the financial district of the city.[52]

The first public bank not connected to a particular family was the *Wisselbank*, the Bank of Amsterdam, established in 1609.[53] A great concern of its founders was to replace the multitude of debased coins issued by assorted rulers with a common currency in which everyone had confidence and which merchants could use in expanding their trade. But the *Wisselbank* also attracted deposits and before long merchants across Europe opened their own accounts. Since figures now could be moved between the columns of the same accounting books, transfers and payments were easy to effectuate and virtually costless. In 1683 the bank began to accept deposits in silver and gold, and the receipts the depositors received in return were readily transferable and tradable as money.[54]

Another Dutch institutional invention which was widely copied across Europe was the *Beurs* built in 1611.[55] As we briefly discussed above, corporations had already for a long time financed themselves by issuing stocks. What was new, however, was the creation of a market where these papers could be traded. At the *Beurs* shares were bought and sold by people less interested in the activities of the company and the profits they could bring than in the movements of the share price. The existence of this secondary market made investments more liquid and this provided entrepreneurs with better terms; people were more likely to buy shares since they knew they easily could dispose of them. In addition, the *Beurs* was a clearing house for everything from government bonds, insurance and foreign exchange to freight services and assorted commodities. And while many of these services had been available also at the medieval fairs, the *Beurs* had the advantage of continuously being in session. It was a 'one-stop-shop' for entrepreneurs, and throughout the seventeenth century it was the nerve centre of the entire world economy.

At the end of the seventeenth century all these institutions – collectively referred to as 'Dutch finance' – were imported into England and the result has gone down as 'the financial revolution.'[56] In 1694 the Bank of England was established and in the following year the Royal Exchange, but stocks were also traded at Garraway's and Jonathan's coffee-houses on Exchange Lane in the centre of the city.[57] While the Bank of England lent money to the government and pursued a conservative policy, institutions such as the Sword Bank lent money liberally and to the broader masses. This combination of easy money and the prospect of speculative gain led to a number of financial upheavals of which the South-Sea Bubble in the summer of 1720 is the most notorious. 'It seemed at that time as if the whole nation had turned stock-jobbers,' as Charles Mackay described the scene in his *Extraordinary Popular Delusions and the Madness of Crowds*, 1841. 'Exchange Alley was every day blocked up by crowds, and Cornhill was impassable for the number of carriages,'

> innumerable joint-stock companies started up every where. ... Some of them lasted for a week or a fortnight, and were no more heard of, while

others could not even live out that short span of existence. Every evening produced new schemes, and every morning new projects.[58]

Even though this particular bubble was rather brusquely deflated, the universalisation of credit in the eighteenth century continued to fuel demand for stocks as well as for consumer items. In the end it was liberal credit and not just the fact that people worked harder which boosted the fashion industry at the end of the eighteenth century.

The universalisation of credit had far-reaching social consequences.[59] When everyone was given access to credit it was suddenly possible for people without any social standing to borrow money, to invest it, and in this way to rise in the world. As one would expect, traditional elites reacted strongly to this possibility, even if the critique largely was phrased in terms of moral admonitions.[60] The fear was that people would start living on borrowed money; spend it extravagantly – especially when egged on by their wives – or engage in overly risky business ventures. But as its defenders strongly insisted, credit did not encourage recklessness at all but rather frugality and hard work; once gained credit had to be maintained and if at all possible augmented. Credit, as Defoe pointed out, 'will keep Company with none but the Industrious, the Honest, the Laborious, and such, whose Genius, the Bent of their Lives, tends to Maintain her good Opinion.'[61]

Yet this did not mean that all obstacles were removed. Even if credit had become more common it was not as widely available as some would have wished. Poor but brilliant entrepreneurs, as Defoe bitterly pointed out, were still given a hard time by the bankers.[62] And credit could also be restricted by state regulation, such as the time-honoured rulers which determined ceilings on interest rates. Artificially restricting rates, as the British government did until the early nineteenth century, was as Jeremy Bentham explained in his pamphlet *Defence of Usury*, 1787, a great obstacle to projectors. Truly entrepreneurial projects can bring great rewards only at the cost of great risks, he argued, and for that reason they require high interest rates if they are to find a financial backer. If rates are restricted, many projects will never get funded:

> it condemns as rash and ill-grounded, all those projects by which our species have been successively advanced from that state in which acorns were their food, and raw hides their cloathing, to the state in which it stands at present: for think, Sir, let me beg of you, whether whatever is now the routine of trade was not, at its commencement, project? whether whatever is now establishment, was not, at one time, innovation?[63]

An entrepreneur of particular importance is the state. The state famously lays claims to a monopoly on the legitimate use of violence, and as such it potentially wields an awesome power. The machinery of the state can be used for guaranteeing the security of the citizens, their right to independence and self-determination, or for any of a long range of assorted social goals.[64] Naturally all of this costs money and the question of how to finance the activities of the state has always been a prominent political concern. Taxes are the easiest answer, but taxes take time to raise – and are for that reason difficult to rely on in an emergency – and they are often highly unpopular. An alternative is to borrow money, but potential creditors are often reluctant to lend to the state since, as a sovereign power, it can cancel its debts at its own convenience.[65]

New financial institutions addressed this issue as well. The creation of a central bank put public finances on a new footing. The Swedish *Riksbank* was founded in 1656, the Bank of England as we said in 1694, and the various Dutch cities all established their own banks in the course of the seventeenth century.[66] The basic idea was simple enough: a group of creditors got together a large sum of money which they lent to the state; in return they were given shares in the bank and the shares could be sold in the stock market. The advantage for the state was that its debts in this way could be permanently funded and at a lower interest; the advantage for the creditors was that they could get their money back whenever they wanted. As if by magic, a large, long-term, loan had been constituted from many small sums of money lent on a short-term basis.

Part IV
Pluralism

10 A world in pieces

For change to be possible, we said above, self-reflection and entrepreneurship are not enough, neither alone nor when taken together. Once the world is reflected on from a number of alternative perspectives it will necessarily come to seem hopelessly diverse. The visions do not relate to each other in any straightforward fashion and many contradict each other as well as the established orthodoxies of the age. The universe cannot, for example, simultaneously have the sun and the earth at its centre. Likewise it is not possible for all entrepreneurs simultaneously to realise all of their projects. Once they start putting their ideas into practice, space, time, and other scarce resources will quickly start to run out.

Contradictions and competing claims on resources both have a tendency to produce conflict. New visions are often highly seductive and the people who have them are unlikely to forget what they have seen. Naturally they will insist that they are right and that people with competing visions are wrong. Similarly entrepreneurs have a tendency to fall in love with the projects they pursue and insist that they be given priority when it comes to the distribution of limited resources. The question is how such conflicts can be resolved without resorting to violence. Somehow society has to be protected and disagreements worked out by peaceful means. A modern society needs a way of dealing with the problem of pluralism.

A first instinct – historically, and perhaps also psychologically – has been to repress pluralism in the name of peace. In this way the European civil wars of the sixteenth and seventeenth centuries were dealt with by sovereign states that drastically sought to reduce the diversity of social life. Similarly, in the middle of the twentieth century, many leaders of newly independent states concluded that although democracy perhaps was a good idea in theory, it was, given the diversity of the societies concerned, also a 'luxury' that they could ill afford.[1] And the instinct to repress pluralism has not gone away. Unity, we are still constantly told, is better than division; united states, nations or farm workers are said to be strong, divided ones are said to be weak. The fact that unity requires conformity to a common norm and hence the repression, or at least silencing, of diversity is less often mentioned.

Hence also the peculiarly modern temptation of fundamentalism. Instead of learning to live with contradictions, the fundamentalists choose, deliberately, to restrict themselves to only one single view. Instead of celebrating the death of god, the fundamentalists recreate religion, literally, or in one or another of its many secular versions. Since they cannot allow truth to co-exist with error, fundamentalists are compelled to silence those who hold alternative, that is inferior, views. The result is a world filled with fanatical Protestants, Muslims, Communists, Freudians, and defenders of furry animals.

In the end neither repression nor zealotry is going to work. Pluralism can only be contained to the extent that reflection and entrepreneurship can be contained, and in a modern society where both activities are thoroughly institutionalised this cannot be done. Instead all modern societies have come up with some way of dealing with pluralism. Somehow pluralism must be translated from a violent competition into a competition carried on by some other means. Easy as such a solution may appear, it has as far as Europe is concerned taken an excruciatingly long time to arrive at. During the last 500 years wars and repression have been far more common than toleration, and fundamentalism has constantly reappeared in one or another of its ever mutating guises. The aim of this chapter is to briefly tell the story of modern pluralism as it emerged after the year 1500 and to discuss the repressive reactions to it. The aim of the subsequent two chapters is to discuss the solutions which the Europeans eventually arrived at.

The unity and diversity of the Middle Ages

To an observer from a neater and more rationally organised era, medieval Europe necessarily appears as a confusing place, full of idiosyncrasies and exceptions. There was a diversity and colour to social life which no later age has been able to rival. And yet this was also a time of extraordinary religious and cultural homogeneity. The Church imposed the same creed, the same rituals, and the same set of values on all societies everywhere. Both pictures are consequently correct. It is possible, depending on how one adjusts one's analytical lenses, to describe the medieval world either as one or as infinitely many. There was unity but also diversity; homogeneity co-existed with the most far-reaching particularism. Surprisingly given this tension, the social order of the Middle Ages was extraordinarily resilient, lasting for close to 1,000 years.

The origin of European unity is best traced to the Roman empire and its institutional legacy.[2] At one time or another most parts of the Continent had been a Roman province, and even once the empire was long gone many continued to claim some form of descent from the *populus romanus*.[3] Hence it is not surprising that when Charlemagne in the eighth century briefly united large parts of Europe, he did so in the name of 'Roman emperor,' and that Otto I took the same title when he in 962 brought various German speaking territories into the same political structure.[4] From the fifteenth century onwards this creation came to be known as the 'Holy Roman Empire of the German Nation,' or simply as 'the Empire.'

Above all, however, it was the Church that constituted the great unifying force of the Middle Ages. During the decline of the Roman empire the Christian religion gradually gained in strength and when Rome eventually fell the Church was the only institution left standing. The medieval Church had pretensions that were both universal and all-embracing. Uniquely among all European institutions it also had the means to carry out these intentions. In canon law, based on Roman imperial law, the Church had an instrument through which it could enforce its claims to secular power; and in Latin, the only written language, it had an instrument through which it could exercise a monopoly on elite culture and learning.[5]

Organisationally speaking the Church resembled a gigantic business corporation.[6] It had its headquarters and a CEO in Rome, regional offices and middle-level management in cathedral towns throughout Europe and sales representatives in branch offices located in each parish. The products marketed by this corporation were remarkably uniform and its sales figures were impressive; the Church was a monopoly-holder operating in a captive market. Or, in the jargon of the time, Europe formed a single *res publica Christiana*, a commonwealth of Christians which included everyone except the Muslims outside the gates of the republic and the Jews in its midst.

Despite its ideological control and its impressive organisational resources, the Church never attained a position of complete hegemony. If nothing else its claims had to be reconciled with the counter-claims of that other universal institution: the Empire. In matters of religious doctrine the Church may have ruled supreme but the emperor had serious pretensions to political power, especially in Germany.[7] The confrontation came to a head in the so-called 'Investiture Conflict' concerning the appointment of bishops and other higher clerical officers. According to the agreement reached in Worms in 1122, the emperor retained an important influence over appointments in Germany while the pope reasserted his rights in Italy and Burgundy.

Yet medieval life was not only surprisingly homogenous but also profoundly heterogeneous. Roughly speaking it was on the universal level that Europe was all the same and on the local level that Europe was all different. In the end of course the far larger part of medieval life was local. Since there were few means of communication and since news travelled slowly and human beings often not at all, every valley, even every village, came to evolve more or less according to its own logic.[8] As a result local customs, folklore, languages and laws were to a large extent unique. People were not only rooted in a particular place, however, but also in a particular social position. Medieval society was steeply hierarchical and social groups were rigidly separated. The life of a peasant had little in common with the life of a nobleman, a burgher or a priest.[9] With each social position came a unique set of duties, even a unique way of dressing, carrying oneself and relating to others.[10] There was little social mobility between these groups.

This rootedness in place and in position meant that although medieval Europe was highly diverse it was only rarely experienced as such. The lack of communications is what brought about diversity but it also made it difficult for people to become aware of the diversity that actually existed. It was only the occasional traveller – the exile, the merchant or the pilgrim – who was in a position to notice the richness and colour of the fabric of social life. A partial exception was the medieval town where various social groups lived side by side with each other. Consequently medieval towns offered an exotic mixture of fraternities, guilds, *societas*, estates and orders. And yet these groups were also closed off from each other with the help of strict membership rules, secret rituals and jealously protected privileges.

This in the end is how the problem of pluralism was dealt with and why the social order of the Middle Ages turned out to be so remarkably long-lived. Pluralism after all is only a problem if competing claims can be made regarding the same resources, the same rights or the same status. Yet as long as you rarely encounter people who are different from yourself such claims are difficult to make. In medieval Europe the fact of diversity did not lead to conflicts since everyone and everything was confined to its own, largely independent, sphere. Medieval society was highly segmented and this is in the end how pluralism was combined with unity.

The legal system was one of the instruments through which this segmentation was maintained. In the Middle Ages there were few generally applicable laws, no common realm of jurisdiction and no universal human rights. The point of the law was not to arbitrate between rival claims as much as to isolate social groups from each other. Hence the idea of *privus leges*, the 'privileges' or 'private laws,' which far from pertaining equally to everyone instead pertained only to one particular group. By law people were both separated and made unequal, and this is how conflicts were avoided.

In order to describe this social and political world the metaphors of the 'chain' and the 'ladder' were commonly employed.[11] All of nature, medieval theologians declared, could be described as a 'great chain' or a *scala naturæ* on which all beings great and small could find their appropriate positions. At the bottom of the ladder was inanimate matter such as stones and mud and at the top were the angels. Man was somewhere in the middle, an entity made up of matter and yet also a spiritual being endowed with an immortal soul. What made these metaphors particularly appealing was that they allowed the most radical diversity to be contained within a single conceptual scheme. As the metaphors affirmed, everything was different from everything else but everything also belonged inextricably together.

This was also the attraction of the body metaphor.[12] The Middle Ages was over-populated with bodies of all kinds: the Church was a body of which Christ was the eternal head and the pope the temporal; the state was a body of which the king was the head, the aristocracy the arms, the clergy the heart and the burghers and peasants the stomach.[13] Similarly the multitude of societies, fraternities and guilds were all understood as corporations – 'bodies' – or perhaps as *corpusculæ* – 'small bodies' – lodged inside other larger bodies. In this way it was easy to allow for the emergence of new groups. When, for example, some new social or religious movement appeared it could easily be assimilated – 'incorporated,' as it were – into some old well-established body.[14] This is how religious orders such as the Franciscans and the Dominicans came to be formed. And yet ultimately all of medieval life was an integral part of the universal body – the body of bodies – which was the Church.

Just as the great chain or the ladder, the body metaphor provided an ingenious conceptual means of dealing with the problem of pluralism. Although its parts all look different and have different functions, a body still operates as an organic unit. In fact it is precisely the differences between them that make it necessary for the body-parts to work together; if all body-parts looked the same there would be no point to their integration. Similarly since the various parts of society were functionally specific and hierarchically organised, they had to be mutually interdependent. The lords needed the serfs and the serfs needed the lords just as the head needs the stomach and the stomach the head. Far from being a source of conflict, difference made unity and peaceful co-operation both possible and required.

Dismemberment

In the course of the sixteenth and seventeenth centuries this universal body was suddenly dismembered in a series of rapid cuts. The reasons behind this disfigurement we have already implicitly discussed. The new pluralism was the inevitable result of the revolutions in reflection and entrepreneurship which by now were well under way. When the world was reflected on from a number of new perspectives it turned out to be not one but many. Since there no longer was an absolute vantage point from which the totality of the whole could be observed, there was no way of telling how the individual perspectives could be combined. Similarly the activities of entrepreneurs produced a plethora of new economic, political and religious entities, many of which laid claims to the same scarce resources. After the year 1500 there was no longer only one God, one Emperor, one language of learning or one *res publica Christiana*, instead there were many.

Chronologically speaking the first of these cuts was that through which the vernaculars came to be established as separate, written, languages to replace Latin. Beginning in the fourteenth century, authors throughout Europe found that they could reach new audiences when writing in languages they previously only had spoken.[15] After the invention of the printing press, the vernacularisation of culture proceeded at a rapid pace. As book publishers soon discovered, it was through vernacular languages that the large book buying audiences could be reached.[16] And what readers seemed to enjoy more than anything were stories drawn from their local, rather than the pan-European, tradition. Recycling material from medieval folk culture, François Rabelais, William Shakespeare and Miguel de Cervantes helped to define what it meant to be French, English and Spanish. Smaller languages too – Swedish, Polish or Hungarian – soon developed a vernacular literature of their own. As a result culture became increasingly national, that is to say limited, in scope.

Hardly surprisingly, the biblical story of the Tower of Babel became a favourite motif among artists in the fifteenth and sixteenth centuries, painted again and again, among others by Hendrick van Cleve, Peter Balten, Abel Grimmer and Pieter Bruegel the Elder. As it would seem to contemporaries, just as in biblical times God had once again 'confused the earth's languages' and made it impossible for people to understand one another.[17] Although scholarship continued to be carried out in Latin well into the eighteenth century, its chief proponents were now provincial intellectuals who never stood a chance of communicating with foreigners in their own tongues.[18] By now more prominently located writers used their native French, English or German, and demanded, self-confidently, that the rest of the world should make the effort to understand.

The second cut into the medieval *corpus* was that through which the notion of a pan-European political community finally was killed off. As we briefly discussed above the political map of the Middle Ages had been exceedingly complex. Power had been shared between a few universal institutions and a large number of local ones in an intricate pattern of overlapping loyalties. This conceptual geography was now radically simplified as the state inserted itself between the universal and the local levels and made itself independent of both. The new state called itself 'sovereign,' meaning that it acknowledged no rival claims to power and that neither popes or nor feudal lords were in a position to challenge its dominance.

Invoking such doctrines, the French church attained a large measure of independence by the middle of the fourteenth century and soon afterwards the king of England seized control of Church revenues and ecclesiastical appointments.[19] In northern Italy the intense competition between popes and emperors meant that the many small city-states were given a choice regarding which of the two authorities to pay allegiance to. In practice however they often asserted their independence of both.[20] Hence the system of city-states which became the political backdrop for the extraordinary achievements of the poets and painters of the Italian Renaissance.

Yet the idea of sovereignty was always more of a myth than a reality. Few statesmen, even in the small republics of northern Italy, had the ability to actually control what was going on within the borders of their realms. What sovereignty referred to in the end was instead the rather more limited notion that one country should refrain from interfering in the internal affairs of another. But in practice even this was difficult to achieve. The existence of a plurality of states who all called themselves sovereign placed some very real limits on their independence and in the end a state could do no more than what other states let it get away with. In order to consolidate their power and to fend off enemies each state began raising taxes and men for armies and developed increasingly efficient administrative machineries.

The third cut chronologically speaking was the Reformation through which the religious body of the Middle Ages was dismembered. What was unusual about Martin Luther, Jean Calvin and their many epigones was not their reformist zeal – Saints Francis or Dominic had been no less reform-minded –

but rather the determination with which they set out to break with the universal Church. Luther and Calvin were openly presenting their congregations as bodies foreign, and hostile, to the Church. Before long the Lutheran churches had formed their own alternative body, the *corpus evangelicorum*, which was separate from Rome.

What was unusual about the new religious movements was also the next to instantaneous success they enjoyed. Luther posted his 95 theses on the church door in Wirtenberg on October 31, 1517, and only 15 years later large parts of Germany, all of Scandinavia and England, were dominated by Lutheran churches. A few decades subsequently Calvinism spread equally quickly from its origin in Geneva. Even before the death of Calvin in 1564 there were Calvinist communities in France, England, Scotland and Holland, and before long also in colonial territories in North America and South Africa. In subsequent centuries the number of converts multiplied together with the number of new sects, and before long the universal Church, the body of bodies, was referred to merely as the 'Catholic' church and just as one denomination among others.

The war of all against all

What was unprecedented, and frightening, about this proliferation of languages, states and creeds was the incompatibility of the entities concerned and the radical demands made on their behalf. The many new bodies did not rest peacefully within one another, instead they rejected and repelled each other. It was as though the hands of the body had begun fighting each other or the stomach rebelled against the arms and the head.

The obvious solution was to look for a way of stitching the various body parts together again. Several such attempts were also made. Throughout Europe many a shrewd ruler – Henri IV of France comes to mind, or Johan III of Sweden – looked for ways of combining the new faith with the old. As it seemed at the time, political success belonged to the one who could unite all subjects behind the same throne and the same altar.[21] The Babylonian diversity of languages could also be addressed, scholars such as John Wilkins and G. W. Leibnitz insisted, by designing an entirely new language which all Europeans could start speaking.[22] For the same reason many had great hopes for the discipline of international law simultaneously being developed by lawyers in Catholic and Protestant countries.[23] Perhaps a common legal framework would allow the Europeans to sort out their differences.

As it turned out such attempts amounted to next to nothing. Syncreticising political leaders all came to a bad end; none of the artificial languages ever caught on; and international law was immediately rejected the moment it came to contradict with the imperatives of *raison d'état*. The idea of a united Europe seemed hopelessly anachronistic. The Treaty of Utrecht, 1712, was the last occasion on which a peace concluded between European states included references to the '*res publica Christiana*.' And while the Holy Roman

Empire would hang on for another 100 years, it was by the time it finally was abolished in 1806 as the joke went, neither holy, Roman, nor much of an empire.

The new era demanded people of a different ilk. The new cleavages forced everyone to take sides and to commit themselves wholeheartedly to their chosen causes. Europeans had to make up their minds regarding which language to write in, which king to fight for, and which religion to belong to, or their minds had to be made up for them. To pick one of these alternatives was to exclude oneself from all the others. Given this competitive social climate, no one could afford to be less than fully partisan. Intellectual positions hardened and people as well as institutions became far less tolerant. Suddenly all of Europe seemed to be filled with followers of sects, parties and factions.

Consider, for example, the position of the Catholic Church which became noticeably more combative after the Council of Trent 1563.[24] What previously had been a doctrine tentatively entertained now became an official dogma, and many ideas that hitherto had been freely discussed were banned. The Inquisition set to work rooting out heresies and one author after another was placed on the *Index* of forbidden books. Thus while Copernicus had been in the employ of the Church when he published his *De Revolutionibus* in 1543, Galilei ended up in prison for his theories a bit more than half a century later. The Church which in the Middle Ages had encompassed life in all its multicoloured diversity now became reactionary and for the first time 'medieval.'[25]

The critics of the established religious and political order – the reformers and the revolutionaries – were at least as dogmatic. In the vocabulary of the time they were often referred to as 'enthusiasts,' from the Greek *entheos* denoting a person 'possessed by the divine.' Enthusiasts were radical and dangerous since they paid no attention to traditional authorities but instead acted on superior commands. Enthusiasts were people on a mission from god and fully prepared to destroy the world for the sake of a victory for their particular vision of it. 'Enthusiasm,' according to the English philosopher Henry More's *Enthusiasmus triumphatus*, 1656, was founded in a 'distemper' that 'disposes a man to listen to the Magisterial Dictates of an over-bearing *Phansy*, more than to the calm and cautious insinuation of free *Reason*.'[26] 'Enthusiasts,' David Hume noted in 1777, are even rejecting morality

> and the fanatic madman delivers himself over, blindly, and without reserve, to the supposed illapses of the spirit, and to inspiration from above. Hope, pride, presumption, a warm imagination, together with ignorance, are, therefore, the true source of ENTHUSIASM.[27]

Enthusiasts, in short, were people guided by principles rather than by self-interest. This had devastating consequences since principles have to be universally applied whereas self-interest usually is more limited and parochial.[28] As Edmund Burke noted in 1790, 'the effect of the Reformation was to introduce other interests into all countries than those which arose from their locality and natural circumstances.'[29] The enthusiasts would stop at nothing except ultimate victory for their own side.

Enthusiasts who cannot agree with one another can only fight and next to permanent warfare – between religions, states and nations – characterised European history from the sixteenth century onward.[30] The religious conflict undermined the political order in Scandinavia, the Baltic provinces and in Poland, and it split Germany in half, first through civil wars and then through the Thirty Years War. Between 1618 and 1648 some 15 to 20 per cent of the population of the Holy Roman Empire died.[31] In France the religious wars raged continuously between 1562 and 1598. On the night of St Bartholomew, August 14, 1572, thousands of Protestants were massacred, and in 1628 the Huguenot community at La Rochelle gave up after a siege in which some 15,000 people perished.

In England the conflict between Catholics and Protestants led first to protracted struggles regarding the right of succession to the throne and later to the Puritan revolution and the civil war. In the conflict between king and parliament which began in 1642 tens of thousands of people died and in 1649 the king himself, Charles I, was beheaded. Three years later, although writing about an imaginary state of nature in *Leviathan*, Thomas Hobbes obviously had contemporary events firmly in mind. In the absence of a state, Hobbes explained:

> there is no place for Industry; because the fruit thereof is uncertain; and consequently no Culture of the Earth; no Navigation, nor use of the commodities that may be imported by Sea; no commodious Building; no Instruments of moving, and removing such things as require much force; no Knowledge of the face of the Earth; no account of Time; no Arts; no Letters; no Society; and which is worst of all, continuall feare, and danger of violent death.[32]

The state and its war on diversity

Among the various entities produced by the break-up of the medieval body, the state was the only one with credible pretensions to secular power. If order was to be restored, it would have to be through the agency of the state. In the end Europe returned to peace only once the idea of sovereignty had become more of a reality. In next to all cases, however, pacification meant repression. The state declared war on diversity and replaced the conflicting wills of conflicting groups with the imperatives of its own superior reason. As a result, from the latter part of the seventeenth century onward all countries became less rather than more diverse.

Consider first the notion of *raison d'état*. According to writers such as Niccolò Machiavelli and Giovanni Botero there were imperatives of statecraft that rulers ought to follow regardless of whichever policies they privately favoured. The most important such principle concerned military preparedness.

Only by strengthening its armies and assuming the worst could the state defend itself effectively against its enemies. Understood as a principle which could be calculated in a calm and methodical manner, *raison d'état* contrasted sharply with the passions that guided the many enthusiasts of the era. Far from following reason, these partisans and sectarians acted on impulse and as a result they did short-sighted and foolish things. Avoiding all enthusiasm, statesmen should instead, as Machiavelli explained, combine the ferocity of a lion with the slyness of a fox.[33]

This was also the way to assure domestic peace. According to the *raison d'état* doctrine, whatever maintained the peace was good and whatever threatened the peace was bad. This was the case even if the actions required by the prince in no way corresponded to the traditional precepts of morality. Sometimes the prince was required to break his word, to lie, or even to commit murder. In relation to other states princes could legitimately resort to violence and in relation to their own subjects they could resort to repression. In the end the only way to secure peace was to make sure that the interests of the parts were replaced by the interests of the whole; that the state imposed itself on the warring factions and disarmed them.

Unappealing as repression may appear to people from a more tolerant era, it had an obvious attraction to those who had lived through the turmoil of the religious wars. One such person was the French jurist and philosopher Jean Bodin. As he argued in *Six livres de la république*, 1576, peace required that all powers be vested in one person. Sovereignty is indivisible and the first prerogative of the ruler is to lay down the law to his subjects. If the people are allowed to dictate their own laws they will no longer be subjects and they will no longer obey; if power is shared it will immediately be contested and contestation will mean war.[34] 'I conclude then that it is never permissible for a subject to attempt anything against a sovereign prince, no matter how wicked and cruel a tyrant he may be.'[35]

In England Thomas Hobbes – he was also a civil war veteran – arrived at similar conclusions. What is needed, he explained, is a state with sufficient power to stop people from killing one another. He called this state 'Leviathan,' and he compared it to a 'mortall God' who maintained the peace by keeping men 'in awe.'[36] Sovereignty could not be divided, Hobbes agreed with Bodin, '[f]or what is it to divide the Power of a Common-wealth, but to Dissolve it; for Powers divided mutually destroy each other.'[37] For this reason all factions should be banned and no parties or intermediary groups should be allowed that could gather in opposition to the state or to each other. Instead of being members of factions, men found themselves alone and it was alone – as one man to another – that they were to be reunited in and through the state.[38]

As Hobbes knew, however, repression was not likely to be enough. For peace to be secure people had to learn to accept their powerlessness and their subjugation. To this end Leviathan had to manipulate people's minds not just their bodies. The state had to control which books that were printed and what people read and in this way to pre-empt sedition. In addition, Hobbes suggested,

Leviathan should embark on a programme of education.[39] He envisioned weekly assemblies where people would get together to praise God but also the state and where the laws of the country would be read and the duties of the subjects expounded on. In this way, Hobbes hoped, the people would learn to love Leviathan and never 'to argue and dispute his Power, or any way to use his Name irreverently.'[40]

Although no European ruler ever quite lived up to these absolutist ideals, peace was eventually restored more or less in the manner which Bodin and Hobbes had suggested. In France the Edict of Nantes of 1598 had given the Huguenots the right to practise their religion but when the liberal king Henri IV was assassinated in 1610 the policy of toleration came to an end.[41] Under the influence of the cardinals Richelieu and Mazarin the agreement was progressively whittled down until in 1685 it finally was completely revoked. From this time onward France was a country which at least in the official propaganda was united behind *un roi, une loi* and *une foi*.

In Germany the Reformation had not only pitted the many small statelets against one another but also divided them internally. Here there was no strong central state that could impose a uniform religious creed on the warring factions and instead the power to homogenise the population was itself decentralised. In 1555 the Treaty of Augsburg established the principle of *eius cuius, eius religio*, according to which the religion of the people in any given territory had to follow the religion of their ruler. It did not matter what people believed, in other words, as long as they all believed the same thing. Those who did not freely conform to this demand were either expelled or converted by force.[42]

Meanwhile in Austria the Habsburgs moved in a similar direction. Despite sizeable Protestant communities among mine workers, craftsmen, and among the Czech nobility, the emperors enforced an increasingly pro-Catholic line. During the Thirty Years War Vienna was the leading proponent of the Counter-Reformation and in 1658 the emperor Leopold I took it as his personal goal to root out all non-Catholic heresies.[43] As a result some 100,000 Protestants fled, much to the economic detriment of the country. Jews too were expelled and the synagogue in Vienna was turned into a church. By the year 1700, there were only Catholics in Bohemia, Moravia and Austria.

In northern Europe the kings basically followed the same *modus operandi*. Here one version of Protestantism was elevated to the status of official state religion and all rival creeds outlawed, including rival Protestant ones. In England the Act of Supremacy of 1549 made King Henry VIII into the head of the Anglican church and forced his subjects to pray to god according to a state authorised ritual. When during the reign of his daughter the question of royal succession came to be defined as a matter of religious allegiance, to belong to the wrong sect was not only to commit a religious but also a political crime. The solution was similar in Sweden.[44] Here all clergymen were on the state's payroll and all the king's subjects were forced by law to attend church. Not surprisingly the Sunday sermon proved to be an indispensable instrument of state propaganda and as such quite close to the educational ideal which Hobbes had envisioned.

In fact, in addition to overt repression, all European states began dabbling in Hobbesian style indoctrination. Although it only paid off in the slightly longer term, the moulding of minds was likely to be less costly than the controlling of bodies, and eventually also more successful. Through education, a love of king and country was to be instilled and people convinced to put aside their differences and instead to look at the many things they had in common. A popular strategy was to elevate one particular way of life to 'national' status while making other ways of life 'provincial' and thereby of lesser worth.[45] In most cases the national culture came to be the one associated with the political elite in the capital city. Languages were unified in the same manner as scholars began compiling national dictionaries and grammars. Suddenly there was a linguistic standard that the state could insist on and traditional ways of expressing oneself were no longer just different but grammatically and socially incorrect.

New institutions were put in place to police these new cultural standards. In 1635 for example the Academie Française was established with the aim of restoring order to the French language. In the patent granted to the academy by the king, the parallel was explicitly drawn between the confusion brought about by religious and political diversity and by the diversity of languages.[46] By making all people talk in the same manner, the hope was that they would come to think the same way. Following the French lead all European countries established a number of similar, homogenising, institutions: cultural academies, theatres and museums, and, in the nineteenth-centurym also systems of public education.[47]

The eventual result of this combination of repression and indoctrination were countries that were far more homogenous than they ever previously had been. At the same time, however, Europe as a whole became far more diverse. From the seventeenth century onward pluralism was banned from each state but it reappeared instead in the interstices between states.[48] Within each unit power was supposed to be absolute but between them power was definitely relative. The Treaty of Westphalia signed in 1648 symbolised this solution. Simultaneously rejecting the universalism and the localism of the Middle Ages, the states were declared sovereign but also powerless in relation to each other. During the following 350 years inter-state wars raged more or less continuously across Europe. Instead of people dying for their personal beliefs as they had during the religious wars of the sixteenth and early seventeenth centuries, they now died for their countries. As the kings and the many apologists for the state insisted, this represented real progress.

11 The polite alternative

The eventual solution to the problem of pluralism was to provide individuals with rights that were institutionally protected and policed. Once institutionalised, conflicts between competing claims could be adjudicated through rules which were procedural rather than substantive. By never consistently favouring any one party, the rules convinced people to play fairly and to act tolerantly. People were loyal not only to themselves but also to the institutions through which their conflicts were resolved. Although this solution may seem obvious enough, it took an exceedingly long time before it became universally accepted. Throughout Europe state repression and indoctrination continued well into the nineteenth century and it was only in the latter part of the twentieth century that all authoritarian regimes finally were discredited. But even today not everyone is a pluralist and, as we discussed, fundamentalism constantly reappears in one or another of its ever mutating guises.

Since this institutional answer seems obvious to us it is tempting to believe that it was inevitable. It is the most reasonable solution to the problem of pluralism after all, and since we like to think of ourselves as reasonable people we are not surprised that this is the solution we eventually arrived at. And yet as we discussed in the introduction, institutions do not emerge simply because they are needed. Institutions develop for all kinds of reasons, most of them completely unrelated to the functions that eventually come to justify their existence. Thus even the most reasonable of institutions can be the product of processes that have no rational pedigree. And as far as the reasonableness of the Europeans themselves is concerned, the causal relationship is most likely the inverse. Our institutions are tolerant not because we are, but rather, we have come to be reasonable because our institutions have taught us tolerance.

The aim of this chapter is to provide a more acceptable historical explanation of the emergence of these institutions. This is essentially the story of politeness and of the political culture of polite society, especially as it developed in the course of the eighteenth century.

Machines vs. organisms

In the eighteenth century a resistance movement of sorts developed among members of the new middle classes, although the aristocracy too played a prominent part. Considering the dominant socio-economic position of these groups, combined with the fact that they were almost completely excluded from political power, the demands of this movement were surprisingly moderate. Often no political demands at all were expressed. If one had eavesdropped on one of their gatherings, one would instead have heard a mixture of society gossip, impromptu reviews of the latest opera or play, and occasional attempts at philosophical witticisms. Conversations on such topics were the preoccupation of what at the time was known as 'polite society,' and it was through their very socialising rather than through any explicit political activities that they came to constitute a radical alternative to the repressive state.

The location of these gatherings is itself significant. Members of polite society met in coffee-houses, Masonic lodges, reading rooms and secret societies or in the drawing-rooms and *salons* of the *haute bourgeoisie*.[1] What places such as these had in common was an ambiguous social position somewhere between the public arena of the state and the privacy of the home. They were public in the sense that they allowed people to socialise outside of their immediate families, but they were private in that they were located outside of the purview of the state. They were places where people could meet up with strangers but in an informal, even intimate, fashion. Here people could reach out to each other without exposing themselves to intimidation; they could talk politics and make friends without the state ever finding out. They were protected above all by the fellowship created through the conversations they managed to strike up.

Etymologically speaking, 'politeness' is derived from the Italian *pulitezza* or *politezza* denoting 'cleanliness,' but in the Renaissance the word increasingly came to refer to the kind of 'polish' a person would acquire as a result of rubbing shoulders with people of manners and good breeding.[2] However, those who lacked the opportunity to learn directly from their social superiors could learn polite behaviour from books.[3] One example is *Il Cortegiano* from 1528 in which Baldesar Castiglione provided extensive advice on how young men and women should carry themselves if they ever were to find themselves at court.[4] Another example is Erasmus of Rotterdam's *De civilitate morum puerilium* from 1530, where the children of the upwardly mobile middle-classes were taught everything from table manners to the importance of controlling the body, its movements and urges.[5]

To have mastered these rules was to be 'civilised,' from the Latin *civilis*, derived from *civis*, meaning city.[6] Just as city-dwellers often think of themselves as superior to country bumpkins, members of civilised society thought of themselves as superior to uncouth peasants and the urban poor. In addition the word *civilis* was full of references to classical Greek and Roman ideals.[7] To be civilised was necessarily, as Aristotle and Cicero had taught, to exist with and for others; it was to be a social being rather than an atomised individual sufficient onto oneself. And politeness was the code which made such a social existence possible; a knowledge of the code allowed people both to get along and to get ahead.

Today politeness and sociability are not commonly regarded as subversive qualities but in the eighteenth century they were, and the reason is that they highlighted the stark differences that existed between the ethos of civil society and the ethos of the repressive state.[8] From the point of view of the authorities, associations of whatever kind were potential threats to the social order and sociability was for that reason regarded with utmost suspicion. Sociability meant concerted action and concerted action, as the history of the sixteenth and seventeenth centuries had demonstrated, meant civil war. The repressive solution was thus to break up all associations, to isolate individuals from each other and to reunite them only in and through the state. As the members of polite society saw it, however, this was no life fit for a human being. '[A] life without natural affection, friendship or sociableness,' as Anthony Ashley Cooper, third Earl of Shaftesbury, put it in his *Characteristics of Men, Manners, Opinions, Times*, 1711, 'would be found a wretched one, were it to be tried.'[9]

> Nothing is so delightful as to incorporate. Distinctions of many kinds are invented. Religious societies are formed. Orders are erected, and their interests espoused and served with the utmost zeal and passion. . . . the associating genius of man is never better proved than in those very societies which are formed in opposition to the general one of mankind and to the real interest of the State.[10]

What we have are thus two competing conceptions of what it means to be a human being. Or perhaps better put, one official version and one subterranean. The official conception which Hobbes and Bodin presented – and which Defoe popularised and Rousseau and Kant further developed – saw man as autonomous, self-sufficient and utility-maximising. The subterranean version, advocated by Shaftesbury and by the members of polite society – as well as by all enthusiastic members of eighteenth-century consumer society – saw man as fundamentally sociable, always dependent on others, and ready to defer to the common judgement. And people today are of course still torn between the same two conceptions. Curiously, however, we rarely notice the tension between them and manage somehow to simultaneously embrace both.[11] Formally we sign up to the official version but secretly we know that our lives would be unbearable unless we based them on the subterranean.

In this respect members of polite eighteenth-century society were more consistent. They rejected the Hobbesian individual as a superficial exaggeration and they despised the Hobbesian state. The problem with the repressive solution as they saw it was that it was far too mechanical.[12] People were combined by means of legal obligations enforced by an all-powerful state machinery but as a result their union lacked any form of sympathy or social commitment. The choice of metaphor was not coincidental. In the seventeenth century there was a great interest in mechanical devices of all kinds and it was common to compare the state to a 'clockwork.'[13] In several respects this metaphor simply replicated the worldview conveyed by the traditional metaphor of society understood as a body. Just as a body, a clock was a unified entity which consisted of many hierarchically ordered parts, each one with its separate functions. In contrast to the body however the clockwork was a mechanical device rather than an organism and as such it was fully determined by physical forces.[14] The state-as-machine was far more repressive and more ruthless; it had no willpower and no soul and it was impossible to appeal to or reason with.

As the apologists of the mechanical state made clear, all subjects of the king were parts of this machine and they were forced to carry out their duties with perfect precision or the clockwork would immediately break down. As far as the king himself was concerned, he was the machine's master yet as such he was nothing like the arbitrary rulers of the previous era. The king too was constrained by mechanical imperatives; he was, as Frederick the Great of Prussia had said about himself, 'merely the first servant of the state.'[15] Or to be more precise, the king was the operator who serviced the machine, polished its parts and applied oil to any wheels that happened to be squeaking. To successfully carry out such tasks he had to become something of an expert in mechanical engineering.[16] While statecraft in the Renaissance had been a matter of stagecraft, it was now, according to this interpretation, all a matter of political technology.

The rules according to which the mechanical state operated were exclusively those of *raison d'état*. Understood as a mechanical device, the state had no particular purpose or agenda apart from the one overriding aim of keeping the peace. The one obligation on the part of the ruler was to make sure the clock kept ticking and whatever action that served this purpose was considered acceptable. Yet the state was amoral rather than immoral; it advocated no particular ethical standards and was in theory at least neutral between competing political and religious goals.[17] In this way public actions came to be sharply separated from private beliefs and the power of the state came, often quite explicitly, to be based on hypocrisy. From the point of view of the king it never really mattered whether people were Catholics or Protestants as long as they were one or the other and as long as they united, faithfully, behind the crown. In the end people could even be free to disagree as long as they never acted on their convictions. 'Argue,' as Frederick the Great put it, 'but obey!'[18]

In all these respects polite society constituted a radical contrast. Polite society was not understood as a mechanical device at all but instead as an organic unit. Its members were not united through contracts but instead through natural affinities and shared social bonds. Far from being sufficient onto themselves, individuals were only something when acting and interacting together with their fellows. Instead of lies and hypocrisy, polite society was a realm of honesty and truth, and instead of moral blindness there was moral purpose. In addition to pleasant company, sociability cultivated a sense of civic virtue.[19] Given the obvious appeal of these many honourable qualities, it is easy to understand why the representatives of the mechanical state were worried.

As far as resistance movements go, polite society was of course extremely badly organised and its political programme was nothing if not diffuse. Instead its power lay exclusively in the alternative it provided and the example it set.

By merely meeting and talking together it highlighted the shortcomings of the mechanical state. At the same time, since the meetings took place in private – or, as with the Masons, in secret – they were impossible for the state to control.[20] Shielded from the repressive power of the state, people were free to speak their minds on whatever topics they wished. The way these conversations were conducted embodied a new vision of social life. Although polite society was understood as an organic unit, it was not a hierarchically ordered entity like the medieval metaphor of the body. Instead the members were all on an equal footing; among friends in the *salon* or the coffee-house everyone was a brother and a friend.[21] In all these respects – embracing the notions of *liberté*, *egalité* and *fraternité* – polite society became a model for how society could be organised if only the mechanical state somehow could be overthrown.[22] When towards the end of the eighteenth century the demands for change became increasingly vocal, and when the *anciens régimes* eventually fell, it was in the image of the polite alternative that the new states were erected.

Learning how to get along

Although freedom, brotherhood and equality are attractive qualities, they do not by themselves make the problem of pluralism go away, and polite society was always at least as exposed to the threat of conflicts as ever the mechanical state. The way this threat was dealt with was, however, far more sophisticated. The most obvious difference concerned politeness itself. To be polite is to know how to get along with others and how not to do or say things that might offend. To be polite is to recognise others as worthy of respect and to listen to their opinions even though one profoundly may disagree with them.[23] Politeness, that is, requires acceptance; in polite society dissent was not repressed but tolerated.

Consider for example the informal rules that govern the art of conversation.[24] As a participant in a conversation there are certain things you can and cannot do. For example: you are supposed to make other participants feel at ease, to include those who sit silent, and if at all possible to give everybody the sense that their particular contributions matter above the rest. It is impolite to interrupt others when they are talking and you are not supposed to monopolise the topic of the conversation or to take it in a direction where others are unwilling to go. For the conversation to flow smoothly it is important not to give offence but it is equally important not to take offence too easily. Everybody should have a chance to talk and everybody should be obliged to listen.

Since the members of polite society spent such a lot of their time talking, they were naturally all familiar with such rules. And those who failed to follow them were given social rather than physical punishments. No heavy-handed repression was required, a raised eyebrow or a humorous reproach would usually be enough to set the offender straight.[25] But for the most part, the rules were self-policing. Conversations resemble games and just as games they force their participants to develop a double set of loyalties. You are required, simultaneously, to assume a particular and a general point of view.[26]

On the one hand, participants in a conversation want to express their opinions and make their points as forcefully and persuasively as they possibly can. They want, in short, to win the argument. On the other hand, they also want to make sure that the conversation keeps going and that the other participants do not fall silent or walk away. To cheat in a game is to deceive your fellow players but it is also in a sense to deceive yourself. And exactly analogously, to win an argument by breaking the conversational rules is to undermine the very notion of a victory.

From a conversational perspective, pluralism is not a problem or a threat but instead something of a requirement. For a conversation to really take off, it must include different kinds of people with different kinds of experiences and outlooks on life.[27] If everybody sees things the same way after all there are no views to exchange and nothing to talk about. All good conversationalists are aware of this fact and adjust their contributions accordingly. If the conversation matters to you, your own – 'real' – opinions matter less than whatever opinions you are required to express by the situation in which the flow of the conversation places you. Often you will end up playing the devil's advocate or gently disagreeing just to make the exchange more engaging. But just as often self-regulation operates in the opposite direction. Instead of exaggerating their opinions, people moderate them; complete disagreement is after all just as much of a threat as complete agreement. Those who care about the conversation will consequently calibrate their views to prevent both outcomes. In the vocabulary of the eighteenth century, this moderated, calibrated, opinion came to be known as a *sensus communis*, the considered judgement – the 'common sense' – of a community taken as a whole.[28]

As the participants in polite society went on to explain, common sense also provided protection against the kinds of enthusiasm that had overcome people in the seventeenth century. From a polite point of view, the partisans, sectarians and ideologues had not been wrong as much as uncouth and badly mannered. Since they already knew the truth, they had no reason to listen to others or to exchange views, and a conversation was understood only an opportunity to convince others of the correctness of their own firmly held positions. This made them strident, judgemental and preachy; enthusiasts were quick to walk off in a huff and they never cared if they gave offence. Socially they were bores and politically they were fanatics.

As the members of polite society concluded, bad manners and fanaticism were both the results of an insufficient exposure to social life.[29] It was only sad and lonely characters who became enthusiasts. Robinson Crusoe's conclusion, quoted above – to the effect that life alone was 'better than the utmost enjoyment of humane society in the world' since solitude allowed him to 'converse mutually with my own thoughts' – was from a polite perspective completely perverse.[30] Thinking only with and of themselves these self-sufficient Robinsonians never developed the ability to see the world from other people's point of view. They were easily carried away since they belonged to no social context that could keep them in place; never for a moment would they suspend their judge-ments. Not surprisingly Defoe himself was a Presbyterian educated at Morton's Academy for Dissenters, a hotbed of enthusiasm.[31]

Contrast this conception of the person with the ideal of the English gentleman or the French *homme de lettres*.[32] Both lived profoundly social lives, constantly engaging with others, talking, making jokes and showing off. As both firmly believed, freedom was not to be found in the absence of others but instead in their presence; only social beings were able to develop their full human potential. Hence social success and personal development both depended crucially on a person's ability to get along with others. Principles and views, stubbornly adhered to, were only obstacles in this regard. Instead gentlemen and *hommes de lettres* were often cynics; they never held any firm opinions of any kind or took nothing for granted except their own social position.

The conversational ideal was equally opposed to the mechanical ideology of the Hobbesian state. Understood as a conflict resolving device, politeness was not only more attractive than state repression but it was also likely to be more effective. Since people were moderating their views by themselves, fanaticism could be held at bay and no Leviathan was needed to keep order. In fact from a conversational point of view, the Hobbesian state was at least as repugnant as ever Hobbesian individuals, and much for the same reason.[33] By isolating its citizens from one another, the state made it impossible for them to benefit from the interaction with their fellow man. As isolated, people were unable to talk to one another and in this way, instead of dealing with fanaticism, the state provided the preconditions for it.

The fundamental problem with the mechanical state, just as the fundamental problem with the enthusiasts, was that it was impossible to engage in conversation. The aim of the state, as Hobbes had argued, was to keep its subjects 'in awe.' Awe, however, is a kind of stupor which numbs and dumbfounds us, and as numbed and dumbfounded we are unable to fulfil our obligations as members of polite society. A person struck by awe cannot talk.[34] For this reason, the Hobbesian individuals were 'awful' in the precise, technical, sense that the state 'filled them with awe,' thereby overwhelming and pacifying them.[35] Instead of enthusiasts who always talked, and a state that never listened, a solution to the problem of pluralism required people who could do both.

From civility to civil rights

Despite its many attractive features the polite alternative eventually failed. Or rather, while it continued to define the culture of a small, socially cohesive elite, it never managed to solve the problem of pluralism in society at large. There are several reasons for this failure. On the most basic level there was a problem of size. For a conversation to flow naturally the number of people engaged in it can never rise above a certain limit. As more and more participants are included, it becomes increasingly difficult for each person to make a contribution and after a while it is even difficult to hear what others are saying.

For this reason alone social life as a whole could never model itself on polite society.

There were also social obstacles. Like most groups, polite society had quite specific criteria for membership, determining who could be included in its ranks and who excluded.[36] By their very nature such rules were discriminatory. Notions such as 'civility' and 'civilisation' always had the function of keeping the lower classes out, or for that matter people living in non-European societies.[37] Membership in polite society equalled more than anything membership in the European upper-classes. The *salon* and the gentleman's club had no place for uncouth workers in dirty overalls or for naked natives with bones in their noses. Equally, the coffee-houses never accepted customers who could not afford to pay for their drinks.

As far as the members of polite society were concerned this was of course just as well. Workers, the poor, and anyone from a non-European part of the world often seemed very angry and they usually made all kinds of unreasonable demands. Often they had no respect for the rules of polite conversation and preferred instead to fight for their beliefs, if need be with weapons in hand. They were not cynical, they were not witty, and not self-deprecating; instead they believed in things, above all in the justice of their own chosen causes. As such they were exactly the kind of enthusiasts that polite culture always had sought to exclude.

Differently put, polite society in its eighteenth-century version was always far too culturally specific. This solution to the problem of pluralism depended on the mores of a particular social class living in a particular time and place but it could not be extended much further. It worked well as long as the ruling class was small and cohesive but once people outside of the establishment began making political demands it quickly became irrelevant. As a cultural solution unique to a specific group politeness was never able to deal with conflicts occurring across cultural divides. Once anti-colonial and working class movements began formulating their demands towards the end of the nineteenth century, all talk of 'civilisation' was quickly revealed as a racist or a classist ploy. And before long all the problems of pluralism, enthusiasm and conflict, reappeared.

Instead the eventual solution to the problem of pluralism was far closer to Hobbes' original suggestion. The solution was to vest people with rights and to enshrine them in a legal code.[38] Compared to the informal rules governing conversations, formal legal codes have many advantages. Rights are universal, given equally to everyone, and limited only by the stipulation that the right of one person should be compatible with the rights of others. Rights, furthermore, are clearly spelled out and explicitly enforced. We know what is required of us and what happens if we refuse to play by the rules. As bearers of rights people are entitled to do or to say whatever they want and to be whichever kind of person they like. If someone infringes on our rights we can take them to court and lawyers will settle the matter on our behalf.

From the point of view of the members of polite society this solution was obviously quite unacceptable.[39] As they saw it talk of rights was simply a way of legitimising a Hobbesian state; the whole ethos of the legal system was focused on the separation of bodies and on crowd control. The bearers of rights had no reason to be polite to each other or to moderate their views; everyone could scream and no one could tell them to be quiet. Actually there was no reason to even talk. You could just go about your own business, do your own thing while letting others do theirs, and then trusting the legal system to deal with any disagreements. Conflicts between rights were resolved in the courts rather than through the careful self-calibration of a *sensus communis*. The rights solution, just as the Hobbesian state, was mechanical and hopelessly impolite.

Not surprisingly perhaps this kind of legalism was more commonly associated with repressive states than with those of mixed or republican government.[40] It was in repressive states above all that human beings were atomised, equalised and separated from each other, and it was here that legal systems in the course of the eighteenth century were introduced as a means of organising the state machineries. As Baron de Montesquieu pointed out, republics require their citizens to be virtuous and to dedicate themselves to the common good, and as long as this is the case they have less need for laws.[41] Monarchies, on the other hand, have no common good and require no civic virtue, instead it is legal provisions that keep them together. Laws are the way in which monarchies make up for the fact that their subjects lack sociability.

And yet a compromise of sorts was eventually arrived at. The rights that had mattered in the seventeenth century – we discussed this above – were primarily property rights. It was by establishing and securing property rights that markets came to flourish. In the eighteenth century, however, the emphasis was rather on what came to be known as 'civil' rights: on rights of free speech, rights of assembly, freedom of the press, freedom of access to information, and so on. Obviously rights such as these do require a measure of sociability; they presuppose communication and a sense of community. Although the language in which they were couched was quite uncouth, civil rights could be seen as concessions to polite ideals. They were an institutionalised expression of the values of polite society but cast in the idiom of rights rather than cultural norms. The obligation of a conversationalist to listen now became a right to speak; the obligation not to give offence became a right not to be offended; the obligation to include everybody became a right of participation. Once institutionalised in this manner the public conversation could – in theory at least – include many more people, and people derived from more diverse social backgrounds.

12 Institutions dealing with conflicts

The shortcomings of the polite solution were more than anything determined by the limitations of its own logic. The culture of a particular group can only be relied on to deal with problems of pluralism to the extent that the culture in question is granted a pre-eminent status. It is only if one culture stands above all the others that it is able to mediate between them.[1] For a while the polite upper-class culture of eighteenth-century society was able to impose itself in this manner but by the nineteenth century this was no longer the case. If we deny that there are superior cultures – and we do – the problem of pluralism can have no cultural solution.

This is where legal institutions, briefly discussed above, came to the rescue. Institutions are far more robust than cultures. It is easier to portray them as impartial and they suffer fewer social constraints; institutions can accommodate more, and more diverse kinds of, people. In the course of the eighteenth century civil rights were added to property rights and all rights were then integrated into a legal system which was policed by the state. The legal system operated according to procedural rather than substantive rules. The question was not which belief, view or interest that was the best, but rather which beliefs, views or interests that could be integrated with which others. In principle every belief, view or interest was allowed which did not infringe on the rights of others.

While this worked well enough in theory there were bound to be problems with the application. Above all a legalistic solution to the problem of pluralism is associated with prohibitively high transaction costs. It is expensive for the state to define the law and to police it and for individuals it is often a waste of time and money to defend themselves in court.[2] Lawyers, as we all know, have a way of getting their cut. In order to bring down the cost of conflict resolution a way had to be found for people to settle their differences without constant recourse to the law. Ideally the execution of justice should be decentralised, automatic and instantaneous. In order to avoid both lawyers and renewed conflict, people should somehow be convinced to police themselves. And yet, as the experiences of the preceding centuries had demonstrated, such self-policing was often impossible to establish. Decentralised and instantaneous justice had often been just another name for civil war. In the latter part of the eighteenth century, however, such a solution was indeed discovered, both within the sphere of politics and the sphere of economics. This aim of this chapter is to briefly tell the story of how this came about.

Self-regulating mechanisms

Again the conversational culture of polite society provided the prototype for the solution. When engaged in conversation, we said above, people are sometimes required to exaggerate their views and sometimes required to moderate them; sometimes we agree even with views we find objectionable and sometimes we disagree for the sake of disagreeing. In this way the various contributions to the discussion will naturally come to balance each other, extreme opinions will be eliminated and the conversation as a whole will converge towards a commonsensical mean. Conversations, in short, are self-balancing and self-regulating. Thus understood, a conversation can be compared to a device like a float-level regulator, a thermostat or a pressure cooker with a safety valve.[3] The point of these devices is to maintain a constant output of water, heat or pressure even as the input is dramatically raised or dramatically lowered. The conflicting forces are set off against each other as a push in one direction triggers an automatic pull in the opposite direction which restores the balance. Just as in a conversation, equilibrium is not a result of harmony but of the interaction of opposing forces.

Today people are used to seeing self-regulating mechanisms everywhere in nature and in society but this is a thoroughly modern predilection. As it turns out the idea of self-regulation was only discovered sometime towards the end of the seventeenth century and Isaac Newton is one of the first to have discussed it.[4] In his *Principia*, 1687, Newton described how the planets in our galaxy form a system kept together by nothing except the planets' own gravitational pull. Fascinated by such self-government, Adam Smith, in an early essay on the history of astronomy, talked about 'the invisible hand of Jupiter.'[5] Similarly in 1752 David Hume discussed the curious way in which water always remains at level; if raised in one place, he pointed out, 'the superior gravity of that part not being balanced, must depress it, till it meets a counterpoise.'[6] A similar observation was made by the botanist Carl Linnæus when travelling through the southern Swedish province of Småland in 1746.[7] The peasants use churchyard soil for their cabbage patches, he noticed, and in this way 'human heads turn into cabbage heads which turn into human heads, and so on.'

Self-balancing mechanisms were not only discovered, however, but also invented. The first was probably the thermostatic regulator constructed by the Dutch alchemist Cornelis Drebbel in the early seventeenth century in order to keep the temperature constant in chicken incubators.[8] Similarly, in 1681, Denis Papin approached the Royal Society in London with his invention of a safety valve intended for controlling the steam pressure in a boiler. A few years later the philosopher G. W. Leibniz proposed a self-regulating solution to the problem of how to adjust the pace of rotating machines such as windmills. The most famous self-regulating device, however, was the governor that controlled the speed of the steam engine. Here, as the rotation of the engine increased, weights attached to the shaft made sure that the supply of steam was cut, effectively reducing the engine's speed. From *kubernetes*, the Greek for 'governor,' the term 'cybernetics' was eventually coined for this science of communication, feedbacks and control.[9]

Understood as a metaphor the self-regulating system had obvious advantages over the metaphor of the clockwork.[10] The clockwork was at the same time too deterministic and too static; it left far too much power to the original clock-maker and not enough power to the clock's constituent parts. The clock was always prone to breakdowns, and when they occurred it was never quite clear what to do. Once society came to be understood as a self-balancing device, however, much more freedom was given to individuals and groups. There was no need for a central authority that directed social life and repressed diversity in the name of peace. People could act passionately, even selfishly or aggressively, as long as the passion, selfishness and aggression of one party was counter-acted by that of another. The differences complemented each other or cancelled each other out and the aggregate pattern that emerged was one of concord rather than discord.

In a conversation, we said, participants are guided by two ostensibly contra-dictory goals. While they want to make their points, they also must make sure that the conversation continues. In an exactly analogous manner, rights can only successfully be defended by people who acknowledge the validity of the system of rights as a whole and the authority of the courts to enforce it. Success-ful conflict resolution will in this way always presuppose a double set of loyal-ties: both to oneself and to the system as a whole. Such double loyalty would never come naturally to Robinsonian individuals who never considered anyone else's interests but their own but to the civilised members of polite society the requirement was obvious.[11]

While the ingeniousness of this solution never was in doubt, the question was whether actual examples of self-regulating devices could be put together and, if they could, whether they really would work. There are two prominent examples both launched at the end of the eighteenth century: a system of self-regulating politics and a system of self-regulating economics.

A system of politics

In politics the idea of cybernetics was first applied to relations obtaining between states. Ever since the state began making claims to sovereignty the question had been how to deal with the problem of competing sovereignties. *Raison d'état* required each state to look after its own interests but as a result there was no one looking after the interests of the system taken as a whole. The result was a perpetual threat of war, all too often replaced by actual cases of warfare.

The solution first discovered among the many small city-states of northern

Italy was to balance the power of one state against the power of another.[12] By concluding alliances and by pooling resources with others one's enemies could be convinced to refrain from attack. In this way peace could be maintained without common decisions, central direction or overt repression. Peace was instead the unintended result of states pursuing their own interests.[13] If a state suddenly began to grow too powerful, the logic required the relatively less powerful states to gather together to oppose it. Or if a state suddenly began losing power, the logic identified it as an increasingly attractive partner in an alliance. And while the balance of power thus understood failed to prevent some wars, the assumption was that there were far more wars that it prevented.

In this way, during the Thirty Years War in the seventeenth century – a conflict ostensibly fought for religious reasons – Protestant Sweden joined together with Catholic France to oppose the armies of the Habsburg Empire. In fact the Swedish king went as far as holding talks with Muslim leaders about an anti-Austrian alliance. And by the time of the peace treaty concluded in Westphalia in 1648, the balance of power was a universally recognised principle of statecraft. Half a century later, the Treaty of Utrecht, 1713, was explicitly dedicated to ordering and stabilising the peace and tranquillity of the Christian world through 'a just balance of power.'[14]

Yet balances of power could also help preserve the peace within a country, and proposals to this effect had already been suggested by the ancients. As both Aristotle and the Greek historian Polybius had argued, power had to be divided so as not to end up in the hands of only one social class.[15] In Aristotle's preferred scheme – known as the *politeia* – a strong middle-class would moderate the inevitable opposition between the rich and the poor, and in Polybius' *monarchia mixta*, the aristocracy maintained the balance between the king and his subjects.[16] Polybius in particular was widely read in the Renaissance and he was a direct inspiration when the Venetian statesman Gasparo Contarini in 1543 described the constitution of his native city as 'equally balanced, as it were with a pair of weights.'[17] In seventeenth-century England references to a 'balanced constitution' were common among monarchists and republicans alike and even in Sweden classical authors provided intellectual support for a 'mixed' regime.[18]

And yet what these classical references and their domestic applications referred to was not actually a self-regulating device.[19] A scale after all does not balance itself. Lacking a feedback loop and an equilibrating mechanism, scales have to be balanced by someone or by something. In its rhetorical use the metaphor would thus often simply imply that one social class should be given more power at the expense of another. This is why apologists for unlimited monarchy also occasionally used the same language.[20] After all, if a society really was 'off balance,' a king may be the only person capable of bringing it back to equilibrium. Contrast this with the way the mechanism worked in relations between states where balances were supposed to be achieved automatically and without the intervention of a balancer.

It took a long time before notions of self-regulation began to be consistently applied in the domestic arena. Instead well into the eighteenth century traditional metaphors describing the state in terms of a body or a clockwork continued to dominate. Politically speaking, self-regulation must have appeared as a thoroughly perilous project. Self-balancing did away with the notion that people and groups had a given place in society and that social positions were hierarchically ordered. As decentralised and independent of each other, individuals and groups were instead each other's equals. Self-balance also seemed to imply that society was rife with divisions and that no unity or consensus could be reached. Indeed, self-balance seemed to require conflicts and thus to create more problems than it solved.

This is how we best should understand the perennial fear of parties. The etymology of the word illustrates what was at stake.[21] Derived from the Latin *partire*, 'to divide,' a party was a part, a faction, or a section of the whole. And while parts of course had existed in both bodies and in clocks, they had always, when properly assembled and directed, functioned together with other parts. The whole was prior to the part and the part had no function except as a part of the whole. Parties by contrast were partisan, they seemed to care little about the common good and instead only about their own interests.

Not surprisingly, parties were universally condemned by the voices of the establishment. In England, Jonathan Swift defined a party as 'the madness of many, for the gain of the few,' and Viscount Bolingbroke referred to them in his pamphlet *The Idea of a Patriot King*, 1749, as 'numbers of men associated together for certain purposes and certain interests, which are not allowed to be, those of the community by others.'[22] Actually anti-establishment groups were often equally critical. Even the most utopian of political tracts, such as those written by the Diggers, Levellers and other seventeenth-century radicals, defined the good society as one without parties.[23] And while settlers in the North American colonies became revolutionaries in 1776, they were partisan only on behalf of the unity of their new republic. When he addressed the convention assembled to ratify the new constitution in 1788, Alexander Hamilton hoped 'to abolish factions, and unite all parties for the general welfare.'[24] Similarly George Washington devoted a large part of his farewell address of 1796 to solemnly warn his people against 'the baneful effects of the spirit of party.'[25] Come to think of it, 'bipartisanship' is still considered a great virtue in an American politician.

And yet as Aristotle had declared, and as members of polite eighteenth-century society constantly reiterated, man is a social animal and it is for that reason surely impossible to suppress the desire to associate with others. In Lord Shaftesbury's words, the spirit of faction 'seems to be no other than the abuse or irregularity of that social love and common affection which is natural to mankind.'[26] While we would like to identify with universal goods or with the interests of society as a whole, this is in practice next to impossible to do. Instead we identify more easily with others the smaller and more intimate the group. This is how we end up as party members. Or, as even Washington was forced to concede, the spirit of parties 'unfortunately, is inseparable from our nature, having its root in the strongest passions of the human mind.'[27]

Having reached this point, a common conclusion was to praise one's own sociability while condemning the sociability of one's opponents. Thus the members of polite society would always see themselves as above partisanship and guided only by the general interest while everyone else – the uncouth and the impolite – were defending their own narrow points of view.[28] Similarly, leading politicians would sometimes dream of establishing a party that would unite everybody under its banners and once and for all do away with the need for parties.[29] Needless to say the problem of pluralism could never be resolved in this fashion. The disinterested opinion of one group would inevitably be contradicted by the opinion of another group, claiming to be equally disinterested. And the party to do away with all parties never remained unopposed for very long.

Society was thus facing a dilemma. Parties were not only evil but also necessary, and from the end of the eighteenth century it was as necessary evils that they came to be discussed. By this time, however, people were far better acquainted with practical examples of self-regulating devices and, as it seemed to many, the cybernetic metaphor could indeed be applied also to domestic political life.[30] Although parties could not be abolished, they could be pitted against one another and in this way their noxious consequences could be rendered harmless. All each party needed to do was to try to maximise its own power. If the radicals came to power, they would be opposed by the conservatives, and if the conservatives came to power they would be opposed by the radicals. Parties would continue to clash but only within the framework of a system of parties which itself remained in balance.

In the course of the eighteenth century a rudimentary party system of this sort came to be established for example in Sweden.[31] Here one party, the Hats, was associated with the court whereas another party, the Caps, was associated with the liberal opposition. Between 1719 and 1772 the two parties took turns controlling the executive. In Britain too there was an increasingly orderly succession between Whigs and Tories.[32] And once the constitution of the newly independent United States came to be written, the idea of self-regulation was enshrined as a basic principle of government.[33] Afraid of repeating what they saw as European mistakes, the founding fathers divided the power of the state between the executive, the legislature and the judiciary. In this way the power of one branch of government was to be balanced against the power of another, and the state would never be powerful enough to encroach on the freedom of the individual. Or, as later critics asserted, the government would never be powerful enough to effectively respond to popular demands.[34]

In all these cases self-regulation implied the same kind of double-vision as the conversations maintained in polite society. Each party, indeed each individual, had simultaneously to be guided by self-interest and by the interests of the political system taken as a whole. While they all fought to gain power, this could only be done in accordance with rules which themselves were more important than any temporary political victory. Thus, if they lost, it made far more sense to bide one's time, gather one's forces and to try again. The idea of a 'loyal opposition' captures this tension. The job of the opposition was to oppose, but only loyally so, that is, within the generally accepted rules of the political game.

A system of economics

The economic sphere represents what to many is the most obvious example of self-regulation. Today we are repeatedly told that government interference with market forces leads to inefficiencies and waste.[35] The state should keep its hands off the economy and leave the market participants to their own devices. Since economic actors know their preferences far better than any central authority, a well-functioning economy will require individual, local and moment-to-moment, decisions. If only supply is allowed to meet demand, markets will clear at the most efficient level.

In addition, however, this *laissez-faire* system can also be understood as a conflict resolving device. Instead of trying to reach common decisions, the decision making can be left to the market.[36] When the market decides, the difficult issue of who to support and why will never become the subject of political debates. Instead those perspectives and entrepreneurial projects for which there is a demand will be supported and the rest will be rejected. Conflicts will be resolved in an automatic and decentralised manner as a result of individuals pursuing their own self-interest. As long as everyone agrees on the rules of the market economy those who fail to attract a sufficient number of customers have only themselves to blame.

When considering this proposition it is worth pointing out that it only was towards the end of the eighteenth century that 'the economy' came to be seen as an independent sphere of social activity.[37] Before this time economic pursuits had always been given a moral or social significance. People looking mainly to their own profits had been condemned by medieval Aristotelians and in the eighteenth century they continued to be vilified by the polite elite.[38] In England the new class of projectors that appeared at this time was often compared to the religious fanatics who had wreaked such havoc in the seventeenth century. Both groups consisted of enthusiasts and both were guided by their private passions rather than by considerations for the common good. The single-minded pursuit of profits made them crass and egotistical, and if they ever took a moment off to sit down and talk, they would surely only talk about themselves.

And yet as eighteenth-century writers like Baron de Montesquieu began to argue, the pursuit of profits could also have a mellowing and softening effect on human passions.[39] People who are trying to make money for themselves cannot after all simply follow their most immediate impulses but must also learn to plan ahead and make compromises and trade-offs between competing goals. Far from making people dogmatic, profit-making encouraged flexibility and rewarded those who were able to defer gratification. By defenders of commercial pursuits such as Montesquieu this was understood as a self-regulating device which balanced short-term interests against long-term interests. In this manner man's greed came to be moderated and rendered less noxious to society at large.

Once each person had been pitted against him or herself it was a short step to start pitting people against each other. Bernard Mandeville may have been the first to explicitly do so in his *The Fable of the Bees*, 1714.[40] Mandeville had little time for politeness and made fun of the curious customs of the gentlemanly elite. Civic virtue was rare, he pointed out, and if politeness was required in order to bring about peace, society would constantly be at war. The answer is instead to take human beings as they are and to look for ways of using their self-interest to achieve common goals. And yet Mandeville himself never quite arrived at the idea of self-balancing. Instead, as he saw it, any balancing would require some kind of external intervention.

It did not take long, however, before a number of self-balancing mechanisms were discovered also in the economic realm.[41] David Hume, for one, found such a device regulating the flow of specie across borders.[42] Imagine, he said, that four-fifths of all money in Britain were destroyed, what would the consequences be? Surely it would mean that the price of labour would go down in equal proportion. But this in turn would lower prices and as a result foreigners would start buying more British-made products. In this way money would before long start flowing back into the country. The contrary effect would take place if the British money supply suddenly was multiplied: things would become dearer and money would flow out. Or, as economists have argued ever since, the economy is always 'aiming towards equilibrium.'[43] In his *Essai sur la nature de commerce en general*, 1755, Richard Cantillon, an Irish banker living in Paris, took the example of a hat maker:

> If there are too many hatters in a city or in a street for the number of people who buy hats there, some who are least patronized must go bankrupt; whereas if there are too few, it will be a profitable enterprise, which will encourage some new hatters to open shop there; and it is in this way that entrepreneurs of all kinds proportion themselves to the risk in a state.[44]

All that remained was for Adam Smith to put these scattered references together into a coherent doctrine of the economy understood as a self-regulating system. Ironically, he wrote in *The Wealth of Nations*, 1776, self-interest is better at serving common goals than any amount of selfless dedication. Economic development requires the clashes between conflicting goals. Competition keeps prices down, qualities up, and assures a steady stream of innovations:

> It is not from the benevolence of the butcher, the brewer, or the baker, that we expect our dinner, but from their regard to their own interest. We address ourselves, not to their humanity but to their self-love.[45]

The individual said Smith, invoking a metaphor he already had employed decades previously, 'is in this, as in many other cases, led by an invisible hand to promote an end which was no part of his intention.'[46]

A precondition for this solution to work was only that the delicate self-balancing mechanism would not be tampered with. The state in particular, Smith believed, should carefully avoid all interference with the free interactions of consenting adults. As a result many of the state's traditional preoccupations could be dismissed as irrelevant or even as detrimental to a successful society. Instead of forcing people to get along and cracking down on those who did not, the state should simply step back and let people find their own way of working out their differences. A successful economy could be maintained as long as everyone involved stuck to the rules of the game.

It all seemed too good to be true, and to some extent it certainly was. In the end of course there were still plenty of people who failed to play by the rules. Most obviously this was the case with all those who had relatively few things to trade. For the poor and the disadvantaged self-regulation was an insult since they knew that their contributions never would weigh very heavily in the overall balance. And yet, as the leaders of various reformist parties explained, what was unfair was not the self-regulating economy *per se* but rather the vast discrepancies in resources it both produced and legitimated.[47] Redressing such discrepancies required periodic redistribution and redistribution required intervention by the state. In this way an active balancer was reintroduced, if for social rather than for strictly economic reasons. Once again common decisions had to be made regarding common goals and once again there was conflict. In the end the self-balancing economy could only be accepted if regulated by the self-balancing political system.

Part V
European paths to modernity

13 Institutions and revolutions

The previous chapters have documented the ways in which reflection, entrepreneurship and pluralism were institutionalised in Europe from the Middle Ages onward. This was how the non-modern era gradually came to give way to the modern; this is how modernity happened. A modern society, we said, is a society which always changes, and change is a result of the translation of potentiality into actuality. Change is the outcome of people discovering new things and acting on their discoveries but it also presupposes a way of dealing with the conflicts that reflection and entrepreneurship inevitably produce. In modern societies all three moments are institutionalised and by combining the one set of institutions with the other, a piece of social machinery is put together which is able to overcome the inertia inherent in all social life. Change takes place automatically, relentlessly and progressively not because someone wished it or consciously sought to bring it about but because change is institutionalised.

Admittedly this is a gross simplification of a historical process which was infinitely more multifaceted and complex. This is the world as described by a historical sociologist rather than by a proper historian. If we really wanted to be serious about history, it could be argued, we should 'let the facts speak for themselves' and refrain from putting them together into a picture of such high level of generality. And yet there is no need to apologise too profusely. We are indeed less interested in the facts than in what the facts mean but this is inevitable as long as we are trying to understand a large-scale historical process. People in modern societies have always wanted to know how they came to be the way they are, and the preceding chapters presented an answer.

There is another shortcoming, however, which we at least could begin to address. Until now we have talked about 'Europe' as though there really was an entity by that name which easily could be described through a few overall characterisations. To some extent no doubt this is indeed the case. European societies – including the extra-European colonies in North America – certainly have a lot of features in common. From the legacy of the Roman empire and the Catholic church to the various reactions to the Reformation and the Enlightenment, the Scientific and the Industrial Revolutions, European societies have been influenced by much the same forces. In addition, the military and economic competition between them have operated as a socialising mechanism.

Since they constantly have been at war with each other, European countries have always been forced to copy the most successful practices of their neighbours.[1]

But of course there is also considerable variation. Today all European societies may be modern but this is not to say that they all have modernised at the same pace or in the same manner. On the contrary, some societies have continuously changed while others have remained far more stagnant; in some countries change has been automatic while in others it has come in short, revolutionary, spurts. As we would expect given the framework of this book, the road to modernity has been smooth wherever there have been plenty of institutions able to accommodate change, and the road has been far more bumpy – or temporarily blocked – in cases where such institutions have been lacking. The aim of this chapter is to provide a sense of this variation.

The smooth path

As a way to separate the dynamic societies from the less dynamic, consider what at first must appear as a rather questionable method.[2] If it indeed is the case, let us say, that change has happened smoothly and without major upheavals, one would expect many features of a society to appear rather old-fashioned. The traditional institutions stay in place since they still serve identifiable purposes or since there simply is no reason to abolish them. In his book *The English Constitution* from 1867 Walter Bagehot made this point in relation to the remarkable longevity of the House of Lords. The puzzle for Bagehot was why this obvious remnant of the Middle Ages had managed to survive into the modern era.[3] The answer is that it never constituted an obstacle to change, and the fact of its survival proves the point. 'So long as many old leaves linger on the November trees,' he says,

> you know that there has been little frost and no wind; just so while the House of Lords retains much power, you may know that there is no desperate discontent in the country, no wild agency likely to cause a great demolition.[4]

Perhaps we could call this the 'November Tree Principle,' according to which the institutional structure of a society is more modern, more transformative, the more remnants of old institutions it contains. And conversely, the more up-to-date the institutions, the more urgent the need must have been to replace their predecessors. In countries with a lot of old institutional leaves, in other words, we would expect change to have been smooth, while in countries where all leaves are brand new, we would expect a far more turbulent history of modernisation.

For an example of the former process consider England. To early modern Continental authors, England was a curious case – it was 'a government stormy and bizarre' – and a particularly intriguing feature was the institutional pluralism that characterised the country.[5] In France of the *ancien régime*, society played no role in politics and the king was the only public person; in Britain, by contrast, the king shared his power with a parliament both in theory and in practice. But the plethora of institutions extended far further, including the judiciary, the universities, the press, the financial system and so on. As conservative Continental politicians saw it, pluralistic arrangements of this kind were a threat to unity and peace, yet Anglophiles at the time, and people today, are more prone to see this institutional set-up as a guarantee of political liberty and economic dynamism.[6]

Take the reflective institutions. The English parliament dates from the thirteenth century and it was soon after that it was established as a place of real political deliberation.[7] Already in the sixteenth century the English parliament was seen to make law rather than merely to discover it; law, that is, was not considered as given by nature or by God but instead the outcome of public deliberations. The parliament was where the business of government was discussed by gentlemen of independent minds and sources of income. This was not a democracy by any means and not all decisions were the best ones but the parliament nevertheless constituted an institutional setting where the country's rulers were forced to give reasons for their actions and inactions. However unwisely it was carried out in practice, power was exercised on reflection.[8]

But there were many other reflective institutions. The universities – Oxford and Cambridge – are perhaps the most famous, if not the most dynamic, examples. Until the middle of the nineteenth century the two were above all institutions where future members of the clergy were educated.[9] The English press is a better example. Already from the earliest years of the eighteenth century the press was where political debates were held; the press was in the contemporary parlance the 'palladium of all liberties.'[10] In fact the notion of a 'public opinion' is largely an English invention, at least as it pertains to opinions formed on political issues. English courts were also highly reflective.[11] Already in the Middle Ages there were guilds of legal experts at the Inns of Court in London who had a largely independent position. The legal system was not laid down by the king as on the Continent but instead based on precedents as they accumulated over time. Contrasting and comparing these various cases was always a deliberative task not simply an administrative.

There were also ample institutional provisions made for entrepreneurs. The constitutional monarchy enshrined in England's non-existent constitution provided guarantees for both economic and political actors.[12] Above all the existence of a parliament meant that there was a check on the avarice of the king. Property rights were safe when the king could not simply cancel his debts or seize the property of his subjects. In addition, England after the financial revolution of the late seventeenth and early eighteenth centuries had excellent ways of providing funding for new projects. The establishment of the Bank of England brought down interest rates across the board and the establishment of a stock market in the City of London provided means of inviting new investors to share both risks and profits. In addition, insurance companies such as Lloyd's helped entrepreneurs deal with risks and the Statute of Monopolies, 1624, regulated patents.

Much the same goes for the problem of pluralism. Culturally speaking toleration was embodied in the ideal of the English gentleman, a social type which developed as a contrast to the religious fanaticism which had characterised the revolutionaries of the seventeenth century.[13] Instead of dogmatic zealots, society was to be populated by people who were polite, witty and conversational; good humour and a sense of fair play should replace strongly held convictions. And while this gentlemanly ideal certainly was exclusionary, it also provided the cultural setting for the development of a range of civil rights which later were extended to a far broader stratum of society. Not surprisingly the idea of self-regulation developed earlier and further in England than on the Continent.[14] Newtonian cosmology was a cybernetic system, but so was Adam Smith's description of the economy and the parliamentary seesaw between Tories and Whigs.

Together these institutions and institutions like them provided what may be the best example of a piece of social machinery capable of continuous self-transformation. Take a case of political change. In England a new proposal could be launched in parliament where it was moderated, further deliberated on and reconciled with other initially contradictory demands. The press added the voices of the politically under-represented to this process of deliberation. The proposal could then be acted on by the state according to constitutionally guaranteed procedures and thanks to sound public finances, or by private political actors protected by a legal tradition which emphasised privacy and individual rights. Political conflicts were moderated by a sense of fair play and resolved through elections, through parliamentarism, and if need be through an independent judiciary.

Or take a case of economic change. In England, technical inventions were actively encouraged by scientific academies, funded by stock-markets and protected through patents, insurance policies and well-established property rights. Conflicts between competing economic interests were defused as they were taken off the common agenda and reduced to problems settled by the interplay between supply and demand.

England was not alone, however, the Dutch Republic is another example of a transformative state but consider instead the less known case of Sweden.[15] Contemporary Sweden takes considerable pride in its status as a modern, indeed a 'progressive,' country, and given this self-perception it is surprising to find that the country, judged by the November Tree Principle, easily can be placed in the same category as England.[16] Sweden too has had institutions which have allowed rather than blocked transformations and as a result the stresses and strains of the modernisation process happened smoothly and without violent conflicts. It is striking, for example, that the Swedish Diet remained in its medieval four estate format up until as comparatively recently as 1866; that the Swedish constitution, together with the American, was the oldest in the world until it finally was altered in 1974, and that the Swedish monarchy survives to this day. Rather than referring to Sweden's institutional make-up as 'medieval,' however, one could think of it as remarkably ahead of its time. The *Regerings-form* promulgated in 1634 is for example often regarded as the world's first constitution; the central bank, Riksbanken, founded in 1668, preceded the Bank of England by almost 30 years and it was the first European national bank to issue paper currency; the world's oldest newspaper is *Post- & Inrikes Tidningar* which has appeared daily since 1645.[17]

Looking more carefully at these institutions, consider first the Swedish Diet which retraces its history to 1435, and which at least from the 1520s functioned as a forum for political deliberation. Just as in England, the parliament was generally strengthened rather than weakened by the incessant warfare of the early modern era since it made the kings ever-more dependent on taxes as a source of revenue.[18] The Swedish Diet consisted of four estates rather than three which was the rule on the Continent, and also the peasantry – representing as much as 90 per cent of the population – was allowed to participate in the proceedings. There is no doubt that this fact improved the quality of the decisions reached. When the Swedish empire eventually collapsed in 1719, the result was not chaos but instead a smooth transition to a period of sovereign parliamentary rule.[19] During this so-called 'age of liberty,' the rudiments of a two-party system emerged, although many politicians no doubt were thoroughly corrupt. In 1766, extensive legislation was enacted guaranteeing the freedom of the press and the freedom of access to information. Both provisions proved invaluable to the operations of newspapers.

Despite this impressive institutional set-up, which preceded and went further than the English in some respects, the Swedish model operated rather differently. Above all the Swedish state had a far more dominant position in relation to society than the English. A good illustration is provided by the notion of a public sphere. In England the public sphere was independent of the state – indeed often in opposition to it – but in Sweden the public sphere was always state-organised and state-managed. Thus while parliaments, universities and academies provided important venues for reflection also in the Swedish case, they were all state institutions; what mattered was not the 'freedom of thought' as much as the service of the common good.

Much the same could be said about entrepreneurship.[20] In a poor peasant society with a small population and large distances between villages and towns, there were few and badly developed markets for produce and little by means of an indigenous merchant class that could take the lead in commercial or industrial enterprises. From the Middle Ages onward commerce was instead in the hands of foreigners, Germans in particular who provided the core population of the first Swedish towns. Industrial enterprises as they began to appear in the seventeenth century – above all in mining and the bourgeoning armaments industry – were similarly often set up by foreign experts invited by the king. In addition the state was an important entrepreneur in its own right, and already in the seventeenth century the state bureaucracy came to be organised according to rationalistic ideals. Constitutional documents assured that bureaucrats were governed by rules and by the scrutiny they were held up to in public.

Swedes, in short, were often deferring to the state but they were also included in the state, and this combination of co-optation and co-determination provided a means of dealing with the problems of pluralism.[21] In Sweden the parliament was always seen as a locus of power to which people had some means of access, and hence as the main forum for presenting political demands. Although Sweden never had much by means of civility or a gentlemanly culture, the very rusticity of its public discourse embodied a profoundly egalitarian ethos.[22] Just as traditional peasant society, modern Sweden excluded both the geniuses and the misfits while including everybody deemed sufficiently normal. The result is a very decent society which combines a commitment to change with a fear of anything radical, including too radical changes.

The revolutionary path

Contrast the relatively smooth path travelled by countries such as England, the Dutch Republic and Sweden with the historical experiences of societies where reflection, entrepreneurship and pluralism were temporarily blocked or seriously impaired. In this latter set of cases, the traditional, medieval, institutions could not adjust and as a result change did not happen automatically, continuously or progressively. Instead change took place in short revolutionary bursts. Since the old institutions could not adjust, they had to be abolished; the weather was always too stormy, in other words, and by November the old institutional leaves had all blown off.

One source of revolutionary upheavals is to be found in differences in the way various sets of institutions operate. If, for example, there is a lot of institutionalised reflection but only little by means of institutional support for entrepreneurs, we can guess that while new ideas will emerge easily people will find it difficult to realise them. The outcome is likely to be a deep sense of frustration. Or imagine the opposite situation where it is easy to act but where there are few new ideas to act on. Here there will be endless imitation yet little by means of transformative change. Or consider cases where reflection and entrepreneurship are well provided for institutionally but where there are few institutional means of dealing with the conflicts they produce. Before long demands will be raised for 'justice' and 'freedom,' and if convincing changes are not introduced, chances are the whole institutional set-up will blow up.

Consider France. The fundamental problem of the *ancien régime* was that there was too much reflection and not enough institutional support for entrepreneurs or mechanisms for resolving conflicts. This is not to say that the French state did not also try to control reflection. There was a parliament but between 1614 and 1789 it did not meet. Universities existed of course – Sorbonne was the intellectual centre of the European Middle Ages – but as François Rabelais and other Humanists pointed out with scorn, they were hopeless bastions of Scholasticism.[23] Moreover, anything that came off a printing press was closely monitored by state officials. Apart from the official paper of notifications – the *Gazette de France* started by Cardinal Richelieu in 1631 – all newspapers were banned.[24]

And yet a considerable amount of reflection continued to take place behind the authorities' back. When the Huguenots were expelled in the 1680s, a clandestine press, printing in French, was established outside of the country and both newspapers and books quickly flowed back across the porous borders.[25] The Enlightenment was fuelled by printing material of this kind. The famous *Encyclopédie* for example was largely printed in Neûchatel in Switzerland and then smuggled back to its avid readers. In addition there were institutions such as the *salons*, maintained by members of educated society in Paris and throughout the country, where people met to go over the latest social and cultural events.[26] To a considerable extent the reflective judgement formed in these private discussions compensated for the reflection which failed to take place elsewhere.

Entrepreneurship met with more obvious obstacles. As far as politics was concerned, all official venues were closed.[27] The affairs of state were exclusively reserved for the king, the only public persona, and they were off limits to private individuals. There were no consultations, no public reasons, no accountability. Economic entrepreneurs hardly received more support. Property rights were insecure since the king repeatedly cancelled his debts; interest rates on the state loan were high since no one trusted the king and this increased interest rates in the country as a whole.[28] In addition no financial revolution took place in Paris as it did in Amsterdam and London; there were no proper banks and only poorly functioning markets for stocks and bonds, and the insurance industry was roughly a century behind that of England.[29]

As far as the problems of pluralism are concerned, the main institutional mechanism was the coercive machinery of the absolutist state which in theory at least operated according to a perfectly Hobbesian – or rather Bodinian – logic. Conflicts were hidden or repressed rather than resolved, especially once the Edict of Nantes was revoked. Under the *ancien régime* there were no universal rights belonging equally to everyone but instead only private laws pertaining exclusively to particular groups. Rather than letting economic and political interests counter-balance each other, rights to particular outcomes were assigned by the state and by tradition. There was little tolerance for clashes between factions and parties.[30]

And yet, a revolution is not by itself much of a solution. Revolutions dismantle existing institutions but the question still remains what to replace them with.[31] Given their essentially destructive nature it is surprising that revolutions often have been regarded as pivotal to the success of the modernisation process. Without a revolution, scholars have declared, modernity will not happen.[32] Yet from the perspective of this book revolutions are best understood as misunderstandings of what a truly modern society requires. Revolutions take place where change cannot happen in other more flexible and more continuous ways; revolutions are quick-fix alternatives to processes of gradual institutionalised change.

And as all quick fixes, revolutions are likely to go wrong – often horribly wrong.[33] The history of revolutionary change from the French Revolution onwards is largely a history of chaos and terror. Revolutionaries have typically sought to implement some grandiose plan or blueprint for a new and better world, and although the plans often have looked good on paper the process of implementing them has quickly revealed the flaws. The implementation of a plan requires the suppression of alternative plans, and before long the struggle against 'enemies of the revolution' – real and imaginary – has become an all-consuming passion. Just as in the famous print by Goya, the revolution begins by devouring its own children and then everything else in its way.[34]

The problem, slightly crudely put, is that all revolutions since the French have focused on matters of substance rather than on matters of form.[35] Instead of trying to achieve certain substantive outcomes what the revolutionaries should have done is to spend their time on institutional design. While the development of history cannot be specified in advance, and cannot be forced, change can be more or less encouraged. Once the debris of the old regime had been cleared away, the revolutionaries should have looked for ways of institutionalising reflection, entrepreneurship and pluralism. Rather than trying to reconstruct the world in the image of their ideals, they should have constructed a social machinery capable of self-transformation.

A group of revolutionaries who came far closer to this ideal were the North American settlers who rose up against the English in 1776.[36] The American revolutionaries had no master-plan for a utopian society and instead their policies were strictly speaking reactionary; above all they reacted against what they regarded as the oppressive practices of the colonial metropolis.[37] Their policies were reactionary also in the sense that the society they sought to create was placed in the past rather than in the future; the revolution, they imagined, would restore the 'ancient rights of the English.' As a result of this outlook, the American revolutionaries spent far more time than their French counterparts on questions of institutional design. Hence the drawn-out process which produced the constitution and the elaborate legal framework which has surrounded it ever since.[38] The American institutions were better thought-through, better supported by various factions of society, and better implemented. As a result they have lasted far longer.

Not surprisingly for a band of revolutionaries with reactionary aims, the kinds of institutions they put in place were not all that different from the ones they already knew from England.[39] And as we already have discussed, the institutional set-up of eighteenth-century England was one in which reflection, entrepreneurship and pluralism were well supported. The subsequent development of American society was also similar to that of England itself. Ironically for a regime set up to recreate the past, in the United States change began happening rapidly, relentlessly and automatically.[40]

Part VI
China

14 Reflection

Although largely ignorant of each other until the early sixteenth century, the history of Europe and the history of China have always run in close parallel.[1] On opposite sides of the Eurasian landmass the two parts of the world have developed in remarkably similar ways. The Warring States period corresponds both in time and in character to ancient Greece; the Han dynasty resembles the Roman empire; and the Ming dynasty, ideologically dominated by Neo-Confucianism, reminds us of the European Middle Ages, ideologically dominated by the Church. As the first European travellers to China discovered, China was at least as prosperous, powerful and sophisticated as their own continent and as such radically different from other parts of the world. Although the parallels seemed to have stopped when Europe in the nineteenth century suddenly surged ahead, China has been busy catching up ever since. Despite much contemporary American triumphalism the twenty-first century may yet turn out to belong to the Chinese.

The puzzle to be considered in this and the subsequent three chapters is why these parallelisms obtain but also how to account for the many differences. The question is why China managed to change much in the same manner as Europe but also why Europe was first to modernise and the first to go through developments such as the Industrial Revolution. The hypotheses are the same as in the chapters above. What determines the pace of social change, we will argue, are reflection, entrepreneurship and pluralism, and the degree to which these three are institutionalised in society. Developments in Europe and China well resemble each other to the extent that reflection, entrepreneurship and pluralism are equally encouraged and equally institutionally embedded. They will differ to the extent that there are differences in these regards.

Obviously an inter-continental comparison of this nature imposes some rather particular demands on our investigation. It would for example be completely out of order to make Europe into the standard by which Chinese developments are measured.[2] A Eurocentric perspective is singularly inappropriate for understanding world history and only Europeans whose self-confidence is matched by their historical short-sightedness can convince themselves that this is not the case. As far as our investigation is concerned this means that we must open our eyes to different alternatives. What we are interested in are reflective, entrepreneurial and pluralistic functions but clearly such functions can be carried out in quite different ways in different historical settings. As we saw above this was the case within Europe and it is even more likely to be the case when comparing Europe and China. As a consequence we will in this and the subsequent two chapters discuss the Chinese case without constantly drawing parallels with Europe and European developments. Only in the subsequent chapter will the two parts of the world be properly compared.

Potentiality and change

The question of change has been a constant preoccupation of people through-out Chinese society. Already the *I Ching*, the *Book of Changes*, dating from around the fifth century BCE, showed a world in a perpetual state of motion.[3] And as next to all subsequent Chinese philosophers, scientists and social reforms have agreed, the *I Ching* and its 64 hexagrams describes all possible states of affairs obtainable in nature and society as well as all possible alterations between them. What accomplishes the move from one state of being to the other is the transformative power generated by the tension between *yin* and *yang*, between Heaven and Earth.[4] It is this interaction of opposing forces that brings forth all life, all patterns, ideas, systems and cultures.

> Tao produced the One.
> The One produced the two.
> The two produced the three.
> And the three produced the ten thousand things.
> The ten thousand things carry the *yin* and embrace the *yang*, and through the blending of the material force they achieve harmony.[5]

This was an outlook shared by Daoists, Confucians, Moists, Legalists and even by Buddhist scholars.

Not surprisingly given this precocious interest in questions of change, people in China have from the earliest times onward been preoccupied with reflections on the potentialities inherent in life, in Chinese known as *shi*.[6] The object of philosophical speculation has not been what things are as much as how they came to be; that is, which disposition of *shi* that produced them. And the philo-sophers have been joined by people of a more practical bent – statesmen and businessmen for example – who have wanted to know how best to benefit from whatever situation they have found themselves in. What they have tried to dis-cover, that is, is how *shi* could be manipulated to their own advantage.[7] This is why the *I Ching* from the beginning was used as a manual of divination. By learning about the potentiality of things, one would learn about one's fate but also hope to learn how to control it.

However, the way in which investigations into the potential were carried out in China differed considerably from the way they were carried out in Europe. In China change was always regarded as a creative process which was inherent in nature itself and not as something which happened as a result of outside intervention. Change was never the responsibility of a transcendent god and it was not something for which human beings could be held responsible. Instead change simply happens by itself; nature and society are pregnant with propensities which continuously and quite automatically come to reveal themselves. All human beings need to do is to learn how to read the situation in which they find themselves and to adjust themselves to the configuration of *shi* it contains.

This understanding of the potential permeates also Chinese æsthetics. A common aim of calligraphy, landscape painting, poetry and drama is to point to the propensities inherent in nature or in society.[8] This is why a good work of art never is self-sufficient, never closed or completely finished. Chinese art has few straight lines and few straightforward plots, instead curves are always meandering, mountain ranges are always craggy and poems take unexpected twists and turns. Or compare the Chinese fascination with the motif of the dragon which, just like life itself, has no determined form, cannot be grasped or penned in, but unfolds and coils up according to its own logic.[9] What is captured by a painting or a poem is not an image of what things are as much as a trace of an ongoing movement, and to the extent that the work is successful the movement should continue in the mind of the audience that perceives it.[10] 'When the feelings are stirred,' as the seventeenth-century artist Wang Yüan-ch'i put it, 'a creative force arises,'

> and when that force arises, it is manifested as rules and order. The fruition [of this process] never goes beyond the original perception, but has the potential for inexhaustible change.[11]

This understanding of change explains the remarkable this-worldliness of Chinese culture.[12] Since all sources of change are taken to be internal to the existing, there is no need to speculate about external sources. There is for example little need for a belief in a transcendental being who created the world and who actively intervene in it. Although such a notion of god did exist in the Shan period, some 4,000 years ago, it disappeared already in the first millennium BCE. Ever since there has been no proper notion of a personal god to whom people can turn with prayers and sacrifices.[13] Instead the supernatural has constantly been naturalised and the metaphysical reduced to a matter of physics. This this-worldliness has also meant that Chinese culture has had remarkably little to say about ultimate questions.[14] 'If we do not yet know about life,' as Confucius put it, 'how can we know about death?'[15] Rather than as an other-worldly location inhabited by gods or by dead human beings, heaven was understood only as a regulative principle. Heaven is the necessary counterpoint to an earth with which it constantly is in creative tension.

The natural point of view

While all Chinese schools of thought can be said to share in this general outlook, there are still fundamental differences between them. For the Daoists, for example, the focus was always squarely on the propensities inherent in nature.[16] For this reason Daoist monks and scholars spent a lot of time contemplating natural sceneries, and painters and poets inspired by Daoist themes never stopped portraying the life of birds, trees and mountains.[17] Landscape paintings had a particular philosophical significance since they were thought to show something akin to a snapshot of the forces of creation at work. A good painting should not portray nature realistically, from the outside as it were, but instead show the 'vital breath' which animated it from within.[18] Similarly, in geomancy – the *feng shui* of Hollywood fame – the point was above all to locate the 'lifelines' running through a landscape where the forces of creation were thought to reveal themselves most vigorously. Not surprisingly, *shi*, potentiality, was the name the Chinese gave to these lines.

The naturalist perspective on life meant that many Daoists took an active interest in minerals, wild plants, animals and parts of the human body. They also engaged in alchemical experiments, in sexual therapies, and made several path-breaking scientific discoveries.[19] In addition the natural perspective equipped them with alternative views on society, and usually they were highly critical of what they saw. The Confucians, the Daoists complained, focused too much on social conventions and not enough on human nature and its relation to the natural world. And the imperial state in its hierarchical authoritarianism deviated radically from the natural egalitarian order which the Daoists believed had preceded it.[20] Throughout Chinese history, from the revolt of the Yellow Turbans in the third century CE to the Taiping rebellion of the nineteenth century, social rebels were often inspired by Daoist ideals.[21]

The physical location of many Daoist critics facilitated such reflections. They usually thought of themselves as outsiders; often they were former civil servants who had been dismissed from their posts or who voluntarily had resigned in protest against some official policy.[22] Sometimes they would live out their days as hermit scholars, engaged in meditation and æsthetic pursuits. A favourite motif in the ink paintings they composed, with an obvious reference to their own predicament, was the defiant old tree, scraggly and withered, which survived against all odds on some barren mountain-side.[23] For additional protection, the Daoists would often cultivate various eccentricities. The poet and philosopher Ruan Chi of the third century CE was for example commonly regarded as 'mad.'[24] When he was not engaged in 'pure conversation' with his friends in the bamboo groves outside of the capital

> he stayed shut up in his room studying books of several months on end, without ever going out; sometimes he went up into the mountains or to the waterside, forgetting for several days to return home. ... He was a great drinker, an accomplished performer on the lute, and skilled in whistling. While he was following out a train of thought, he would quite forget about the outside world.[25]

Under the impact of Daoism even the Confucians were eventually forced to start considering the world from more of a natural point of view. In the eleventh and twelfth centuries in particular the doctrines first formulated by Confucius in the fifth century BCE were reformulated into the grand synthesis known in the West as Neo-Confucianism.[26] Yet nature as the Neo-Confucians understood it was always curiously abstract. What mattered to them was above all the basic principle, *li*, underlying the cosmic order – 'the Great Ultimate' – and not messy empirical facts. And this abstract understanding of nature rein-forced a very conservative theory of statecraft. As the Neo-Confucians explained, the Emperor had a personal responsibility for maintaining the balance between Heaven and Earth and the responsibility of everyone else was to subject themselves to the imperial rule. From this time onward most of the emperor's time was taken up with various rituals designed to assure this end.[27]

Astronomy was an interest which Daoists and Confucians shared and for both schools alike the study of celestial phenomena was a way of reflecting on politics.[28] The Confucians studied astronomy in order to discover whether a given government was organised in accordance with the requirements of Heaven. To this end the state maintained a team of imperial astronomers whose only job it was to keep their eyes on the evening sky. Unusual sightings were immediately identified as portents and vested with huge political significance. Astronomy was for this reason regarded as a political science and as an *arcanum imperium*, a secret of the state.[29] Soon however the official science found its counterpart in a subversive astronomy guided by anti-establishment motives and often pursued by renegade Daoist monks.[30] Just as the official astronomers they kept their eyes on the sky, but what they wanted to know was rather how long a particular emperor was going to last or whether an uprising they were planning was likely to succeed. If Heaven was seen to grant its approval, the rebels were ready to strike. Naturally the imperial state did everything it could to hide such astronomical knowledge and ordinary people were for this reason banned from making observations.[31]

The historical point of view

In general however the Confucians were always far more interested in social than in natural phenomena.[32] For them the regenerative principles of Heaven and Earth were most obviously on display in the unfolding of society over time. Hence history was always their primary object of reflection; by investigating the past, they believed, they could investigate the *shi* inherent in the present. This is why, once a new dynasty was established, a group of historians would start working on a history of the previous regime.[33] In this way it was hoped they would learn the secrets of its rise and decline and avoid the mistakes which became its undoing.

Yet the past was not only studied but also thoroughly idealised, and in China this idealisation began before most other societies had even accumulated much by means of a history. Already in the first millennium BCE personages from pre-vious eras exercised an extraordinary power over the collective imagination.

One constant point of reference were Yao and Shun, the semi-mythological founding fathers – the 'Sage Kings' – of the first Chinese dynasty.[34] In the eyes of the Confucians, Yao and Shun had been paragons of virtue and good government. Similarly, in the case of the arts, painters and poets were from the earliest times advised to emulate the examples of 'the ancient masters.'[35] The highest praise imaginable was to say that a painter's work perfectly mimicked the style of some illustrious predecessor. Old cultural practices had the same canonical status. Already in the third century BCE, the Confucian moralist Xunzi would for example repudiate all institutions, rituals, food, utensils, music, colours or garments not explicitly prescribed by 'the ancients.'[36]

To Europeans, particularly from the nineteenth century onward, such constant harkening back to a remote past has been taken as proof of the inherent conservatism and stagnation of imperial China. And yet there is no doubt that the historical consciousness of the literati constituted a powerful source of creativity.[37] The long and well-documented unfolding of Chinese history contained a vast storeroom of examples with which the present could be compared. Such comparisons were never mindless or automatic since the historical examples always had to be carefully chosen and alternative interpretations considered before they could be refuted. Rather than slavishly following precedent, history was always reflected on before it was used. The point, said Confucius, is to 'review the old so as to find out the new.'[38] Echoing these words, Chairman Mao 2,500 years later agreed that '[w]e have to learn from the past to serve the present.'[39]

Take the example of the *Spring and Autumn Annals*, a chronicle of the state of Lu covering the period from 722 to 479 BCE, and once thought to have been compiled by Confucius himself.[40] In and of themselves these chronicles provide only the most basic information – short sentences mainly, recording the precise events of individual reigns – and as such they have about as much literary or philosophical merit as an average telephone directory.[41] Yet their skeletal structure is precisely what made them useful for later interpreters. Rather than laying down any precise teachings, the annals yielded their lessons only once creatively reimagined. To scholars of the Song period, for example, they demonstrated the importance of 'revering the emperor and expelling the barbarians,' while in the nineteenth century the same texts yielded a doctrine of limited, constitutional, government.[42]

Rather than proving the conservatism of imperial China such creative use of the past demonstrates how political discussions necessarily must be framed in a society where history is free from the metaphysical illusion of progress.[43] Chinese utopias were never located in the future or in other non-Chinese places but instead always in the remote past. For this reason it is difficult to make a clear separation between a return and a renewal. Radical opinions and alternative political programmes were necessarily couched in terms of the example set by some ancient ruler and revolutionary action was conceived of as a restoration of an earlier era rather than as a break with the past.

Consider the case of Huang Zongxi, a Confucian scholar of the early Ch'ing dynasty.[44] Huang, like so many of his predecessors, saw a reestablishment of the institutions of the Sage Kings as the only model for a virtuous government, but far from making him into an arch-conservative this historical awareness turned him into a radical critic. The Sage Kings had ruled in the interest of the people and at their own expense, Huang explained, but recent emperors had inverted this principle. To restore the past would thus necessarily be to break with the imperial tradition. Among the reforms he advocated was the establishment of a universal public school system where people could come to form opinions about political matters and learn to participate in public discussions.[45] Similarly, Huang continued, under the Sage Kings there had been no private ownership but land had instead belonged to the king who had distributed it equitably so that everyone had had enough to meet their needs. How very different were the contemporary rulers who allowed some people to grow immensely rich while others were starving.[46]

There were however also those who were far more sceptical of this reliance on history examples, above all the Legalists, a group of scholars of the third century BCE who have become notorious for their defence of authoritarianism.[47] To make himself omnipotent, they explained, the power of the emperor must always be greater than the power of the past. And yet, given the way in which political discussions were framed in imperial China, even the Legalists were often forced to make their points in terms of historical examples. To them history demonstrated above all how a Confucian obsession with 'humanity' and 'benevolence' allowed far too much room for dissent.[48] Rather than being kind, an emperor could maintain himself in power only through the harshest of laws and the most draconian of punishments. The Sage Kings, the Legalists argued, were the first illustrations of this thesis. As the Legalist scholar Li Si explained:

> That the wise rulers and the Sage kings were able to long maintain their exalted position, hold on to awesome power, and monopolise the benefits of the world was not due to any exotic methods but by making decisions alone, implementing careful supervision, and instituting harsh penal punishments.[49]

In his official capacity as Prime Minister of the first imperial dynasty Li Si had ample opportunities to practise what he taught.[50] The most infamous policy, implemented in 212 BCE, was to bury hundreds of Confucian scholars alive and to burn all the books in the country, except the official chronicles of the current dynasty and select technical treaties. As Li Si explained in a memorial to the emperor Qín Shi Huángdì:

> Those who dare to talk to each other about the *Odes* and *Documents* should be executed and their bodies exposed in the marketplace. Anyone referring to the past to criticize the present should, together with all members of his family, be put to death.[51]

Incidentally emperor Qin Shi Huangdi is reputed to have been the long-standing role model of Chairman Mao Zedong, proving that in China even the most revolutionary of leaders can be influenced by figures from the remote past.[52]

Technologies of reflection

As far as technologies of reflection are concerned China was well provided for. For example, already in the earliest times divinations were carried out with the help of oracle bones.[53] Tortoise shells were heated over a fire and the configuration of cracks that appeared on the surface was then interpreted for signs regarding the disposition of Heaven and Earth. In the first millennium BCE, sticks made out of yarrow stems were used for the same purpose. Depending on the combinations of odd and even stems, continuous or broken lines could be drawn and these patterns eventually formed the basis of the hexagrams which made up the *I Ching*. Reflection on these basic patterns was the starting point of all of the sciences and all philosophy in the Chinese speaking world.

From early on in its history China was also a literate society. The first ideographs appeared about 4,000 years ago and in the first millennium CE more Chinese people than any others were able to read and write.[54] The existence of writing was a precondition for the unification of the country. Since people were literate they could communicate over long distances and in this way efficiently co-ordinate their activities. But writing also facilitated reflection. Just as in Europe, but in contrast to societies in Africa and the Americas, arguments, ideas and proposals could be written down and thereby spread both across time and space.[55] The first compilations, such as the *Spring and Autumn Annals* and *The Odes* – the latter a compilation of speeches, harangues, oaths and descriptions of ritual dances – go back as far as to the eighth century BCE.[56]

Other European technologies of reflection were present in China as well – or rather, in most cases, they were Chinese inventions in the first place.[57] The mirror is one example.[58] Large bronze mirrors were manufactured as early as 1200 BCE, and already in the fourth century BCE technical manuals explained the differences in the optical qualities of plane, convex and concave mirrors. In addition the mirror had a philosophical significance. It was used as an image of the cosmos and to the Buddhists it was a metaphor of the peacefulness of the enlightened mind.[59] The mirror was also a metaphor for political reflection. Consider the monumental *Complete Mirror for Aiding Government* by the historian Sima Guang of the northern Song dynasty, which was read both as a historical encyclopædia and as a *Fürstenspieghel*.[60]

Art was another reflective technology. From earliest times there were both professional and amateur artists, various schools and academic conventions. What was taught within each tradition was not a technique or a style as much as a distinct way of seeing the world. In addition there was a long-established tradition of connoisseurship and Confucian scholars would often assemble around an art collection, drink tea and discuss the comparative merits of various works.[61] From the Song period onward such reflection concerned more than anything the depiction of nature. The golden age of Chinese landscape painting – from the tenth to the fourteenth century – corresponded to the emergence of Neo-Confucianism and its interest in the principles underlying the natural world.[62] But also here there were subversive traditions, notably the 'Southern School,' influenced by Chan Buddhism, which regarded nature as spontaneously ordered rather than as rule-governed and which rejected the conventions of the academic style in favour of highly individualised expressions.[63]

In addition to such high-brow traditions pictures were available also to people of little or no education.[64] With the invention of paper made from mulberry bark in the second century CE, and the invention of woodblock printing in the eighth century, images of all kinds became easy to produce and reproduce. In contrast to the ink paintings of the literati, prints intended for the mass market were in colour and they represented the world realistically, not philosophically or metaphorically. The colour and the realism served to instil a sense of wonder in the viewers.[65] The extent of the demand for pictures is obvious from the burgeoning mass market for prints as well as from the inevitable complaints from the literati of a 'dumbing down' of the visual culture.[66]

From woodblock printing it is of course only a short step to the printing of books. The technology seems to have been invented by Buddhist missionaries and the first printed book, the *Diamond Sutra*, appeared in 868.[67] By the year 900 printing was in general, commercial, use and all kinds of books were published: manuals in the occult sciences, almanacs, Buddhist texts, lexicons, short encyclopædias and manuals, collections of model compositions and historical works. Before long printing became a concern of the state and various state-sponsored projects of popular education were launched.[68] The *Nine Classics* – comprising canonical texts on history, philosophy and ritual – were printed by imperial command between 932 and 952 but so were many treatise on divination, acupuncture, arithmetic and metallurgy. The first pharmacopœia appeared in 973, detailing the use of no fewer than 1,748 basic drugs, and *Diagrams of the Internal Organs and Blood Vessels* was published in 1113. Many works were on agriculture, written in a simple language which even the relatively uneducated could understand and illustrated with pictures of tools and appliances.[69]

There were newspapers too, or rather an official paper of notification which circulated widely among members of the elite. Already during the Tang dynasty officials throughout the country were required to report on events taking place in their prefectures, and in addition the military kept a separate 'Courts for the Forwarding of Memorials.'[70] During the Song dynasty these documents began to be printed and soon they appeared as the world's first national newspaper, subsequently and by foreigners referred to as the *Peking Gazette*. By the late Ming this was a common source of information for government officials who regularly cited it in their memorials. In fact some emperors are said to have been reluctant to deal with matters of state since they knew that information about their actions would end up being publicised.[71] Despite its obvious limitations – above all the fact that it was read by such a small circle of people – the *Peking Gazette* was an invaluable source of news. As its regular readers, top Chinese bureaucrats were probably better informed about the state of their country than any of their colleagues elsewhere in the world.

Institutions that reflect

In addition reflection in imperial China was always a highly institutionalised activity. Rather than leaving individuals in charge, deliberations were carried out by institutions responsible for the gathering, collating, and comparing of various ideas and perspectives. The primary examples of such institutions are the Confucian state machinery, the educational system and the civil service exams.

When applied to matters of public administration Confucian thought became a doctrine of benevolent rule carried out by a virtuous elite.[72] The ideal was a rigidly ordered society where harmony and peace prevailed and where people were well-fed and content. Such a society was only possible, the bureaucrats believed, as long as the best men – that is, themselves – were in charge. This was also indeed the case for over 2,000 years, from the year 136 BCE when Confucianism was made into the official state ideology until the abolition of the examination system in 1905. Although in practice, it should be said, the cynical principles propagated by the Legalists always had a strong influence on emperors, military leaders and power-hungry eunuchs.[73]

According to the official Confucian doctrine the state was best described as a hierarchical structure of personal relationships which started with the emperor and ran through to the very bottom of society.[74] The most important of these relationships were those between father and son and between emperor and subject. These bonds imposed obligations on both parties: above all the requirement that superiors be compassionate and inferiors obedient, and that everyone should be considerate of the feelings of others. There were a large number of rituals through which these relationships were confirmed, and the Confucians were convinced that social harmony would prevail as long as only the rituals were correctly performed. Confucianism was explicitly anti-legalistic: government was constituted by men rather than by rules, and good government depended on the nature of its officials rather than on the nature of its regulations.

From the time of Confucius in the fifth century BCE, these ideas were added to by thinkers such as Mengzi, Xunzi and Dong Zhongshu, and already in the early Han dynasty a number of set texts had been established in this way, often summarised as the *Five, Six, Nine* or up to *Sixteen Classics*.[75] It was knowledge of this canon that was tested in the examination system organised by the state.[76] The institution itself was established during Tang, but it was during Song that it became universal and from the Ming dynasty onward success in the examinations constituted the only available means of gaining access to the administrative elite.[77] There were three levels of exams, prefectural, provincial and metropolitan, and they were ferociously selective: less than one in ten succeeded at the prefectural level and less than one in ten at the provincial. In the end only a few hundred people out of China's millions made it to the very top.[78]

Although candidates could be tested in a long range of different subjects the literary exam had by the Ming dynasty become by far the most prestigious. Most notorious was the so-called 'Eight Legged Essay,' a piece of literary composition on a classical theme of ethics, æsthetics or statecraft.[79] In order to prepare students for the exams the state established schools throughout the country, and although they never had anything like a universal coverage – for one thing, no girls were allowed – a larger proportion of students were educated here than elsewhere in the world.[80] Given the all-determining importance of the state exams, however, the schools rarely ventured outside of the official canon.[81] This was true also of the many private schools. In short, the educational system became a kind of prep school dedicated to the single purpose of helping students enter the administrative elite.

At the peak of the intellectual establishment was the Hanlin Academy, an imperial institution which served as the official keeper of the Confucian faith.[82] This was where the best scholars in each field resided and it was to them that the emperor turned whenever he required particularly sophisticated advice. In addition the Hanlin scholars served as Grand Secretaries at the palace, that is, as a kind of ministers. They also held public lectures on themes drawn from the Confucian canon.[83] With the emperor in attendance they reminded the court of the duties of the Son of Heaven and the importance of maintaining the highest possible moral standards. They were also expected to criticise the emperor, and scholars who merely used the occasion to flatter him were considered disloyal. In some cases they were even dismissed.

More intellectual freedom characterised the many private academies that were established from the Song dynasty onward.[84] Often they were organised around a particular teacher or group of intellectuals, perhaps with a disaffected former bureaucrat as its *primus motor*. The extent of the activities varied considerably depending on the academy. Usually there was a library, a few scholars in residence and perhaps a reading club or a set of informal seminars. As independent intellectual centres the academies were occasionally given a harsh treatment by the authorities, at least whenever the security police suspected them of engaging in subversive political activities.[85] And yet, at least as far as the choice of subject matter was concerned, the private academies operated thoroughly within the established, Confucian and humanistic, tradition.

Turning next to the institutions which made up the imperial state, they too had considerable reflective capabilities. According to the Confucian ideal the imperial state was to be collegially run.[86] Although the emperor was the supreme ruler, he was not supposed to initiate policy but instead mainly to confirm the decision proposed by the Grand Secretaries or reach agreement on a different decision after consultations with them. The emperor was also supposed to lead debates at general court audiences and engage smaller groups of high-ranking officials in policy discussions. Here each participant would have an equal voice and a right to vote on the proposals before them. Unanimity was hoped for and when it was achieved custom dictated that the decision was binding also on the emperor. The administrative regulations of the Ming dynasty explicitly forbade the making of any important policy decisions without recourse to such deliberative procedures.

A similar concern for reflection characterised the state bureaucracy. A tremendous amount of time and resources were spent collecting information and making sure that the administrative machinery operated in accordance with official stipulations. There was even an official Censorate in charge of policing the imperial administration.[87] They scrutinised memorials and budgets in search for any improprieties, and officials in the capital were evaluated every six years. In addition the censors made surprise inspections of government agencies at various levels and parts of the country. Their powers were as wide-ranging as they were feared. On one occasion in the late Ming dynasty no fewer than 2,000 officials were dismissed from their posts.[88]

In addition the right to remonstrate was an explicitly recognised institution with a long and impressive pedigree.[89] Formally this right belonged to all imperial subjects. Beginning in the Tang dynasty, a petition box was located outside of the gates of the Forbidden City and all people needed to do if they had a complaint was to go there and drop off a letter. The officials themselves had the same right to react to objectionable practices but there was also an official institution, the Imperial Remonstrance Office – a kind of licensed critic operating inside the bureaucracy – whose only task it was to come up with critical perspective and alternatives to the official policy. Custom dictated that officials should be circumspect in their views but there were still acceptable ways of forwarding even strong forms of criticism.

In practice, however, these institutions never quite worked quite the way they were intended.[90] When it came right down to it a virtuous administration was not necessarily easier to establish in China than elsewhere, and a government by men rather than by rules often left too much to chance. Corruption was for example rife, especially in the Ming period when the salaries of officials declined precipitously.[91] Similarly the 'parliament of the court' was an ideal construction which only functioned as intended to the extent that the emperors decided to go along with it. Often they did not, and those who did not could entirely bypass the deliberative process. For years on end some emperors completely ignored the affairs of state and no new decisions at all were made.[92] Instead actual power often slipped into the hands of the eunuchs.[93] As the only men allowed into the emperor's private quarters, the eunuchs were in a unique position to exercise power, and since they had made their careers outside of the examination system they had little respect for Confucian morality. At the height of their power there were some 20,000 of them within the gates of the Forbidden City.

Institutions like the Censorate and the Imperial Remonstrance Office can also be given a rather more sinister interpretation. As the Legalists had insisted, access to information – the way it was gathered and disseminated, withheld and distorted – was an important source of power for the emperors. Information, that is, did not only allow for wise decisions to be made but it also provided a means of manipulating the imperial subjects.[94] The Censorate was after all a way of detecting conspiracies and the Remonstrance Office allowed malcontents to identify themselves to the authorities.[95] Although it was against the rules, many remonstrating officials were punished – usually flogged – and while at first they had been allowed to wear protective padding, during the later Ming dynasty they went through these ordeals naked. Not surprisingly the institution of the Imperial Remonstrance Office seems to have atrophied from the middle of the fifteenth century onward.

15 Entrepreneurship

The classical Chinese understanding of reflection has implications for the position of human beings in the world and thus also for how entrepreneurship is pursued. The innate resistance to metaphysics and the lack of a notion of a personal god have from the first millennium BCE put the emphasis squarely on human beings, their actions and interactions. Hence the humanism and moralism of Confucius and his followers. Since there is no hope of divine intervention, men, not gods, are responsible for the state of the world. Clearly this understanding served to empower Chinese entrepreneurs. Since there is no reason to wait for outside assistance, we have to act on our own. Moreover, our actions will be judged not in an unpredictable afterlife but instead right here on earth according to well-established precedents.

At the same time the lack of a belief in an omnipotent creator has meant that entrepreneurship always was quite differently conceived in China than in Europe. The fantasy of the individual-as-demiurge was never embraced by the Chinese. Instead change happened ceaselessly through the interaction of the generative powers of Heaven and Earth, *yin* and *yang*, and successful entrepreneurs had to find a way of working with rather than against these forces. In addition, people in China were always reminded of the social character of their actions. Individuals were never regarded as self-sufficient and self-determining but instead as deeply embedded in relationships to particular others. Entrepreneurship took place within this relational context and entrepreneurs could achieve their goals only by working together with others. And while this is true everywhere else in the world, the explicit recognition of this fact meant that Chinese entrepreneurs had a far more realistic appreciation both of the opportunities and the challenges facing them.

As a result Chinese entrepreneurs came to require the support of quite different kinds of institutions. Or, as commonly was the case, people in China expressed a deep suspicion of formal institutions of all kinds. As far as political entrepreneurship was concerned, we said, it presupposed the virtuous actions of good men rather than the impartiality of good laws. And as far as economic entrepreneurship was concerned it relied heavily on personal connections and informal networks. Instead of trusting universal commitments, people tended to trust only the people they themselves knew. As we will see this informal, personalised, way of dealing with challenges made entrepreneurship simultaneously both easier and more difficult than in Europe.

The action of inaction

Given the ideas about the relentlessness of change and its thoroughly this-worldly nature, the job of a Chinese entrepreneur was first and foremost to watch and to wait. As all the classics had affirmed, change is happening all around us, it is happening by itself, and the key to success lies more than anything in our ability to understand its force and direction. It is a mistake to impose our preferences on the world and try to manage it imperiously by our actions.[1] Instead we should simply go with the flow of things and let ourselves be carried along as the world pleases. The *shi* inherent in every situation can never be worked against but there are a number of clever ways of using it to one's own advantage. Rather than being 'pro-active,' in other words, the trick is to keep one's cool, keep one's options open, and when conditions are right to settle the issue as expeditiously as possible.

From a European point of view this may perhaps appear as more of a managerial ideal than an entrepreneurial. People seem to be managing things that already exist rather than creating new things that previously did not exist. This, however, is the wrong conclusion to draw, and it is wrong because it is based on a European metaphysic which sees creation only as a result of the exercise of a personal will. The relevant choice is not whether to create or to manage but rather whether to act flexibly or inflexibly.[2] For much of the time maintaining one's flexibility may mean to reflect on a situation, to gather information, or to keep things quietly humming while secretly planning one's next move. The impression of normalcy which such activities give rise to can appear managerial but as soon as the right opportunity arises the manager is quickly replaced by the entrepreneur.

This, incidentally, is why there are such few heroes in Chinese mythology and no proper notion of tragedy.[3] The hero as conceived of in ancient Greece was a man who thrived on antagonism. He confronted superior powers which he valiantly fought against and ultimately defeated. In the tragedy this battle was lost beforehand as the actions of the main protagonist took him ever closer to his preordained end. The protagonists of a Chinese story however would always work with rather than against the forces which determined their fate. There was no agonistic struggle – no head-to-head confrontation – and hence no heroic victory. Instead the final outcome once it was achieved looked both straightforward and easy.

These were the lessons taught by Chinese strategists of war such as the famous Sun Zi of the fifth century BCE whose doctrines today are endlessly bastardised in various self-help books for middle-managers.[4] Wars are not decided on the battlefield, Sun Zi insisted, but instead when first organising and directing one's military positions. Rather than pitting force against force – as in the hoplite armies that clashed in ancient Greece or the citizen armies of total, post-Napoleonic, wars – the key to military success lies in postponing engagement with the enemy. This is a cold war of manœuvre and stealth and it requires endless revisions of one's tactical deployments; the aim is to mislead the enemy, to catch him off guard or to take him by surprise. For this reason the true strategist will only appear to win easy victories. 'For a man who is expert at using his troops,' as Sun Zi put it, 'this potential born of disposition may be likened to making round stones roll down from the highest summit.'[5]

Such ideas are easily applied to other fields of entrepreneurship. Translated into a theory of statecraft for example it became the Daoist notion of *wu wei*, the theory of 'no action.'[6] According to this doctrine a ruler should engage in few overt actions but instead always pull strings behind the scenes. As Lao Zi explained the best government is the one that governs least.

> I take no action and the people of themselves are transformed.
> I love tranquillity and the people of themselves become correct.
> I engage in no activity and the people of themselves become prosperous.
> I have no desires and the people of themselves become simple.[7]

Or as the Daoists were fond of saying: 'to rule a large state is like cooking small fish – stir as little as possible.'[8]

Other schools of thought expressed the same idea, not least the Legalists. This is perhaps surprising given their enthusiastic apologias for unlimited government, yet it fits perfectly with their love of secrecy and their emphasis on the arts of deception. According to Hanfeizi a successful ruler must learn to exploit the weaknesses of his opponents and to turn their own forces against them.[9] Rather than confronting his enemies directly he should pit them against each other and watch them annihilate themselves. To this end the gathering and manipulation of information are crucial. The emperor ruled more than anything through his secret police, through the spreading of gossip and the telling of lies. This paradoxically is the context in which the Legalists emphasised the role of law.[10] The law as they understood it was the codified expression of the ruler's will and there was nothing objective, universal or moral about it. When backed up by harsh punishments, the law established a naturalised social order which the ruler could manipulate at will. Repression, and the fear of repression, kept people in line. As long as everyone followed the law thus understood the emperor could afford to do nothing.

In practice however far from encouraging idleness on the part of the state, the *wu wei* doctrine often required considerable activity. Egged on by their Legalist advisers the emperors were busy burning books, burying Confucian scholars and building great walls to keep the barbarians out. They would also periodically engage in legislative reform or what was referred to as 'changes of law.'[11] By fundamentally revising the set-up of the administrative system they would radically change the official agenda of the state. Again the aim was to out-manoeuvre their opponents rather than to confront them head-on. By altering the rules of the game they hoped to catch their enemies off guard. One example of such changes were the Han dynasty reforms that abolished the independent feudal aristocracy and made all elites dependent on the state.[12] Another example was the way the peasant population was divided into more easily supervised groups of ten households which had collective responsibility for the actions of their members.[13]

Despite their profound differences in other respects, the prescriptions advocated by the Confucians were strikingly similar. For them too *wu wei* was preferable to overt action. The legendary emperor Shun, said Confucius, took no action and yet the empire was well governed. 'What did he do? All he did was to make himself reverent and correctly face south' [that is, sit on his throne].[14] This is also in the end what the Confucians meant by the 'Mandate of Heaven.'[15] To successfully maintain himself in power, we said, the emperor had to make sure that Heaven and Earth were in harmony with each other, but as long as this was the case there was nothing in particular that the ruler had to do. The emperor should lead by example and through rituals rather than by ceaseless activities.

In practice, however, and just like the Legalists, the Confucians interpreted the *wu wei* ideal as a demand for the construction of a certain kind of infrastructure.[16] For the state to be actively non-active, as it were, society had to be thoroughly organised; it was only once the appropriate organisational framework were in place that the emperor could sit back and face south. The construction of such frameworks was therefore the prime task of each new dynasty as it came into power. The case of the Song dynasty is the most striking.[17] In the tenth century CE roads and canals were constructed together with dikes and dams for irrigation; markets were set up and policed, calendars prepared, taxation regulated and security improved; large-scale arms industries, porcelain and silk factories were founded by the state and public store houses for grains were built to protect people against famines. The Chinese state in its Song dynasty manifestation was an architect, an engineer and a teacher. Inevitably however much of this institutional infrastructure then decayed and eventually the dynasty itself was toppled. The job of the incoming dynasty was to restore the framework.[18] This move from institutional renewal to institutional decay described the lifecycle of every dynasty and thereby the political rhythm of imperial China.

The Chinese discovery of Africa

Even though infrastructural projects of various kinds kept officials busy there were undeniable limits to the entrepreneurial ambitions of the imperial state. Above all Confucian officials were unlikely to embark on ventures which they deemed too risky. Most notably the *wu wei* ideal only worked well in situations where the officials had access to plenty of information. The manipulation of information, we said, was the real foundation of the power of the imperial state. Yet in cases where information was uncertain and the risks high, doing nothing was not a feasible option, and for this reason such situations were best avoided. What was precluded in other words were precisely the kinds of actions that

European explorers had embarked on from the fifteenth century onward: intrepid sea-borne adventures into the radically unknown.

True to expectations the Confucian literati were indeed highly reluctant to interact with foreigners.[19] China was the 'Middle Kingdom' after all, the most sophisticated society in the world, and by comparison everyone else was a 'barbarian' and more similar to insects or birds than to human beings. As the scholar-bureaucrats constantly repeated there was nothing whatsoever that the Chinese could learn from such beings and there were hence no reasons to visit them. If by contrast foreigners desired to abandon their uncouth ways and come to China, the Chinese were happy to assist them and include them in their system of tribute-bearing states. They would become satellites to China's sun and bask in the glory which radiated from its civilisation.

Yet there is clearly something wrong with this account since we know that the Chinese during long periods both traded with foreign countries and frequently visited them. The Chinese were at least as intrepid as ever the Europeans. Already before the establishment of the first imperial dynasty in the third century BCE there was trade with Korea, Manchuria and India, and during the Tang dynasty the Chinese ventured even further afield, including in 607 CE to Siam.[20] In the Song dynasty they mastered the monsoon winds and the open sea and embarked on trading missions with countries throughout Southeast Asia, in particular with Java.[21] Chinese merchants bought elephants' tusks, rhinoceros' horns, strings of pearls and incense in exchange for silver and gold. The trade was extensive enough for the authorities to start worrying about the drain of precious metals.[22] In 1219 an ordinance proclaimed that silk and porcelain henceforth should be used in payment for foreign transactions instead of coins.

The most famous of these maritime projects were the enormous fleets dispatched in the early fifteenth century to explore the countries around the Indian Ocean.[23] The leader of these expeditions was the admiral Zheng He who between 1405 and 1433 conducted several expeditions the largest of which comprised no fewer than 62 ships and some 37,000 soldiers. They sailed to Ceylon, India, Persia and Arabia and visited places like Aden and Mecca before continuing southward along the African coast. The Chinese exploration of Africa predated the European by several decades.

The question is why the imperial state embarked on these entrepreneurial ventures despite the official hostility to all things foreign. The answer is that the adventures in practice had little to do with the worldview of the Confucian literati, instead it is significant that Zheng He was a eunuch.[24] As direct employees of the emperor the eunuchs were responsible for supplying the inner court – including the 3,000 or so members of the emperor's harem – with clothes and assorted luxury items. Missions of procurement with this aim had taken place at least since the second century BCE.[25] Zheng He, one could say, went to the Indian Ocean on a shopping spree. As for the literati, they accepted these transactions since they brought tax revenue but also glory to the imperial state by including an ever-larger number of countries into its planetarium of tribute-bearing subjects.

Although they were employees of the palace the eunuchs had not passed the state examinations and they were not part of the regular administration.[26] Often born of poor parents and with little or no formal education they had few of the prejudices of the Confucian-trained elite. If there were opportunities to make money and gain a reputation through foreign trade the eunuchs were ready to seize them. In addition it is easy to imagine that Zheng He's personal background made a difference: he was a Muslim born in the multicultural province of Yunnan in the extreme south. Like many other successful entrepreneurs He was positioned on the threshold between different worlds and for that reason able to respond to alternative logics of action.[27] In fact his father and grandfather, like all good Muslims, had already made the trip to Mecca before him.

But then these expeditions suddenly ceased and all international commerce was outlawed.[28] In fact a state monopoly on foreign trade was put in place as early as in the fourteenth century and from this time onward commerce had periodically been halted. The only reason He's ventures could proceed was that they were considered as parts of the official system of tributes rather than as straightforward trading missions. From the middle of the fifteenth century this ruse was no longer accepted. New imperial decrees were enacted to regulate maritime commerce in 1433, 1449 and 1452, and each one had increasingly severe penalties attached to it. The ban was even extended to coastal shipping so that in the end 'there was not an inch of planking on the seas.'[29] The laws would continue to oscillate in subsequent centuries, periodically allowing certain forms of foreign trade and then outlawing them completely.

As an explanation for these bans the anti-commercial instincts of the Confucians, their xenophobia and ingrained conservatism, are often blamed but there are also several contingent reasons, including the completion of the Grand Canal to Beijing in 1411 which dramatically reduced the importance of costal trade.[30] Yet the main reason for the ban was political, or to be more precise it was a result of the power struggle between the eunuchs and the Confucian literati.[31] In a simplified formula, whenever the eunuchs were in power trade restrictions were relaxed and whenever the literati were in power trade restrictions were tightened. Restricting international trade was a way for the Confucians to impose their outlook on the state but it was also a way to enhance their power at the expense of their despised opponents. As the Confucian Vice President of the Board of the War Office summarised the new consensus later in the fifteenth century:

> The expeditions of the San-pao [Zheng He] to the Western Ocean wasted tens of myriads of money and grain, and moreover the people who met their deaths on these expeditions may be counted by the myriads. Although he returned with wonderful precious things, what benefit was it to the state? This was merely an action of bad government of which ministers should severely disapprove.[32]

This abrupt conclusion to the overseas adventure illustrates nicely the limits of the entrepreneurship sponsored by the Chinese state. As we have seen, far from inactivity, the *wu wei* doctrine required the construction of an elaborate organisational framework which the officials could manipulate to their own advantage. However, where such a framework was impossible to set up, such as in relation to the all-too-unpredictable world of barbarians, there was nothing for the state to do. Here *wu wei* truly came to mean 'no action.' As a result, just as the Europeans were 'discovering' the world, the Chinese were withdrawing from it. If Portuguese sailors had rounded the Cape of Good Hope some 50 years earlier than they did they would have encountered Chinese ships in the waters of East Africa, but when they finally got around to in 1488 the Chinese were already gone.

Supporting private entrepreneurs

Although the imperial bureaucrats disliked foreign trade they hardly liked domestic trade much better. What mattered to them were instead moral values, enshrined in the Confucian canon and exemplified in their own way of life. Commerce by contrast was a degrading occupation pursued by unproductive and dispensable people. What the Confucians liked were farmers who made a living from the sweat of their brow and who knew their proper place in society.[33] At the same time the Confucians knew the importance of keeping people happy and well-fed since economic hardship only too easily could lead to political discontentment. For this reason alone the emperors had an obligation to assure the prosperity of their subjects. Hence the infrastructural and institution-building projects – the land reclamation and irrigation projects, the road and canal building, the book printing and book dissemination – which each new dynasty embarked on. We briefly discussed the reforms of the Song dynasty above but the first Ming and Ching emperors made similar, if ultimately not as impressive, efforts.[34]

The state also made attempts to establish and enforce property rights although it never was completely successful in this regard. The criminal code enacted by the Ming emperors and borrowed by the Ching provided some means of adjudicating conflicts over property but the main provisions were embodied in customary laws and they varied considerably from one part of the country to another.[35] On the other hand, the imperial state constituted no threat to the property rights of merchants and investors. In imperial China public finances were generally in an excellent condition.[36] From the beginning of the Ming dynasty until the crises of the latter part of the nineteenth century, the state participated in few wars and the financial requirements of the state were limited. Hence taxation was light and corvée labour was infrequent. In fact the state relied on money-lenders not for loans but in order to recycle some of its surplus funds.

Encouraged in these ways and others, markets developed vigorously both during Ming and Ching.[37] In the markets for factors of production, labour, land and credit were freely traded with a minimum of government intervention. And markets in consumer items were booming too. People bought rice, cotton, tea and sugar on a regular basis but also silk, pearls, porcelain and jade. As one would expect, the demand for luxury goods was driven entirely by social imperatives.[38] By surrounding themselves with the expensive and the extravagant, members of the elite sought to enhance their status in their own eyes and in the eyes of the rest of society. This is how China became the world's primary supplier of luxury goods; the things the European upper-classes came to value so highly, in other words, were really produced by and for the Chinese upper-classes. To pay for their habits the Europeans extracted silver from the mountains of Peru and shipped it across the Pacific, and this injection of precious metals expanded the Chinese markets even further. In addition several kinds of domestic credit instruments were developed together with bills of exchange.[39] As a result of the commercial boom, and as a measure of it, Chinese towns increased dramatically in size, in particular during the course of the eighteenth century.

Despite such evidence it can still be said that China remained a predominantly agricultural and bureaucratic society rather than a commercial. Markets were highly developed to be sure but they existed alongside subsistence farming and the economy organised by the state. If anything the market and the non-market parts of the economy expanded together, neither gaining relatively on the other.[40] A similar point can be made about urbanisation. Chinese cities were indeed enormous, but the countryside was even more so. By the middle of the 1780s, some 94 per cent of the empire's 290 million people lived in the countryside.[41] Moreover, even during the height of the consumer boom the imperial state remained profoundly sceptical regarding the inherent value of commerce. Economic growth was not a value in itself and it was noticed by the Confucian authorities above all for the social dislocation it brought.[42] It was taken as a sign of decline rather than progress when people left farming to go into business or any of the crafts.

And as we said, entrepreneurship in imperial China was always understood as a profoundly social activity, and this fact determined both the opportunities available to entrepreneurs and the limits facing them. Property, for example, never belonged to individuals but instead to families and lineages, and in many cases regulations stipulated that land could be sold only to other lineage members. Similarly entrepreneurs were fathers above all, *pater familias*, driven by the double ambition of honouring their ancestors and leaving as much as possible to their descendants.[43] After the Ming period all farms and next to all businesses were family-owned, family-run and family-staffed, and there were almost no larger economic units except those organised by the state.[44] Supplied by a very large number of very small producers, most markets were decentralised and ferociously competitive; everyone was a price-taker and no one was in a position to dictate to others. This made markets highly efficient and kept profit margins low but as a consequence large and long-term investments were often difficult to organise.[45]

Loyalty to the family meant that Chinese entrepreneurs rarely faced problems with collective action. Within the family it was easy to see who was contributing to the common endeavour and easy to apply a wide variety of sanctions against non-contributors. At the same time its business-like character meant that the family was more characterised by hard work than by shared intimacies, and the small profit margins meant that people had to work extremely hard in order to survive.[46] This made family firms more efficient than alternative corporate forms since families could exploit their members far more ruthlessly. The most exploited were women, wives in particular who suffered much abuse from their mothers-in-law especially before they had produced a male heir.[47] But children worked hard too and they were often beaten if they refused. The only reward for the children was that they one day would inherit the family business, and the only reward for wives was that they one day would become mothers-in-law themselves.

The familial nature of the entrepreneurial unit meant that it was hard to expand the business beyond a certain size and that advantages of scale often were difficult to achieve.[48] To some extent such problems could be dealt with through the personal contacts the father was able to establish. Personal contacts are important for entrepreneurs in all societies but in the case of China access to *guanxi*, as they were known, often made the difference between success and failure.[49] Not surprisingly people invested much time in creating and maintaining such personalised networks of contacts. Typically they would start by exploring some pre-existing affinity – based on lineage, shared place of origin, education, dialect or last name – and then reinforce this tie through mutual gift-giving and the sharing of meals.

Guanxi networks also provided a means of reducing risks and uncertainties and they gave entrepreneurs access to all kinds of crucial resources. In imperial China such informal support was always more important than whatever formal support the imperial institutions provided. People of the same lineage or locality would organise mutual aid societies and co-operative banks; people of the same trade or craft formed guilds through which working conditions were regulated and measurements and weights standardised; there were funeral societies, secret societies and criminal brotherhoods where the members swore holy oaths to come to each other's assistance in times of need.[50] The arcane lore of these fraternities simultaneously helped protect trade secrets and disseminate innovations. In addition *guanxi* networks were often entrepreneurs in their own right. Lineage associations in particular were large land-owners and it was commonly the case that the members invested in businesses together.

This organisational logic determined the conditions under which also political entrepreneurs operated. In imperial China, as we have seen, there were several official channels through which complaints could be expressed yet independent political entrepreneurs were not permitted. Politics was the prerogative of officials duly appointed by the state. At the same time Chinese history from the earliest times onward is rife with peasant rebellions and other uprisings. Some of them were eminently successful: the revolt of the Yellow Turbans brought down the Han, the revolt of the Red Turbans undermined the Chin, and the Taiping Rebellion prepared the way for the end of the empire in 1911.[51]

The official doctrine of the state acknowledged the legitimacy of these revolts in a roundabout fashion. The eventual success of a rebellion demonstrated that the current emperor's heavenly mandate indeed had been lost and this automatically conferred legitimacy on the new regime.

The best way to organise such uprisings was to rely on some kind of personal networks and in most rebellions secret societies and semi-criminal gangs played a crucial part. Just as in the case of economic entrepreneurs these networks were able to draw on various financial resources, and since they had fewer problems of collective action they could easily draft the manpower required. Often they were inspired by millenarian ideas derived from Daoist mysticism and their ethos would often be radically egalitarian.[52] In the vast majority of cases however the rebellions were ruthlessly suppressed by the authorities and the insurgents unceremoniously disposed of.

16 Pluralism

Consider next the problem of pluralism as it played out in the Chinese setting. The first European travellers to China in the sixteenth century came back with stories of a country that was highly authoritarian.[1] In China, they reported, the emperors ruled like tyrants and everyone was forced to obey their commands; the cruellest and most unusual of punishments made sure that dissent was silenced and social order maintained. For the Europeans the kowtow – the practice of prostrating oneself flat on the ground before the Dragon Throne – became the symbol of what came to be known as 'Oriental Despotism.'[2] In a country where everyone was kowtowing both literally and metaphorically pluralism was not a problem since pluralism did not exist. Standing up for diversity and the freedom of conscience the Europeans refused to engage in this cultural practice, with predictable diplomatic complications as a result.[3]

And yet China was, and is, not a monolith but instead a highly pluralistic society. Rather than comparing it to a single European country it is best compared to the European continent as a whole, with the same diversity and contrasts between various regions and ways of life. Hence the circumstances of a cultured bureaucrat in the capital had next to nothing in common with the circumstances of an illiterate peasant in the countryside but countryside life differed greatly too between north and south or between the eastern seaboard and the western interior. In addition China is and has always been ethnically, linguistically, and confessionally diverse. Although the vast majority of people are Han Chinese – today they officially constitute some 92 per cent of the population – there are 56 officially recognised ethnic groups, seven Chinese dialects and hundreds of minority languages, in addition to religions as diverse as Daoism, Confucianism, Buddhism and Islam.[4]

Diversity characterised also the machinery of the imperial state with a bureaucracy that was split both vertically and horizontally into factions.[5] The conflicts between eunuchs and Grand Secretaries we have already discussed but there were also perpetual power struggles between these two groups and the higher mandarinate in charge of the imperial departments, and between this 'inner court' and the members of the 'outer court' consisting of the members of the regular bureaucracy.[6] Moreover each of these institutions was divided within itself as the officials formed factions based on competing *guanxi* networks. Thus for example the students of, say, the 'class of 1580' stuck together and continued to pay deference to the officials who once had examined them.[7] Informal groupings such as these looked after their own interests, promoted their own protégés and covered up for each other's shortcomings and mistakes.

The European visitors to China were quite simply wrong. In China as everywhere else in the world where reflection and entrepreneurship are institutionalised conflicts will continuously arise between mutually incompatible projects and ideas. Such incompatibilities could not be resolved on an *ad hoc* basis and they could not simply be repressed in the name of uniformity and obedience. The problem of pluralism, also in China, required institutionalised solutions. The aim of this chapter is to briefly discuss some of these.

The fear of chaos and what to do about it

Few societies have been more acutely aware of the problems of pluralism than the Chinese. In the political memory of the country, among the mighty and the powerless alike, this was above all expressed as a perpetual fear of *luan*, or 'chaos.'[8] Chaos meant that the carefully crafted balance between Heaven and Earth had broken down; it meant banditry and famine and massacres committed by imperial troops sent to restore order. Or, in its most grisly manifestation, chaos meant cannibalism.[9] Although cannibalism surely never was particularly common it served as the perfect symbol of the utter collapse of civilised existence. Consequently there are reports of human flesh being consumed whenever *luan* ensued, including most recently during the Cultural Revolution.[10]

Given this troubled history the perpetual question in the minds of all Chinese was how chaos best could be avoided and peace assured. Political thought as it developed from the earliest times onward – including Daoism, Legalism and Confucianism – was more than anything attempts to answer this question.[11] According to the Daoists the fundamental problem was that statesmen and bureaucrats interfered with the natural development of society and imposed their own, and invariably conflicting, policies on it. Instead social life should follow the seasons of the year and the stages of human life and periods of growth and agitation should be replaced by periods of relaxation and silence.[12] Surely an unrealistic set of policies in a world dominated by struggles over power!

As far as practical politics was concerned, the answers provided by Legalists and Confucians were always more influential. The Legalists as one would expect were adamant that chaos only could be avoided with the help of the harshest of possible measures.[13] All subjects were to be tightly controlled; all independent groups to be abolished; and those who engaged in anything that even remotely resembled a crime against the state – or those who failed to report such crimes – were immediately to be put to death. In a metaphor popular with the Legalists the emperor was a huntsman.[14] Some animals he killed and consumed immediately, others he domesticated and kept as chattel. To assist him he had his eagles – the state officials and the secret agents – who tracked down the prey and prepared it for the kill. Among his chief enemies were 'the five vermin of the state,' that is, scholars, freelance politicians, independent knights, persons with connections to senior officials, and merchants and craftsmen.[15] What these groups had in common was the fact that they had access to independent bases of power and for this reason alone they were threats to the state.

In China, however, such overt repression was always going to be an expensive and therefore an inefficient policy. As the peasant proverb had it, 'heaven is high and the emperor is far away,' and in practice there were limits to the power of even the most totalitarian state. Instead effective policing and long-term stability required a far more flexible approach. This is what the teachings of Confucius provided. Instead of destroying all independent bases of power the Confucian suggestion was to look for a way of bringing all diverse groups into harmony with each other. One precondition for this to happen was that people learn to exercise self-control. Desires should be suppressed and a calm, stoical, attitude should be cultivated. Another precondition was that people learn to consider the feelings of others and treat everyone as they themselves would like to be treated.[16] Finally people had to be taught to do their duty. As the Confucians saw it society was a gigantic hierarchical network made up of superiors and inferiors who all had responsibilities towards each other; above all the inferiors had the duty to obey and the superiors had the duty to be benevolent.[17]

If people only followed these precepts no repression was needed nor even much by means of central commands. Instead order was guaranteed through mutual adjustments and compromises worked out in millions of continuous, everyday, encounters. The emperor was the ultimate guarantor of this balance but his power was above all the power of example. In order to keep chaos at bay he too should first of all make sure that he honoured his ancestors and cared for his dependants. 'The character of a ruler is like wind and that of the people is like grass,' Confucius explained. 'In whatever direction the wind blows, the grass always bends.'[18] Conversely the ultimate cause of all cases of chaos was always found in moral failings at the imperial centre. It was a heavy responsibility that rested on the shoulders of the Sons of Heaven, and in order to cope, particularly from the Ming dynasty onwards, the emperors took refuge in an entrenched bias in favour of the status quo.

In cultural terms self-control and a consideration for the feelings of others were often translated into a preference for indirect rather than direct expression.[19] In China people have generally preferred to withhold their opinions or to express them indirectly, in ornate, flowery and non-threatening language. Indirection was regarded as more polite, as a better way of getting along with one's fellows, but also as a wiser course of action in the face of political repression. In addition indirection was understood as a more efficient way to communicate. By speaking around rather than directly about a subject it was possible to say more about it; by taking an indirect route, Chinese thinkers asserted, it was possible to get quicker to one's goal.[20] In a society where people prefer such roundabout routes, there will be fewer head-on collisions.

As a way to summarise these various solutions to the problem of pluralism consider the problem of what came to be known as the 'rectification of names.'[21] In China, just as in early modern Europe, the problem of social order was often blamed on a confusion of language. The reason people constantly were fighting, thinkers of all schools concluded, was that they no longer could agree on the meaning of the words they used. Thus if only the words could be 'rectified' – clearly defined and made stable in their definitions – peace and order would be assured. In this way linguistics became a part of statecraft; *zheng*, 'to govern,' was a matter of *zheng*, 'to rectify.'[22]

This connection was never more explicit than in case of the Legalists who as one would expected looked to the emperor to impose linguistic order on his subjects. This in the end was the rationale for their book pyres and their anti-intellectual campaigns. As Qin Shi Huangdi made clear people should not learn the meaning of words from ancient books but instead directly from his officials. The emperor's word was law and his laws were the only words permitted. Or as he proudly declared on a stele engraved in memory of his deeds: 'I brought order to the mass of beings and put to the test deeds and realities; each thing has the name that fits it.[23]

The Daoists, for their part, rejected all such talk of repression.[24] The rectification of names, as they saw it, was a philosophical and not primarily a political issue. The problem is above all that words never can capture the illusive and ever-changing nature of reality. Words divide the world and for this reason they cannot grasp the unutterable unity which lies beyond all verbal distinctions.[25] Moreover since words often divide reality in a clumsy and arbitrary manner it is not surprising that they divide also human beings and cause misunderstandings and confusion. It follows that conflict, since it is an inevitable consequence of the use of words, never can be settled through verbal means. 'This disordered world can only be reformed by a Sage, but so long as the world is disordered, no Sage can appear.'[26] Instead final peace will require the abolition of all words and all distinctions.

Clever as such arguments may be the Confucians had no time for mysticism. For them the rectification of names was instead a moral imperative.[27] As long as meanings are unstable people will inevitably make mistakes regarding their status and their obligations, and when such mistakes are made no one will be able to act appropriately. Before long social classes will be levelled, generations will be mixed, and chaos will ensue. For this reason it was an urgent matter of the security of the state that words meant what they were supposed to mean. The Confucians agreed with the Legalists that the emperor had a particular responsibility in this regard yet his power rested not in his ability to kill the proponents of alternative definitions as much as in his ability to set a proper linguistic model for his subjects to follow.[28] As always the ideal was government by example rather than by decree. 'If a ruler sets himself right,' Confucius explained, 'he will be followed without his command. If he does not set himself right, even his commands will not be obeyed.'[29]

An orthopraxic society

A curious feature of traditional Chinese society, often pointed to by foreigners, is what appears to be a remarkable ability to live with even the most blatant of contradictions.[30] Consider for example the views of the current Chinese leadership on matters of political economy.[31] There is an absolute contradiction between capitalism and communism – for one thing, capitalism entails private ownership of the means of production while communism requires its abolition – yet this has not stopped Deng Xiaoping and his successors from declaring that China simultaneously is communist and capitalist. To a European this makes no sense. It is either an outrageous example of double-speech – the post-totalitarian disregard even for the formal rules of logic – or a ruse easily revealed as hypocrisy.[32]

On inspection however 'double speech' and 'hypocrisy' turn out to be two venerable Chinese traditions, and this fact should lead us to suspect that something else is going on. Consider for example the stark contradictions that always existed between the philosophical systems of ancient China. Although the differences between, say, Confucianism and Legalism are at least as obvious as ever those between communism and capitalism this has not stopped individual statesmen and teachers from happily embracing both. Or consider religion. There are conspicuous tensions between Confucianism, Buddhism and Daoism, and yet many Chinese have had no problems whatsoever in subscribing to all three.[33] People may visit different temples at different times and for different reasons and never be much bothered by the incompatibility of the beliefs.[34] Even more remarkably, temples in the Chinese countryside would often have a generic nature and combine religious symbols drawn from all available creeds.[35]

In order to make sense of such violations of the basic rules of logic it is important to remember that Chinese religions have had little or nothing by means of an organisational structure.[36] Apart from the ancestral cult which is institutionalised within the family there is no organisational affiliation between temples and worshippers; there are no memberships or membership requirements, no catechisms or tests of the knowledge of the tenets of the faith. As a result there is never a reason to sign up to a particular set of beliefs at the exclusion of all others. All a worshipper needs to do is to show up at the temple and go through the prescribed motions. Religious worship is like a series of casual relationships rather than a life-long marriage. And it works since Chinese gods – in sharp contrast to the Christian – never were particularly jealous.

Similarly contradictions between philosophical systems rarely become obvious since the questions the systems usually are required to answer concern practical matters and not matters of dogma.[37] Statesmen and scholars would shop around for ideas that suited their purposes and assemble them into intellectual bricollages rather than into architectonic structures. In the same way, one could argue, the tenets of communism or capitalism mean less to contemporary Chinese leaders than the fact that the respective systems help keep the country together and them securely in power. This is also the reason why religious wars have been exceedingly rare throughout Chinese history.[38] The crimes that mattered were those directed against the state and the public order but religious dissent never belonged in this category.[39] The simple fact that people embraced a different interpretation of the sacred than the officially prescribed never counted as a sufficient reason to kill them.

Instead of orthodoxy it was orthopraxy that held the country together; what mattered that it was the right ritual rather than the right belief.[40] As long as people participated in the officially prescribed motions it did not matter what, if anything, that went on in their minds.[41] In China the most important rituals were those concerned with the cult of the ancestors, above all the funeral rites, but there were also important rituals for marriage, baptism and the celebration of New Year, and a long series of festive annual events. Although initially these ceremonies may have had an explicit religious content, from the first millennium BCE their moral significance became more important.[42] They were celebrations of life on earth and not life in heaven.

As we briefly discussed above, *li*, 'ritual' or 'ritualism,' was an important instrument of social control.[43] Rituals expressed the meaning of social obligations; rituals provided people with concrete ways of fulfilling their obligations; rituals assured the filial piety of the sons, the faithfulness of the wives, and the loyalty of the subjects. Rituals also helped define social classes and thus to maintain the hierarchical order of social life. More than anything the Confucians believed it was ritual that protected China from chaos.[44] The emperor was the person ultimately responsible for the maintenance of this ceremonial system. It was the rituals the emperor performed that kept Earth in correspondence with Heaven; *yin* in balance with *yang*; and the five elements in harmony with each other.[45] To help him in these arduous tasks he relied on two large departments of the state bureaucracy: the Department of Rites and the Office of Protocol.

The metaphor which best captures the logic of the ritualistic Chinese state is a musical one. The emperor was like a conductor directing a state bureaucracy of musicians and the people were like dancers moving in unison to the beat of their tune.[46] As long as everyone only concentrated on their particular tasks it did not matter what they were thinking and there was no need to monitor and control their minds. Social order was assured above all since none of the performers had a reason to object to the performance in which they were participating; most of the time they preferred to simply lose themselves in the music:

> The dancer's eyes do not look at himself; his ears do not listen to himself; yet he controls the lowering and raising of his head, the bending and straightening of his body, his advancing and retreating, his slow and rapid movements; everything is discriminated and regulated.[47]

Any discordant notes or awkward movements were immediately detected by the other performers. In a state organised in this manner adjustments will happen smoothly and by themselves and no overt repression is required.

Or slightly differently put, the most fundamental reason why rituals work so well as instruments of social integration is that they have no contraries.[48] People may disagree on whether to wear a cap made of linen or a cap made of silk as part of a ceremony, and while these objects are different they are not contra-dictory in the way a belief in an afterlife contradicts a lack of a belief in an afterlife.[49] For this reason it is easier to be tolerant of differences in rituals than of differences in beliefs. Or differently put, the same ritual action can be associ-ated with any number of diverging opinions. Even if they mean different things with the same actions – or indeed, mean nothing at all – people can still get on without conflict. In addition since ritual actions have no contraries, they are impossible to question or to doubt, and for this reason ritualism ruled out criti-cism as a political strategy. In a society where harmony is the highest social goal, and where carefully integrated rituals are used to achieve it, there can be no political dissent, only bad manners.

The advantages of chaos

But as we know harmony was not always achieved. Occasionally the emperor would indeed lose his mandate and chaos would ensue. Although the Chinese always had an innate fear of such times, there are good reasons why we should view them slightly more sympathetically. Or rather, while it is impossible to be positive about warfare, famines and cannibalism, there is no doubt that chaotic times in Chinese history allowed more room for pluralism and as such they often had beneficial long-term effects. Chaotic times and their immediate after-maths were times when China was more open to the outside world and to new influences, when new economic and technological advances were made, and new institutions put in place. It was as a result of chaos that China changed most rapidly.[50]

There are two good reasons why this has been the case.[51] First of all periods of chaos were periods of fragmentation when it was impossible to impose a single political framework on the country as a whole. When there were compet-ing centres of power each one was free to implement their own policies in their own fashion. This allowed more alternative solutions to be presented and more political, social and cultural experiments to take place. Second, during times of political fragmentation there was competition between political units, most obviously in the form of wars or threats of war. Facing aggressive enemies, each state could only survive if it was militarily prepared. Such preparations required developments in military hardware but soon also innovations in many other dimensions of social life, technological know-how, economic organisation and political institutions.

Consider three examples of this logic. The first we have already briefly dis-cussed: the Warring States period prior to the establishment of the first imperial dynasty in the third century BCE.[52] In all respects and by all accounts this was an extraordinarily creative period in Chinese history. What more than anything seems to have driven the innovation was the fierce competition that developed between the assorted statelets that constituted the Chinese cultural sphere. The imperative for all of them as the Legalist dictum put it was to 'enrich the nation and to strengthen the army.'[53] Hence military battles were no longer as in the previous period fought in order to win fame but rather in order to kill enemies and gain territory. For these purposes new weapons were invented – swords, crossbows and cavalry units – and these in turn required new industrial techniques for their manufacture. Already by 400 BCE China produced as much cast iron as Europe would in 1750 CE.[54] Farming techniques developed too and the first major irrigation works were undertaken; metal coins appeared and markets developed, including trade with Manchuria, Korea and even India.[55]

The Warring States period was also a time when the state machineries became far more professionalised. New administrative procedures were put in place and the bureaucracies began to be more rationally organised. The old aristocracy was suppressed by a new generation of ruthless leaders and scholar-bureaucrats took over the day-to-day operations. The intellectual developments of the period were extraordinary. This was the time of the vast outpouring of creative energy associated with the 'Hundred Schools' when all major systems of Chinese thought originally were established. Many of the new ideas – including, most famously, Confucianism – were propagated by scholars who wandered from one court to another looking for interested audiences and royal patronage.[56] The multiple centres of competing power made sure that even unorthodox thoughts were impossible to suppress for long; there was always some ruler somewhere who was prepared to give unfamiliar ideas a hearing.

The second example concerns the Song period and the period immediately before it.[57] In Chinese history this interregna has gone down as the time of the 'Ten Kingdoms' and the 'Four Dynasties,' both labels giving a flavour of the political diversity of the age. But since also the Song dynasty itself was under constant attacks from various central Asian tribes, military competition continued even once the country was unified in 960 CE.[58] In fact in 1127 the Yürchen eventually overran the northern parts of the country. Culturally, intellectually and economically this was another period of great flourishing, and again it was the lack of a stable hegemony and the need for military preparedness which propelled the transformation.[59] During the interregna between Tang and Song, China was wide open to the world; foreign trade was officially encouraged and treaties were concluded with foreign nations on more or less equal terms. Merchants from around Asia visited the country – there was even an Iranian trading mission at Hainan – wandering monks imported Buddhist scriptures from India, and among popular entertainers there were conjurers, jugglers and acrobats from Bahtria in Central Asia.[60] Throughout the interregna Daoism was particularly influential and Daoist ideas led to new developments in both the sciences and the arts. This was when books began to be published and new forms of practical knowledge disseminated. The military competition meant that the warring states were forced to take an active role in sponsoring a long range of infrastructural and industrial projects; armament factories and looms were scattered around the country.

The third example is closer to the present: the chaotic interregna between the end of the empire in 1911 and the founding of the People's Republic in 1949.[61] Unable to establish a central government which could hold the country together the republican regime broke up into rival fiefdoms governed by separate, and interminably competing, warlords. Foreign troops were also a threat, in particular the Japanese who at the Treaty of Versailles in 1919 were granted the right to all previous German concessions in China. Hostilities continued even once the Guomindang unified much of the country at the end of 1928. In 1931 Japan invaded Manchuria and throughout the following decade they committed atrocious acts of genocide; the 'rape of Nanking' in 1938 being the most notorious.

Difficult and insecure as life must have been this was at the same time a socially, culturally and intellectually very exciting period. The old hierarchical order was breaking down and the country was slowly industrialising; women, workers and students were given different roles; people dressed in new clothes and listened to new music.[62] Yet more urgent reforms were required, this at least was the view of the members of the 'May Fourth Movement,' the movement of students at Peking University and assorted sympathisers who on that date in 1919 took to the streets to protest against the outcome of the Versailles Treaty.[63] Many of them blamed Confucianism and 'feudal' traditions for the humiliation the country suffered. Jettisoning the old, China should reform its language and embrace Western science, philosophy and arts. Not content to wait for the reforms to take place, the students experimented with alternative lifestyles and devoured authors like Marx, Freud, Spencer, Darwin and Spengler. When Albert Einstein, Bertrand Russell and John Dewey passed through the country on speaking tours they were everywhere given rapturous welcomes. When the Communists finally came to power in 1949 they not only unified and pacified the country but they also brought an end to this ferment of political opinions and competing social and cultural programmes.

17 Europe and China compared

In the nineteenth century it was common among Europeans to see China as eternally stagnant and as hopelessly behind their own ever-more dynamic part of the world. China constituted a warning regarding what would happen to a country where tradition and authority came to dominate at the expense of initiative and innovation. While Europe surged steadily ahead, China was sinking ever-deeper into the mire of its own past. And yet it is easy to reveal such conclusions as little but Victorian prejudices. If anything change was always a far greater concern in China than in Europe. As nineteenth-century Chinese scholars may have insisted, change was nothing new, nothing modern, it was instead an inescapable feature of all of nature and all of society. The Chinese had already spent more than 2,000 years reflecting on its sources.

What is true however is that change in China never implied progression. Change was not taking Chinese society in any particular direction; instead society was always subject to the same cycles and patterns.[1] The most basic such cycle was the one of the agricultural calendar but there were also political cycles associated with the rise and fall of dynasties. And yet, lest we forget, this was also the traditional European conception of change.[2] Indeed, as we have discussed, the first Europeans to call themselves modern were not looking forward to an unknown future but instead backward to a classical era. In this respect they were no different from Chinese thinkers and social reformers. What all European revolutionaries before 1789 wanted to do was to restore the past rather than to break with it.

At the same time there is no doubt that the conceptual resources available in China differed from those available in Europe. The Christian religion provided an alternative conception of history, a notion that was not cyclical.[3] Jesus Christ had died at a particular point in time and at the end of all time he would return to judge the living and the dead. The history that stretched between these two junctures was linear not cyclical. The Chinese held no similar fanciful beliefs and the reason they did not is itself a result of the way they conceptualised change.[4] In China the sources of change were regarded as internal to the world and change was not the outcome of the application of anyone's will. In Europe by contrast the sources of change were external. It was god who had created the world and who continued to intervene into it. Human beings could have an impact too, except that, as the Church constantly affirmed, they were hopelessly sinful and powerless.

In Europe it was only in the course of the seventeenth century that these various conceptual components came to be put together in a different fashion. Suddenly the Europeans were able to make and achieve things previously never made or achieved. Bacon pointed proudly to gunpowder, the compass and the printing press as examples of the spirit of the new age. In their new-found self-confidence the Europeans began looking forward rather than backward, and as a result 'modernity' and 'revolution' came to take on their contemporary meanings. The progressive view of history is a Christian eschatology for a secular age.

From our perspective however Bacon's examples appear singularly badly chosen. Gunpowder, the compass and the printing press were Chinese inventions after all. If all it took was the invention of these particular technologies China should have modernised far earlier than Europe. But as we have insisted, modern society was never only a consequence of a few scattered inventions. It was not the technologies that mattered as much as the fact that Europe was able to appropriate, disseminate and develop them. These were social achievements rather than individual, or rather they were achievements to be credited to the operations of institutions. It was institutions in the end that provided the basis for the self-confidence of the Europeans. The real achievement, largely accidental and unintended, was the creation of a piece of social machinery able to produce constant change. Conversely the reason why Chinese society was unable to modernise was not the lack of extraordinary individuals, the technological know-how or the entrepreneurial spirit, but instead the fact that a similar piece of social machinery never was assembled.

And yet as a comparison of Chinese achievements with European will make clear, China could easily have gone down a European route. Chinese and European societies were always very similar to each other and this was still the case as comparatively late as in the early eighteenth century. Yet by the middle of the nineteenth century a great gulf seems to have opened up between them, never more dramatically illustrated than in terms of the discrepancies in military hardware. The challenge is to come up with an explanation which simultaneously is able to accommodate both these similarities and these differences.

Reflection, entrepreneurship and pluralism

Around the year 1500, we said, the Europeans attained new perspectives on themselves as a result of the largely unexpected discovery of three new kinds of outsides: classical antiquity, new continents overseas and a limitless universe. But in China too the same kinds of outsides were available and just as in Europe they provided alternative perspectives and new ideas. This was most obviously the case with history. As we have seen history – in particular the mythological golden age associated with the Sage Kings – was both a source of authority and a source of social criticism. Far from clutching the living in a stifling grip, the hand of the Chinese past provided plenty of creative guidance.

Much the same can be said regarding nature which, particularly within the Daoist tradition, constituted an attractive alternative to society and to the imperial state. Sitting on their mountain sides the Daoist hermits formulated a state of nature reasoning far more radical and philosophically sophisticated than anything the Europeans ever came up with. As far as astronomy was concerned it had a curious status in China as a political rather than a natural science, and as such it was a carefully guarded *arcanum imperium*. But there was also a subversive astronomy pursued by enemies of the ruling dynasty, again often made up of Daoist critics. At the same time the fact that Chinese cosmologies were interpreted politically meant that they had few of the existential ramifications of their European counterparts. It is difficult to imagine a Chinese philosopher uttering a Pascalian *cri de cœur*; Chinese philosophers were always thoroughly at home in the world.

As far as geography is concerned it always meant something quite specific in the Chinese context. Although there certainly were periods when the imperial regime was prepared to accept influences from abroad, the main attitude was as ethnocentric as it was xenophobic. Foreigners were all barbarians of one kind or another and they had nothing whatsoever to offer China. The best perspective on the world, all Chinese literati believed, was offered by its centre, by China itself. This was an attitude soon adopted also by the foreigners – the Mongols and the Manchus – who came to occupy the Dragon Throne.[5] On the other hand, China is a very large country which encompasses many different kinds of people and things. For this reason alone there may have been less need of a proper outside.

Just as in Europe reflection was carried out in canonical form, and in China too the canon came to provide an external standard by which the everyday world could be judged. But while Europe turned Christianity into an official dogma, China had several alternative belief systems and this fact allowed more vigorous reflection to take place. There was not, as in Europe, only one kind of truth which everyone was forced to embrace. The dominant canon, Confucianism, would in the twentieth century receive a tremendous amount of flack; by foreigners and Westernised Chinese intellectuals alike it was blamed for all of China's ills – it was 'feudal,' 'backward-looking,' 'anti-science' and 'anti-modern.'[6] And yet compared with Christianity it must be regarded as a wonderfully flexible doctrine, far more generous, accommodating and open to the new and the unexpected. Rather than scapegoating Confucianism it is best regarded as a leaf on a Chinese November tree.[7] The Confucian canon survived above all since there was no reason to abolish it. This was not, let us note, the case with Christianity. The main tenets of the Christian dogma had to be repudiated, in effect if not always in name, before modernity could proceed apace.

A similar argument can be made regarding entrepreneurship. In China there were always plenty of resourceful and innovative entrepreneurs both within the political and the economic sphere. What strikes a European however is above all the entrepreneurial capacity of the Chinese state. The state was rational and meritocratic and already in the first centuries BCE its officials were carrying out assorted grandiose schemes: building great wall, canals and irrigation projects. In this respect the Han dynasty resembles the Roman empire, except that when the Han dynasty eventually fell, the entrepreneurial ethos survived. During Song the state undertook a large number of impressive infrastructural investments, creating and supporting markets, spreading literacy and learning, facilitating agriculture and manufacturing. There was nothing even remotely similar in the European Middle Ages.[8] After the year 1500, however, these roles seem to have shifted. European states became far more active and the Chinese state more passive. European states affirmed their sovereignty, waged wars, and developed a large number of tools with which they proceeded to reconstruct society; the Chinese state, by contrast, focused largely on the maintenance of peace and stability.[9]

But private economic entrepreneurs continued to be active. Although the imperial bureaucracy treated private enterprise with benign neglect – indeed merchants were officially regarded as an entirely unproductive class – there were nevertheless plenty of successful businessmen who made great profits. China was more thoroughly commercialised than Europe and when European merchants began arriving in the early sixteenth century there was absolutely nothing they could teach their Chinese colleagues about the logic of market capitalism. Naturally the periodic bans on foreign trade constituted obstacles to trade but whenever the bans were relaxed Chinese merchants were quick to take advantage of the new opportunities. And even when the bans were in place there were still huge markets to be explored in China itself.

The fact that economic and political agents always were slightly differently conceived in the two parts of the world gave entrepreneurship a unique character. In Europe there were many public agents who were independent of the state and there were many kinds of corporate bodies.[10] In the early modern era horizontal membership organisations quickly expanded to unite people who shared the same interests and outlooks. In the case of China independent bodies and public agents were rare and instead organisations were predominantly made up of personalised networks. This was not least the case with economic entrepreneurs who relied heavily on their networks of families and friends. Briefly put, since they faced fewer social constraints, European entrepreneurs had more freedom of action and potentially they could gather many more people. But this also meant that collective actions became notoriously difficult to organise.

In China by contrast entrepreneurial action was strictly speaking a private rather than a public matter, and while this limited its potential impact, it also made it far easier to organise. In China political entrepreneurs relied on the 'brothers' of their secret societies and economic entrepreneurs relied above all on their families and lineages. Chinese entrepreneurs never regarded themselves as demiurges and they were not heroes pitting themselves against the world. Instead entrepreneurs saw themselves as acting within social contexts, and this provided them both with opportunities and with limits.

Vigorous reflection and active entrepreneurship resulted in conflicts in both parts of the world; there were constant clashes between people with different visions, diverging plans and mutually exclusive demands on the same resources. How such conflicts were resolved determined matters of peace and war but also the pace of social change. The European nineteenth-century cliché, propounded by John Stuart Mill and others, was that Chinese society was conformist and that this was the reason for its stagnation. And within the sphere of politics at least the cliché is largely correct – there was indeed preciously little room for political pluralism. Diverse opinions were tolerated only as long as they did not question the existing political order; political dissent was accepted only in retrospect. And yet similar repressive ideals were common in Europe as well. The metaphors constantly invoked by Hobbes and Bodin were functionally equivalent to those of the Chinese Legalists.

Broadening the picture it is clear that Chinese society was both more diverse and more tolerant of diversity than Europe. For one thing there was no Christian church that rigorously enforced the tenets of an untenable dogma. Instead competing doctrines co-existed peacefully and people often embraced distinct ideational frameworks seemingly without bothering about the contradictions. In China ideas were treated pragmatically, in terms of their consequences, and rituals were always more important than beliefs. What Europeans ended up calling 'Chinese culture' was a ritualistic façade behind which there was little by means of a common content.[11] In Europe by contrast beliefs were everything and the Sunday confession was used as an occasion to inspect the content of people's minds. While Europe was orthodox, China was orthopraxic, and orthopraxy is always a lot easier to enforce than orthodoxy. In Europe as soon as the precarious consensus broke down in the sixteenth century endless religious and ideological conflicts ensued.

A first solution – originally proposed by Renaissance Humanists but perfected in the salons and coffee-shops of the eighteenth century – was in some ways strikingly Chinese. Good manners and polite behaviour were, just as Confucius had taught, a way of dealing with conflicts. Yet it was always difficult for people with widely divergent views to be polite to each other, and in the end the solution worked best within small and socially homogeneous groups. In China, by contrast, politeness was combined with other social virtues, above all a deep-seated preference for indirect expression. Although it would drive nineteenth-century Europeans mad with frustration, indirect expression, once you have learnt to interpret it, is often a more efficient way of communicating, and it can indeed help to maintain social peace.[12]

From a European perspective, however, these were not tenable solutions. Given the preference for indirection there were never enough contradictory forces that could counter-balance each other; social co-ordination took place already before social expression and as a result the surface of society always stayed calm and smooth. Ultimately these Confucian ideals were a cultural solution to the problem of pluralism which never could deal adequately with the stresses and strains brought on by the modernisation process.

Institutionalisation

The comparison above is of course far from complete and much more could be said along the same lines. Even the longest of summaries would, however, reach much the same conclusions. Based on what has been said it is difficult to see why Chinese society should be any less dynamic or transformative than European societies. If reflection, entrepreneurship and pluralism are what determines the pace of social change, China always had plenty of it and from early on in its long history. Although the Chinese solutions are quite different from the European they seem to be more or less functionally equivalent. In fact in many respects China was better positioned than Europe. Chinese culture allowed for more vigorous self-reflection and for more diversity, and there was certainly no shortage of extraordinary Chinese scientists, businessmen and politicians.

When summarised in this manner the puzzle becomes even more puzzling. Why indeed did not China modernise far earlier than Europe, say sometime in the Song dynasty? And why did things slide to the point where China in the nineteenth century let itself be embarrassed by a few foreign merchants and their accompanying gunships? The answer is provided by the general argument outlined above. Reflective, entrepreneurial and pluralistic as Chinese individuals and Chinese society no doubt were they lacked the appropriate institutions. Europe modernised first not because its culture was more conducive to modernisation, or because its inhabitants were smarter or harder working, but only since it happened to be more institutionally blessed. In China, despite its achievements, the mechanics of modernity was never properly assembled; there was change to be sure but it was never institutionalised.

Consider the case of Chinese science and technology. Given its extraordinary precocity it is surprising that the sciences in China never made the same breakthroughs as in Europe. Take the Daoist doctors who manufactured sex hormones as early as in the eleventh century or their contemporaries the surgeons who used datura in order to induce total anæsthesia during operations.[13] Or take the example of the scholar Wu Yu-hsing, whose book *On Epidemics*, written in response to the great epidemic of 1641, took him tantalisingly close to a theory of micro-organisms.[14] Or consider similar puzzling failures among entrepreneurs. Already in the fourteenth century the Chinese had all the technology they needed for the industrial production of cloth; they had the looms, the gearing and the sources of power.[15] And yet from this time onward the technology deteriorated rather than progressed and eventually much of it fell out of use altogether. The Chinese could surely have started the Industrial Revolution some 400 years before Europe but for some reason they did not.[16]

It has been common to blame Confucianism for these failures and it is no doubt true that although the Confucian reflection was deep, it was always exceedingly narrow. Above all the Confucians never cared much for science or industry, and this was particularly true for the Neo-Confucians who dominated the state from the fourteenth century onward.[17] And yet in contrast to Europe, the problem in China was never really that conservative ideas blocked progressive ideas but rather that science and technology lacked the proper venues to develop. There were plenty of innovative people but few ways of combining their ideas and routinising their activities.[18] There were for example no scientific academies. Instead science was an *ad hoc* activity pursued by individual scholars, often Daoists, and the groups of disciples they happened to have assembled.[19] This was not good enough to assure steady scientific progress. It also seems likely that the predilection for indirect expression hindered scientific advances.[20] Since arguments rarely came head to head there could be plenty of conjectures but few refutations.

What Confucian intellectuals cared about more than anything were instead political, social and moral matters. In these fields there were indeed a number of institutions to support them; the bureaucracy and the examination system above all, but also more specific bodies like the Censorate and the Office of Remonstrances. These were impressive institutions to be sure and with their help Chinese top-level bureaucrats soon became the most well-informed and reflective in the world. The problem is only that such institutionalised reflection took place only within the state and almost never outside of it.[21] State power was exercised in public silence; the state never turned to the people, addressed them and sought to convince them; people were never asked to reply, to defend themselves or to argue the opposite case.[22] There was not as in Europe a notion of a public sphere where a public opinion could be formed and deliberation could take place on matters of common concern. There were no parliaments, no press, no middle class with a tradition of discussing politics, and there were no means of exercising public scrutiny or control.[23] As a result the bureaucrats could never speak on behalf of the people and their decisions were never as well informed as they could have been. Political entrepreneurship was the prerogative of an elite.

As far as economic entrepreneurs are concerned they were as we have seen largely left to their own devices and this benign neglect may indeed have done more good than harm. Many merchants made a lot of money and China became a thoroughly commercialised society, and yet this was not simply a consequence of the magic of the free market. Rather the commercial expansion during Ming and Ching took off from a base put in place already in the Song dynasty. This was when the institutional framework was established – the roads, the regulations, the markets – within which all subsequent commercialisation happened. It was thanks to this early institutionalisation that China continued to grow economically even though the state subsequently did little or nothing to support economic entrepreneurs.[24] In fact the commercial expansion took place even though the institutions themselves slowly began decaying.[25] By the late eighteenth century even basic infrastructural services such as roads and canals had become unusable, and commercial legislation and standardised weights and measurements were no longer respected.

The fact that economic activities could expand even under such circumstances is largely explained by the presence of private alternatives to the public institutions. Above all people fell back on their families, lineage or surname organisations, guilds and secret societies. Just as in Europe of the Middle Ages personalised networks such as these provided a modicum of predictability even in an environment of high uncertainty and risk. Instead of trusting the imperial institutions people trusted their families and friends. While this provided an ingenious way of dealing with a society in institutional decay, the solution had obvious limits. Above all support for entrepreneurship was entirely privatised. Without the personal contacts there was very little an aspiring entrepreneur could do to obtain funding or to protect and develop his investments.

Differently put although traditional economic activities continued apace it was difficult to develop new ones; while the turn-over increased in existing markets, few new markets were developed. Chinese capitalism followed Smithian rather than Schumpeterian prescriptions: things were becoming ever more efficiently allocated but markets were not adapting to new technologies or opportunities. This is why comparisons only of levels of economic development are deceptive.[26] The Chinese level of development may have been close enough to the European in, say, the year 1650, but by this time the two parts of the world had already developed along different trajectories for quite some time. The Europeans relied less and less on personalised networks and more and more on impersonal institutions. This is after all what the financial revolution in Holland, and then England, was all about – the creation of public banks, joint-stock and chartered corporations, stock markets, insurance companies and the protection of patents and property rights. The economic consequences of the presence or absence of institutions such as these were not visible to the naked eye in the year 1650 or even in 1750, but by the year 1850 they were embarrassingly obvious to all.

As far as the problem of pluralism is concerned it too was largely dealt with on a cultural rather than on an institutional level. The preference for ritualism and indirect expression meant that it was difficult to even imagine clashes between opposing interests.[27] Despite its presence as a technology self-regulating mechanisms never gained the status of political or economic metaphors and instead a combination of politeness and deference to authority were the continuously reiterated official solutions. Instead of self-regulation musical metaphors were common; people were supposed to follow the official tune and live in harmony with each other. In China the notion of rights was completely missing from the political vocabulary, and since there were no rights people could never argue that a certain status or a capacity was theirs by nature. Hence there could be no institutionalised systems of rights which could operate as conflict-moderating devices. Although it may be tempting to see the *wu wei* doctrine as an early Chinese precursor of the late eighteenth-century European doctrine of *laissez-faire*, the *wu wei* doctrine had political and not economic aims. Whether the economy grew was irrelevant as long as the country was politically stable.

Although there was an innate fear that diversity would lead to chaos in both parts of the world, times of diversity were often moments of cultural and intellectual flourishing. Economically they were periods of spurts in development. War and the fear of war meant that autonomous states and statelets had to prepare themselves militarily, but also politically, administratively and socially.[28] The most successful among them, the ones that eventually won out, were the ones who built the most successful institutions. In many cases, in China as in Europe, these institutions survived once the new dynasties eventually were established.

The reassertion of hegemony limited pluralism even though, as we said, the hegemony of the Chinese state was far more tolerant of diversity than, say, the Catholic church. Confucianism is not to blame, or the machinations of power-hungry eunuchs, or even the xenophobia endemic to classical Chinese culture. The failings were instead institutional. Not that the political authorities ever really saw the point. In China, in contrast to Europe, the idea of *pluribus unum* was never properly institutionalised. The different states did not retain their sovereignty and they did not come to interact in a mutually counter-balancing system of states. Instead hegemony imposed itself on all of them with the reestablishment of each new imperial, and singular, dynasty. One obvious result was that while European military technology developed rapidly under the pressure of military threats, the matchlocks and canons of early nineteenth-century Chinese armies were essentially the very same ones as they had employed three centuries previously.[29]

In a short-hand, China was either united or divided; united it allowed too few competing solutions, divided it allowed too many. Europe was more fortunate in that it developed institutions which allowed it to be at the same time united and divided. And this was not just a more attractive solution on moral or æsthetic grounds, it had concrete social consequences. If one European society temporarily slowed down, there would elsewhere in Europe be another society that continued to change. From the seventeenth century onward European societies seem to replace one another as leaders; when one country slowed down, another country picked up.[30] In the long run reactionary societies lost out in the competition for wealth and power.

Part VII

Reform and revolution in Japan and China

18 Foreign challenges, Japanese responses

In practice of course few direct comparisons were ever made between China and Europe. Although there had been continuous contacts between the two parts of the world ever since the early sixteenth century these were limited by the profound Chinese scepticism of all things foreign.[1] From 1720 onward overseas commerce was a monopoly controlled by a merchants' guild in Canton and requests by Europeans to allow them the freedom to trade were angrily rebuffed by Qing officials. Ever ethnocentric, the Chinese knew preciously little about foreign countries and they had as we have seen no official interest in foreign trade. 'We have never valued ingenious articles,' as emperor Qianlong famously explained in an edict sent to King George III after he in 1793 had been approached by the British envoy George Macartney:

> nor do we have the slightest need of your country's manufacture. Therefore, O king, as regards your request to send someone to remain at the capital, while it is not in harmony with the regulations of the Celestial Empire we also feel very much that it is of no advantage to your country.[2]

The reaction on the part of Japanese officials was initially just as dismissive.[3] What they feared more than anything was the corrosive effect on Japanese society of foreign influences, Christianity in particular. In 1633 Japanese subjects were forbidden to travel abroad and six years later all Europeans were unceremoniously expelled from Japanese soil. Only a small Dutch trading post was maintained in Nagasaki and a few ports were open for trade with China and Korea. The ideal, if not always the practice, was a country hermetically sealed off from the rest of the world.

Behind these closed doors China and Japan came to develop quite independently of Europe and of each other right up to the middle of the nineteenth century. At this point however the Europeans suddenly returned, and this time around they had a clearer set of demands, far more determination, and enough military hardware to exercise real pressure. Measured by this simple military standard, but also by the standards of economic development or industrial capacity there was no question of who by now was the superior. China and Japan were simply not powerful enough to successfully defend themselves.

What the Europeans wanted was access to markets above all; in particular, in the case of the British, the ability to sell their Indian-grown opium.[4] When the Chinese refused to yield to these demands Britain flexed its military muscle and imposed a series of treaties which seriously limited China's sovereignty. The United States and France won similar concessions and soon Germany, Russia and Japan joined the scramble. China descended into civil wars of which the Taiping rebellion was the most traumatic. And then eventually the Qing dynasty itself was overthrown and in 1912 a Chinese republic was proclaimed.[5]

In the case of Japan the story was initially quite similar although it began unfolding slightly later and with the Americans rather than the British in the lead.[6] In 1853 Commodore Matthew Perry sailed into Edo Bay with several gunships and demanded that the Japanese end their policy of isolation, allow foreigners to trade, to settle and to propagate their religion. Subsequent visits by assorted Europeans kept up the pressure. Just as in the case of China the foreigners imposed unequal treaties, and just as in China the political centre eventually crumbled. Unable to defend the integrity of the realm the Tokugawa regime was overthrown in a military coup in 1868.

And yet the story in the case of Japan ends quite differently. Here the final result was not political disintegration and economic malaise but rather a vigorous set of reforms which united the country and set it off on a path of rapid social change. The question is why. Why did the Japanese react so successfully to the arrival of the Europeans whereas the Chinese reacted so belatedly and inefficiently? Why did Japanese society change whereas Chinese society stagnated? Leaving the explicit comparison of the two countries until the next chapter, this chapter looks at how Japan responded to the foreign threat.

The Japanese react

One factor which put Japan at a comparative advantage was the simple fact that the Europeans came to China first. Hence the Japanese were in a position to study the behaviour of both Europeans and Chinese and to draw their lessons from it. It is easier to succeed after all if one first can observe the failed actions of others. Although this historical coincidence surely made a difference it would be a mistake to conclude that Japan's success for that reason was purely coincidental. Rather, as we shall argue, Japan was able to take advantage of the fortuitous timing of events only since it was equipped with the appropriate set of institutions.

Consider for a moment what is involved in observing a situation as it unfolds in a foreign country. Clearly the Japanese first of all needed a way of getting information from China or a way of going there themselves. Furthermore they needed a way to disseminate this information once they had it and a forum in which the news could be discussed and put into a proper analytical framework. Only in this way would they end up actually understanding what was going on and how they best might prepare themselves for the European onslaught. What was required that is were institutions that facilitated reflection. But obviously this is not enough since the Japanese also had to act on the basis of the information they had. Actions requires actors and actors too, as we know, need institutional support. Finally, and as always, there was a need for institutions that could deal with the conflicts that inevitably would arise. In short, while coincidences of different kinds always are likely to occur, and maybe to one's advantage or one's disadvantage, it is only a society that is well equipped institutionally that consistently can hope to seize opportunities and avoid mistakes.

Take the issue of how the Japanese first learnt about the events taking place in China in the early nineteenth century and how they discussed them among themselves. Naturally the fact that Japan only had had limited contacts with the outside world severely limited the flow of information across its borders.[7] And yet the news block-out was far from complete. Some information trickled in through the Dutch in Nagasaki, or through stranded foreign sailors, but above all the Japanese received information from imported Chinese books.[8] These books were carefully read first of all by the Tokugawa censors who screened them for traces of Christian doctrine but before long they reached book-sellers throughout the country. In addition, in the early part of the nineteenth century, defying the travel ban, an increasing number of Japanese subjects did indeed go directly to China to see the unfolding of events for themselves. Invariably they were alarmed. As the samurai leader Takasugi Shinsaku reported in 1862:

> When British and French walk along the street, Chinese move aside and get out of their way. Shanghai is Chinese territory, but it really belongs to the British and the French. . . . This is bound to happen to us too.[9]

But obviously one person sounding the alarm is never going to be enough. What was required was instead the kinds of institutions that could allow the information to be processed by society at large. Fortunately Japan was well equipped in this regard. From early on in its history Japanese society had been highly reflective, at least as reflective as China, and largely for the simple reason that reflective technologies and institutions all were of Chinese origin. With a start in the eighth century CE the Japanese borrowed the Chinese system of writing as well as the printing press, schools, academies and remonstrance boxes, Buddhism, Confucianism, Daoism, Legalism, and all kinds of Chinese sciences and arts. And just as in China this institutional paraphernalia provided the Japanese with a wealth of perspectives from which to view their own and at the time far less developed society. If anything the foreign origin of their viewpoints on themselves only added to the reflective power; they were simultaneously able to see China from a Japanese perspective and Japan from a Chinese perspective.

As a result of all this activity, by the middle of the nineteenth century there were educational institutions serving the children of both samurais and commoners, and perhaps 50 per cent of all boys and 15 per cent of girls had some degree of formal schooling.[10] The level of literacy compared well with that of several European countries. In fact by this time a public culture based on the printed word had existed already for some 200 years.[11] By the late Tokugawa period some 500 to 600 books were published each year, including novels, works on morality and social etiquette, sample forms for letter-writing, maps and lists of famous places, outlines of Japanese history and calendars of annual events.[12] These books were cheap enough to buy but in addition there were also book-lending shops – some 800 of them in Edo alone – and other parts of the country, including remote villages, were often served by travelling book-lenders.[13]

Despite the Chinese origins of this reflective apparatus relations to China itself were always complicated. China was the 'middle kingdom' after all, and the rest of the world, including Japan, was by definition peripheral, that is to say inferior. Some consistent sinophiles, such as the early eighteenth-century Confucian Ogyû Sorai, accepted this world view and self-deprecatingly referred to himself as an 'eastern barbarian.'[14] Others were far less comfortable with such labels and there were even those who openly rejected China and showed nothing but contempt for its venerable traditions. From the eighteenth century in particular an increasing number of ever more vocal writers used China as a foil for a definition of the uniqueness of Japan. As the philosopher Motoori Norinaga put it:

> If one wishes to penetrate still further into the spirit of the true Way, then one must purify oneself from the filthy spirit of Chinese writings and proceed to the study of the ancient texts [of Japan] with the pure spirit of the sacred land. If that is achieved one will come to know, gradually, that we are not obliged to accept the Way of China. But to know this is to receive the Way of the *kami* [god] itself.[15]

This transvaluation, and the new sense of self-confidence which it indicates, may remind us of the way in which Europeans like Francis Bacon at roughly the same time first avidly studied the classics of Greece and Rome and then proudly rejected them.

In the eighteenth century this rejection of China provided the *kokugaku* school, the school of 'national learning,' with new perspectives on Japan itself.[16] Its leading proponents – the father and son, Azumamaro Kada and Kamo, for example – turned their backs on what they regarded as the empty intellectual-ism of the Chinese tradition and defended instead a purer, more innocent and more Japanese, form of sensibility.[17] Chinese culture, they insisted, functioned as a screen which obscured reality while indigenous Japanese traditions represented the world as it really was. Instead of reading old books the nativists spent their time contemplating cherry blossoms, August moons or snow on distant mountains; they preferred Shintoism to Buddhism, the irregular to the regular, and the spaces between things to their essences.[18]

In institutional terms the town of Mito became an important centre for the development of the native tradition.[19] The local lords, despite being closely related to the Tokugawa shoguns, took it upon themselves to sponsor an ambitious research programme into the history of Japan since the earliest times. The historical investigations and inventions engaged in by this group of scholars in the latter part of the eighteenth century provided the foundation for all subsequent visions of the Japanese past. Before long they had denounced the shogun as morally flawed and focused on the emperor as a symbol of all things Japanese. A revived Japan, they decided, would have to return to traditional values of hierarchy and loyalty.

This rejection of China was not necessarily an indication of ethnocentrism, however, and Japanese nativists were often quite prepared to consider alternative intellectual influences. One prominent example was *rangaku*, the 'school of Dutch learning,' the generic Japanese name for all sciences and arts emanating from Europe.[20] Just as the Chinese, the Japanese had first been introduced to European science by Jesuit missionaries in the seventeenth century but in contrast to China this intellectual tradition established indigenous institutional roots.[21] After the closing of the country in the 1630s intellectual contacts with Europe were kept up through the Dutch trading post at Nagasaki whose resident physician was an important source of medical information. And there continued to be a small group of dedicated Japanese scholars who eagerly awaited shipments of Dutch books on topics as diverse as astronomy, geography, botany, physics and chemistry.[22] In the first half of the eighteenth century *rangaku* scholarship even received official encouragement and the shogun ordered interpreters, government-employed physicians and other professionals to visit the Dutch and to absorb whatever knowledge they could get access to.

Given this background it is not surprising that the Japanese were quick to react to Commodore Perry's arrival.[23] They had their own history of dealing with the Europeans after all and in 1853 they already knew about the humiliation which the Chinese had suffered at their hands. Once Perry had left – threatening to return in a year to put even more pressure behind his demands – the shogunate began wide consultations with the daimyos, the various feudal lords, and with the emperor's court in Kyoto.[24] Although this hardly constituted a representative cross-sample of Japanese public opinion, it did constitute the views of a large and heterogeneous elite. Although the advice they gave varied considerably, all Japanese leaders in 1853 saw the presence of foreigners on Japanese soil as a threat to the cultural integrity and the political order of the country. On the other hand, since the military superiority of the foreigners was beyond doubt, the Japanese had no choice but to make some form of concessions. This is how the Treaty of Kanagawa came to be signed in 1864, opening up the ports of Shimoda and Hakodate to foreign trade.

The public debate however did not stop there but continued right through the 1850s and 1860s, and it was as a result of these discussions that opinions eventually came to shift.[25] As soon became clear the foreigners were not going to be content with the limited rights the Japanese initially had granted them but as additional concessions were made the impact of their presence became increasingly palpable. To the horror of the Japanese, Americans and Europeans traded, travelled, proselytised and educated, and before long they demanded access to more ports and more markets. After the additional Harris Treaty of 1858 there was clearly no way of stopping the trend. The shogunate had failed in its duty to defend the peace and integrity of the realm. The question was only what to do next.

The debate on this issue drew on native sources and on the country's Confucian legacy but also on assorted foreign examples. Suddenly quite new demands began to be heard: for a more centralised and bureaucratised polity, for the emperor to be reinstated as the figurehead of the political system, and for the country to completely open up to the outside world. As for centralisation and bureaucratisation, they were said to be necessary in order to strengthen the state in the face of the foreign threat.[26] Feudalism and decentralised responses, the argument went, had made Japan weak and had led to confusion. The ideal was instead a Confucian state of the Chinese mould and this is why the Confucian classics were rediscovered in the 1850s and 1860s and why their ancient arguments often were read as subversive calls for political reform.[27] Ironically this was just at the time when the same model was being undermined in China itself.

The call for a restoration of the emperor could also easily be interpreted in Chinese terms.[28] Just as China, Japan had had an emperor since times immemorial although, as the Japanese pointed out with pride, their emperors were all of the same dynasty. For the previous 1,000 years however these ostensible rulers had quite unceremoniously been tucked away in the imperial palace in Kyoto entirely without political influence and occasionally also without money. Yet as foreign pressure came to undermine the shogunate, the reformers began to see the emperor as a symbol behind which they all could rally. The emperor was the embodiment of uniquely Japanese ideals and the personification of the country's political and cultural independence. Or, in the battle cry of the radicals, the task was to 'revere the emperor and expel the barbarian.'[29]

It was from this position of xenophobia that the country opened up to the outside world.[30] As the reformers argued, if Japan only could become properly centralised, bureaucratised and unified behind the emperor an open-door policy was not really a problem. In fact, as many of them came to realise in the course of the 1860s, a strong Japan could only be a Japan which was open to the world.[31] The country needed military hardware and the industrial capacity to back it up, and foreign markets in turn required access to technology and an industrial base. Coming to learn more about the world the reformers also realised that many of the most successful European countries – Prussia was a commonly cited example – had managed to combine military prowess and political authoritarianism in exactly the way they themselves found attractive. Rather than finding safety in isolation, the reformers began looking for a way of establishing Japan as a fully-fledged actor on the world stage.

The Japanese act

But assorted proposals are not enough to bring about changes unless enough people are prepared to act on them. Reflection must be combined with entrepreneurship for change to take place, and entrepreneurship as always needs institutional backing. It matters greatly for example how various actors are constituted, what degree of autonomy they have, and what institutional resources they can command.

The most obvious actor at the time of Perry's arrival was of course the shogunate. The shoguns regarded themselves as military leaders and as such they were imbued with quite a different spirit than Chinese emperors. Although they never hesitated to invoke the authority of the Confucian corpus in legitimising their rule, the state was not a meritocratic bureaucracy and there were for example no entrance examinations.[32] The Japanese state was small, decentralised, and run by samurais connected to their superiors through personal ties of allegiance rather than through impersonal rules. Japan as a whole was a feudal society and the primary social virtue was not Confucian benevolence but instead personal loyalty; inferiors were expected to stay loyal to their superiors come what may.[33] From the point of view of entrepreneurship this provided a rather unique solution to the problem of collective action. A failure to do one's duty was punishable by death or *seppuku*, whichever came first.[34]

The shogunate had a tradition of political activism inspired by Confucian ideas of moral regeneration and 'self-strengthening,' but also by the examples set by Chinese Legalists. From the middle of the eighteenth century onward all shoguns embarked on their respective attempts to rejuvenate society.[35] What they sought to deal with were above all changes in the economy. Commercial capitalism as it took off in the seventeenth century led to new opportunities for social mobility but also to new inequalities and social tension. Conservative in their instincts the shogun began regulating guilds and money lenders and granting monopolies for the sale of everything from brass, sulphur and camphor to cinnabar, ginseng and lamp oil. At the same time the shogun made sure to improve their own financial positions.[36] They took increasing control over the national rice market in Osaka which all feudal lords relied on in order to convert the taxes they received in kind into readily available cash.

The shogunate was also the first actor to react to the foreign challenges of the 1850s, and while its reactions were predictably xenophobic it too soon came to realise that the unprecedented situation required bold moves. Under duress the shogun signed the treaties that opened up the country to foreign penetration, but it also adopted a far more proactive attitude. By the time it was overthrown in 1868 the shogunate had sent seven official delegations and numerous students and purchasing agents to Europe and the United States, and also established permanent embassies in London and Paris, developed a regular passport system and invited numerous foreign experts to help out with educational and industrial projects.[37] Many of these late Tokugawa reforms were quite successful and their general thrust was the same as that of the famously modernising regime which replaced it.

For a while it even appeared that the imperial court would lend the shogun its prestige. As many argued, the foreign challenge could only be effectively met if all Japanese rallied together for their common defence.[38] In practice however the court stood to gain far more from such collaboration than the shogun. For centuries the court had played no part whatsoever in politics and the fact that its views now were canvassed greatly enhanced its position. But it was the court's rejection of the Harris Treaty of 1858 that turned it into a political actor in its own right and set it off on a course opposed to that of the shogun. In the early 1860s various feudal lords presented themselves as intermediaries between the shogun and the court, but once the shogun came to be regarded as weak and defeatist they all began outdoing each other in pro-imperial rhetoric.[39]

In the end it was these feudal lords that held the future of the country in their hands. The daimyos were sovereign actors who pursued their individual agendas with the help of their independent resources.[40] The institutional guarantee of this independence was the feudal structure of Tokugawa society. Japan, we should remember, was not a nation-state of the European kind and the shogunate was not a central government; nearly all capabilities associated with a sovereign state were instead located in the feudal domains.[41] The 260 plus daimyos had a monopoly on the means of coercion, including their own armies and legal systems; they had their own bureaucracies and educational establishments; their separate currencies and economic policies were often geared to the exploitation of their neighbours. In relation to this diversity Japan as a whole was only a vague notion; it was the 'realm' – the *tenka*, meaning 'all under heaven' – and as such it constituted nothing as much as the uttermost limits of the known world.[42] It made sense to identify oneself as 'Japanese' only for the small elite groups who for one reason or another had dealings with the outside. Everyone else belonged in the *han*, the region governed by the daimyo.

The Tokugawa regime was the custodian of this realm. Or differently put, the shoguns were the ones responsible for the balance of power in the international system of states which was Japan.[43] Institutionally speaking the foremost expression of this balance was the *sankin kôtai* system whereby all daimyos were forced to reside in Edo for half the year and leave their families as hostages with the shogun when they returned home. Yet such harsh measures barely restrained their independence. A few daimiates in the south – Satsuma and Chôshû – were particularly difficult to control. They had become rich from sugar plantations and a lucrative trade with Okinawa and China, and once the foreigners appeared they began acting on their own accord.[44] When the shogun's delegates arrived in Europe in the 1860s they were surprised to find that representatives of the southern provinces already had been there. Rumours were going around about weapons purchases, a permanent Satsuma embassy to be set up in Paris or at least a separate exhibit at the Paris World Fair of 1869.

It was these southern daimyos who eventually overthrew the Tokugawa regime. In 1867 they suggested that the shogun step down and acknowledge imperial authority, and after some hesitation the shogun agreed. Yet in January of the following year mistrustful radicals seized the imperial palace, proclaimed a restoration of imperial rule, and armies from Chôshû, Satsuma and Tosa marched on the capital. A majority of daimyos stayed neutral and the remaining loyalists in the north-east were soon defeated. Soon the emperor moved to Edo, renamed Tokyo, and a very different chapter in Japanese history began.

Dealing with diversity

Given its later successes it is easy to forget how precarious the situation was for the Meiji government in 1868. The new leaders were not universally regarded as legitimate and their military forces were not strong enough to assert the authority of the government throughout the country. The *ancien régime* could have reasserted itself; civil war could have broken out; the country could have fallen apart. In the end of course none of this came to pass. On the contrary, the new leaders defeated the old order, kept the country together, and embarked on a programme of institutional innovation which in retrospect appears as remarkably successful. The question is how they managed to do it.[45]

As far as the old Tokugawa regime was concerned it never really posed much of a threat and there was no bloodshed and few purges. Rather the shogun and his closest allies were simply ordered into retirement and the Tokugawa bureaucracy was largely rehired as Meiji officials. The political fragmentation of the country, guaranteed through the feudal system, constituted more of a challenge. The daimyos had a long tradition of independence, even as we said their own armies, and there was no obvious reason why they should listen to the new rulers. And there were indeed military revolts: in the northeast of the country in 1868 and 1869 and in the southwest in 1877. Yet the political fragmentation also made it difficult for the daimyos to cooperate against the new leaders.[46] Generally they cared more about their own *han* than about united action in the name of the country as a whole. In the end they were all roundly defeated. At the same time repressive measures were combined with a great deal of sensitivity to local concerns.[47] Even though the country was formally unified in 1868, it took several years before the new government actually tried to make the assorted daimyos follow its central directions. The daimyos were not purged but retrained as governors of their respective provinces and their samurai retainers were generously paid off with government bonds.

In addition to such administrative measures order was maintained through the construction of an elaborate new state ideology. Drawing heavily on decades of *kokugaku* scholarship and on assorted nativist ruminations the new leaders constructed a new past for their country and for themselves, a past whose dignified traditions they then proceeded to invoke in support of their claims.[48] The Nara period, for 1,000 years lost in the mist of time, was a particularly powerful reference and the ministers of the Meiji government were all given titles used at the Nara court. Not knowing what any of their titles actually meant they were reportedly seen in Tokyo bookstores busily reading up on the subject.[49] Another reference was the Shinto religion, used as inspiration for an elaborate set of state rituals and eagerly supported by the Meiji government in preference to the more alien Buddhism.[50] For a while Buddhists were even actively persecuted and thousands of temples were closed. Before long however the new leaders realised that maybe they had overdone it. Already in the early 1870s references to the Nara period were quietly dropped and the Buddhists were readmitted to the national fold. A modern Japan required more modern references.

In this respect the symbol of the emperor was more useful. Dusting off hundreds of years of accumulated neglect, the emperor was reinvented as a divine presence and as a personification of the eternal unity of the Japanese people.[51] To be loyal to the emperor required every subject to be loyal to the new regime and to abandon their previous, regional, identities. Particular attention was attached to the idea of *wa* or harmony.[52] Presented as an eternal expression of the innermost feelings of all Japanese, harmony – just as the musical metaphors employed in imperial China – implied coordination, organisation and reconciliation; harmony required people to moderate their views and to defer to the tune and the rhythm set by the collective will as interpreted by the new leaders. In this way a new national consciousness was created for a nation that never previously had existed. The Japanese nation was made from domestic material but at the same time curiously similar to the nations which simultaneously were being created in Europe.[53] The Japanese could be nationalistic too and just as in Europe nationalist sentiments helped to maintain order at a time of rapid social change.

19 Japan and China in a modern world

Yet the story most commonly told about Japan in the nineteenth century does not concern the Meiji Restoration itself as much as everything that happened subsequently to it. This was when Japan embarked on its frantic quest to catch up with Europe and North America. The most immediate aim was to make the country strong enough to withstand foreign pressure but as the new leaders realised military might required an economic base and also radical social reforms. As soon became clear the Japanese were spectacularly successful in attaining these objectives. Even as they were allowed into the country in ever larger numbers, the foreigners were successfully held at bay. The unequal treatise were renegotiated and Japan won wars, first against China in 1895 and then against Russia in 1905. Economic growth took off and Japanese society began changing rapidly.

The question is how they managed to do it. The answer is above all that the Japanese leaders focused on the construction of new institutions. Remarkably, as soon as they had consolidated their hold on power they collectively took off on a lengthy study trip to Europe and North America. The aim was more than anything to investigate how modern institutions operate, and what the Japanese regarded as the most successful examples they took home with them. More, and more specialised, missions followed and foreign experts were also invited to come to Japan as teachers and advisors. Grafting these institutions onto the body of traditional Japanese society the country embarked on decade after decade of continuous change.

Yet this is at best only half an explanation. Although we have no reason to be surprised at the spectacular effects brought about by a given set of modern institutions, the question remains why Japan for such a long time was the only country outside of Europe to modernise. The comparison with China is particularly striking in this regard. Initially in many ways far better positioned than its eastern neighbour, China repeatedly failed in its modernising efforts. Instead of decades of continuous change China experienced decades of foreign invasions, civil wars and chaos, and when order finally was restored it happened under a Communist regime which embraced an entirely different conception of modernity.

Given these experiences the really interesting question is not why it was that

Japan changed so dramatically but rather why it was that Japan managed to implement these institutional reforms. The recipe is fairly simple after all and the puzzle is why only some are able to follow it. Or to be more precise, there are two separate questions here. The first concerns the ability of a society to implement reforms, the second the relationship between the new institutions and traditional society. For a society to modernise, that is, there must be people around who can put the required institutions in place without too much opposition. And yet implementing the reforms is only the beginning. What is required in addition is that the grafting be successful. Somehow the foreign institutions must be made to work together with the traditional ways in which society operates. The task of this chapter is to discuss these questions in the context of a comparison between Japan and China.

Japan: the institutionalisation of change

Study missions abroad were as we have seen not an invention of the Meiji government, yet after 1868 they were led by more high-level people and they became more frequent and more thorough in their work. With the old power structure gone there were also fewer obstacles to implementing their recommendations. As the Meiji emperor had declared when ascending the throne: '[k]nowledge shall be sought throughout the world in order to strengthen the foundations of imperial rule.'[1] In the following four decades some 11,000 passports were issued for overseas travel and in the 1880s in particular foreign models were eagerly studied, adopted and then adapted to Japanese conditions.[2] For a while this process was quick enough for people to talk about a wholesale replacement of Japanese society by foreign models; everything old was to be abolished and everything new was to be embraced.

The most spectacular example is the study mission led by Iwakura Tomomi between 1871 and 1873.[3] Iwakura, one of the leaders of the Restoration, once he safely had established himself in power, took a sabbatical and simply went off abroad together with some 50 of his most senior colleagues. During their 21 months away they visited the United States, England, France, Germany and Russia, and as they immediately came to realise a great developmental gap separated Japan from these countries. The Faustian spirit of the Europeans was impressive, their obsession with material goods was both fascinating and scandalous, and the new Japanese leaders were quick to make note of all the latest advances in military technology. When returning home even the most conservative members of the mission had no doubts regarding the urgent need for reforms.[4] The gap may be great, they all agreed, but it was not unbridgeable.

What the Iwakura mission studied most avidly, and what they more than anything took home with them, were blueprints for institutions. Institutions were also what subsequent missions – such as the one in 1883 led by Itô Hirobumi, the future drafter of the constitution – were asked to study.[5] From each country they visited they borrowed the institutions they regarded as the most advanced: from France the Napoleonic code, the police service and elementary schools; from Prussia the army; from England the navy and the central bank, and from the United States the universities.[6] The criteria behind each adoption was efficiency and rationality and the Japanese were quick to identify the connection between the dynamism of Anglo-Saxon societies and their emphasis on liberal values.[7] Yet political considerations played a role as well. To the more conservatively minded Japanese leaders Germany was a particularly attractive model. Like Japan itself Germany was recently unified, it had authoritarian traditions and it was a newcomer to industrialisation and world markets.

Putting these institutions together a modern society was constructed which at the same time was imported and yet indisputably of native origin. To begin with institutions that facilitated reflection, consider the newspaper.[8] In Tokugawa times there had been no place for public discussions of matters of state and everyone was expected to obey even if they never understood why.[9] This changed after the Meiji Restoration as a new freedom of the press allowed discussions of politics. In the 1870s a host of new newspapers took up the challenge and they quickly found readers. Similarly a modern university, Tokyo University, was established in 1877 and a number of distinguished foreigners were invited as teachers and researchers. Initially the focus was on the humanities and on law but in the course of the 1880s and 1890s departments of engineering, medicine, agriculture and forestry were added. Scientific academies spread as well, first focusing on engineering and the military sciences but soon catering to all kinds of social needs. Among others there were institutes for the study of statistics, economics, psychology and international relations.[10]

As a result of the operations of these institutions Japanese society soon became vastly more reflective. New ideas were easier to publicise, technologies and solutions were more widely disseminated, news about foreign developments reached more people more quickly. The reports produced by the Meiji study missions became bestsellers and the books by Fukuzawa Yukichi, one of the most perceptive of the new globetrotters, reached an audience of millions.[11] Reading about inventions made abroad Japanese companies began looking for ways in which they could get their hands on them. One example is the newspaper trade itself where woodblock prints soon were abandoned for printing presses, but soon French shipyards, English gas lights and American telegraph lines spread across the country.[12] New philosophies and lifestyles spread much in the same way. European-style clothing became compulsory for government officials in 1872, the solar calendar was introduced together with Sundays off from work, and European accounting, medical and educational practices caught on. Translations of Samuel Smiles's *Self-Help*, 1871, and Defoe's *Robinson Crusoe*, 1883, became mandatory reading for anyone who wanted to understand the logic of the new society.[13]

Other institutions facilitated entrepreneurship.[14] From the early 1870s onward people were free to move around and to settle wherever they wanted; they could take up any occupation and farmers could cultivate the crops of their own choice.[15] Moreover commoners were allowed to take surnames and to ride horses, outcast groups like the *eta* were abolished and marriages between members of different social groups were allowed. Markets were further improved when all internal custom duties were removed and the communications network extended. In the course of the 1870s a modern banking system was established, boosted by the bonds that decommissioned samurai received, and soon a nationally integrated structure of interest rates emerged.[16] The corporate form of enterprise was introduced and the corporations began trading their shares in the stock-market; in 1893 a commercial legal code and tax laws were promulgated.[17] And not only economic entrepreneurship was facilitated. The preaching of Christianity was permitted in 1873, political party activities were legalised, and while trade unions were not given an officially recognised status until 1920, their activities were informally accepted.[18]

These reforms acted as powerful incentives to entrepreneurs. After the mid-1880s economic activities of all kinds were booming and while some of these were initiated by the government most were private ventures, often located in the countryside.[19] Before long the economy began growing quickly and between 1886 and 1889 alone manufacturing output grew by 50 per cent. Political, social and cultural entrepreneurs also seized the opportunities the new institutions offered. Various political parties were formed in the early 1880s but political activities also took to the streets with movements such as the League for Establishing a National Assembly. Well-off farmers formed both self-help societies and societies for social improvement.[20]

Taken together this proliferation of ideas and entrepreneurial projects inevitably led to conflicts. Defenders of the old order, although powerless to change the overall direction of society, occasionally resorted to political assassinations or at least to spectacular and well-publicised suicides. Defying the myth that Japanese workers are inherently docile, the labour market was at the turn of the twentieth century in a state of perpetual turmoil.[21] Factories across the country erupted in wildcat strikes and acts of sabotage and many workers simply downed tools and ran away; employers cracked down on such activities with the help of the police or by hiring their own thugs and the government worried lest the armaments industry would suffer. The Meiji leaders also agonised over the activities of political parties and movements which at least the more conservative among them regarded as inherently subversive.

In order to deal with these conflicts a number of European-style institutions were put in place, above all the constitution of 1889. Together with a fully-fledged judicial system the constitution provided for an elected parliament, and parliamentarism gained ground from the 1910s onward. The suffrage was gradually expanded from its highly limited beginnings and became universal for all men in 1925. Rights replaced privileges and they applied equally to all subjects. An important area was occupational health and safety: a Factory Law was passed in 1911 and additional labour related laws were passed in the 1920s.[22] Yet European-style self-balancing mechanisms never really took off. The party system was too corrupt, too focused on the personalities of individual leaders, and for a long time completely overshadowed by the *genro*, the collective leadership made up of the leaders of the Meiji Restoration. Instead of being spontaneously brought about, balances were achieved only through heavy guidance. Much the same applies to the economic system where great conglomerates – the *zaibatsu* – soon established a dominating influence and where the state always continued to actively intervene.

In the last decade of the nineteenth century Japanese leaders increasingly turned their backs on liberal European models, preferring instead the more authoritarian.[23] The freedom of the press was restricted together with the right of public assembly even though neither was ever outright abolished.[24] But above all nationalist symbols and rhetoric made a return. The seminal text, constantly referred to in subsequent decades, was the Rescript on Education of 1890 where all imperial subjects were encouraged to be 'filial,' 'affectionate,' 'harmonious' and 'true,' and in the case of an emergency to 'offer yourself courageously to the State.'[25] Relying on such language Japan seemed to become ever more Confucian the quicker it was transformed. And everywhere there were references to the notion of *wa*, or 'harmony':

> What is *wa*? It is not merely peace achieved on the surface. It is inner and spiritual harmony and peace. This ideal brings about a unity of communal spirit by maintaining not only hierarchical distinctions but also the essential equality of an ethical order. It should be the ethic that will bring forth continuity, integration, and unity in the state.[26]

Japanese workplaces were one setting where the spirit of *wa* was becoming ever more prominent.[27] From the 1920s onward Japanese companies were reinterpreted as feudal institutions where consensus reigned and trade unions deferred to the wishes of the management.

The institutional set-up which the Japanese eventually arrived at was thus quite different from the European, but nevertheless it worked. In a short period of time Japan had changed, modernised, caught up. The victory against Russia in 1905 in particular became a symbol, both in Japan itself and throughout East Asia, of their unprecedented achievements. Not since the days of Genghis Khan had an East Asian people defeated a European. Yet the question remains why it was that these institutions were so successful. If we see the reforms as a process of grafting new limbs onto a traditional social body, the question is why this quasi-Frankensteinian creation functioned so well.

The answer is of course that Japan already had been reflective, entrepreneurial and pluralistic for centuries. Indeed the Meiji Restoration, as we discussed it above, was a perfect illustration of this fact. What the new institutions did was to channel and multiply energies which already existed; they reshuffled people and recoordinated their activities; they unified and codified and made publicly known, but they created little that was not there already. It is thus a gross simplification to say that Japan's success was due to its emulation of foreign examples, that Europe was a teacher and Japan a student, or that Tokugawa

Japan was an obstacle that Meiji Japan somehow magically overcame.[28] Many countries have tried to emulate European models but exceedingly few have succeeded. The reason is that very few of them have been as well prepared as Japan was. Everything was already there, what it took was only the institutional framework which could bring it all together.

There are endless examples of this process of syncretic combination. It is for example true that the Meiji Restoration brought press freedom and industrial printing presses to Japan but at the same time widespread literacy – indeed the very idea of a reading public – were pure Tokugawa achievements.[29] Similarly a European-style system of commercial law may have been put in place in 1893 but the reason it worked as well as it did was that it built on a decentralised and non-codified system of arbitration which already had been in operation for centuries.[30] The new law was certainly more uniform and easier to police, and it thereby provided better protection of property rights, but there was nothing new about the idea of legal arbitration as such. Similarly there were well-developed markets for consumer goods and services already in the seventeenth century and there was even a de facto market in land.[31] The freedom to trade and settle, which was institutionalised in the early 1870s, certainly improved the efficiency of these markets – and added a proper market in labour – but the new institutions were successes not despite the pre-existing practices but because of them.

China: continuous revolution

The last 150 years of Chinese history could hardly be more different. In China instead of continuous social change there was continuous revolution; instead of orderly progress there was chaos. Yet this was not supposed to have happened. At the time of the arrival of the Europeans China was in several respects better positioned than Japan.[32] The country had more physical resources and no feudal institutions; there was more social mobility, better integrated markets and better protection of private property; the Chinese state was profoundly meritocratic rather than patrimonial. The question is why so little came of these initial advantages.

The answer is basically that the Chinese state was far more difficult to reform; the imperial house and the Confucian bureaucracy were too powerful, too self-confident, and there were not enough non-state actors with a capacity for independent action. And yet initially at least the signs looked promising. Already at the end of the eighteenth century various scholars had argued that more attention should be paid to administrative problems and often the critique was couched in the language of Dao eccentrics.[33] In the early nineteenth century intense discussions were held in many private academies, especially in Canton, regarding the evil influence of practices like foot-binding and opium smoking. Foreign books were translated into Chinese: works on European government and history, international law, treaties on mechanics, algebra, differential calculus and astronomy.[34]

During the so-called Tongzhi Restoration of the 1860s, named after the reigning child-emperor, the call for reforms reached the state.[35] With foreign soldiers on Chinese soil the need for some kind of a shake-up was obvious to all and yet the language in which the need was formulated was thoroughly Confucian. As always any crisis was interpreted in moral terms and as such it required above all a moral regeneration, especially at the imperial centre.[36] In addition however, as the leading group of very able imperial bureaucrats realised, China had to embrace European technology, above all as it applied to military hardware. The idea was to combine Western technology and Chinese spirit in a movement of 'self-strengthening' which could allow China to defend its sovereignty. Just as in the case of Japan the required technology was soon imported and put to work. It is reported how Zeng Guofang, a general who had successfully put down the Taiping rebels, 'stood and watched [the machine's] automatic movement with unabashed delight, for this was the first time he had seen machinery and how it worked.'[37] The machine was making guns and cannons.

The Tongzhi Restoration produced some impressive results.[38] A rebellion in Chinese Turkestan in the 1870s was successfully put down and in 1885 a French advance from Vietnam was blocked. Yet in the direct showdown with Japan in 1895 the limitations of the self-strengthening movement became obvious. The Chinese humiliation was not primarily the result of technological backwardness – in some cases Chinese weapons were even more advanced than the Japanese – rather China lacked the proper administrative set-up to co-ordinate, direct, and control its forces. In addition assorted rebellions continued throughout the latter part of the nineteenth century and the presence of foreign armies on Chinese soil – Japanese as well as European – continued to undermine the sovereignty of the empire.

Defeat at the hands of the Japanese led directly to a renewed reform movement, the so-called 'Hundred Days' Reform' of 1898.[39] Here for the first time real attempts were made to radically reorganise the state. There were experiments in constitutional government and regional assemblies were set up, the army was remodelled on European lines, and a new railway network was developed to improve communications and markets. Yet the reforms failed. The regional assemblies encouraged rather than defused the ever more radical demands; conservative groups within the bureaucracy and within the imperial family rejected many of the proposed changes, and regional leaders were furious with the attempt at centralisation. Meanwhile anti-Manchu agitation increased throughout the country.

In 1911 the Qing government was finally toppled in a surprisingly bloodless putsch; a republic was established but it never became secure.[40] Instead the political centre gradually imploded and the initiative passed to regional leaders, before long supported by regional armies. Warlordism characterised the 1920s and the chaos continued even once much of the country was unified under the Guomindang in 1928. In the 1930s the Japanese invaded, the Communist guerrillas grew in strength, and once the Japanese had withdrawn the country erupted in a full-blown civil war, the final outcome of which was the revolution of 1949. The new Communist regime centralised the country, restored its sovereignty and brought peace, and imposed its own notion of modernity. Independent reflection was banned and everyone was instead required to follow the party line; private entrepreneurship in politics, economics and religion was made illegal; and diversity was seen as hopelessly 'bourgeois' and thus as counter-revolutionary. Instead social changes were imposed by the state in a lopsided and erratic manner, accompanied by endless political campaigns and much human suffering.[41]

Comparing China's trajectory in the nineteenth and twentieth centuries with that of Japan it is obvious that the two differed greatly as far as reflection, entrepreneurship and pluralism are concerned, and these differences more than made up for the initial advantages of China's position. A first problem was the limited nature of reflection. The Chinese never cared much about the rest of the world and for most of their history this may indeed have made sense. In the nineteenth century, however, it did not. There was no tradition of adopting things from abroad or even of taking anything foreign into account. Japan by contrast had always mixed various cultural influences – the native, the Chinese and the European – and despite their mid-nineteenth-century isolation they kept their eyes firmly on events abroad.[42] When the foreigners eventually arrived Japan was well equipped to deal with the challenge. While China merely sought to add a bit of military hardware to a political system which was to remain firmly intact, the Japanese realised that technological improvements would have to be accompanied by profound institutional changes.[43] In the end only a modern state could adopt modern weapons.

The two societies differed greatly also as far as entrepreneurship was concerned. In China the political centre was at the same time too powerful and too weak. It was too powerful in relation to other political actors. The imperial state was the all-dominating force and while private businessmen flourished they had no influence whatsoever on politics. At the same time the state was too weak to implement successful reforms. Growing internal and external pressure gradually undermined the political order but there was nothing that could take its place. The reform movements were never radical enough and even these moderate initiatives were fiercely resisted. In Japan, while the shogun was undermined in exactly the same manner, there was a well-established structure of peripheral powers that could step into the eroding centre. There were regional powers in China too but they had none of the experience in self-governance – nor the military capability – which feudalism assured the Japanese daimyos.

In the end China simply disintegrated. While the country became ever-more pluralistic it lacked proper ways of resolving the conflicts which pluralism produced. The first instinct of the elite was to fall back on its Confucian traditions but Confucianism provided only cultural and not institutional solutions. It presupposed that you belonged to a certain group, the Confucian elite, or at least that you aspired to membership in this group. Once the examination system was abolished in 1905 there were no more such people. Similarly the European institutions that were put in place were never powerful enough and they never became proper channels for the expression of political dissent. Instead conflicts were resolved through force.

In Japan by contrast where the emperor was untarnished by the past, the imperial institutions could be wheeled out in 1868 and invoked as symbols of national unity, and in the course of subsequent decades nationalism and Confucianism, while increasingly repressive, helped keep Japanese society together. These are particularly striking examples of the November Tree Principle at work. In China the emperor was discredited and nationalism was unavailable. Instead nationalist propaganda against the Manchu dynasty eventually forced the emperor to abdicate, and while nationalist agitation continued after 1911 it had no political institution to attach itself to.

Japan: institutional failure and restart

This discussion requires a short post-scriptum. In the latter part of the nineteenth century Japan was successfully modernising, we said, yet a few decades later the country embarked on a series of militaristic ventures which culminated with the invasion of Asia and the war against the United States. For our investigation this constitutes a challenge. We have presented the Meiji institutions as highly successful yet the decision to go to war has often been blamed on institutional failures. Or differently put: a sufficiently reflective society should surely have realised the folly of a continental two-front war; public opinion should have alerted the leaders and the political system should have blocked the action. Or, turning the challenge into an advantage, the decision to go to war presents an opportunity to learn more about Japan. There must be something that we overlooked in our discussion above.

Consider briefly how the decision to go to war was made.[44] Strangely enough it was not the outcome of a central decision and it was not discussed and debated in the newspapers or the parliament. Instead the decision to invade Manchuria, the Nanking atrocity, the attack on Pearl Harbor and the war in Burma were all decisions taken by the military without prior consultations. Usually only one branch of the military was involved or even just individual – sometimes surprisingly low-ranking – officers. The fact that these actions once undertaken never were censored by the politicians in Tokyo spurred the military on. It was always far easier to embark on an action than to put an end to one since Japan during World War II, in contrast to Germany or Italy, never had a military dictator and not even much by means of a unified command.

These strange arrangements were in fact not coincidental but on the contrary they had a long institutional history. In feudal times, as shown above, the country was not a unified actor but instead a *tenka*, a system which contained many independent units. And while the Meiji Restoration was supposed to have unified the country and brought an end to this diversity it never did.[45] The real leader after 1868 was the *genro*, the collective body of elderly statesmen whose nucleus was made up of the former rebels from the daimiates in the southwest who founded the Meiji government. For the first decade or so this group acted fairly cohesively but before long it disintegrated into factions organised around a particular statesman and ministry.[46] In the end all vital offices of state were staffed by people who identified with their office and its personnel rather than with Japan as a whole. Often they were not on speaking terms with each other and the policies they pursued were incoherent at best and often outright contradictory.

Despite all the institutional reorganisations which took place after the war this model of decentralised decision-making survived and we find numerous examples of it in the post-World War II era. Japanese corporations have, for example, often been organised this way.[47] Many Japanese companies are networks rather than hierarchical pyramids; the various sections have had a large measure of independence and loyalty is often given to the small team rather than to the corporation as a whole. Political parties in Japan have functioned in much the same manner.[48] The leading Liberal Democratic Party was for example always riven by factionalism and the divisions were never ideological but instead always personal. This is why next to all Japanese prime ministers have been powerless, and usually also colourless, stooges, and why they never have lasted long in office.

This constantly repeated pattern presents us with a characteristically Japanese way of organising reflection, entrepreneurship and pluralism and in concluding this chapter it is worth briefly considering some of its implications. As far as reflection is concerned the networking model represents an ingenious way of building deliberative capability into a collective body. Rather than using the organisation merely to gather intelligence which then is channelled to the top for processing and deliberation, individual low-level teams have their own ability to process intelligence and to deliberate. This can make a corporation far quicker at responding to changes in consumer demands and it can make a military organisation better at responding to the enemy's tactical redispositions.[49] It is also an ingenious way of making bureaucracies entrepreneurial. In a networked organisation individual teams have the power to act and as a result there is no need to sit around and wait for orders from one's bosses. Individual workers and officers are empowered in a way they have not been in traditional European hierarchies.[50] At the same time the network structure is also a way of dealing with the problem of pluralism. The various teams have their independent turfs and in this way the incidences of turf-wars can be minimised. The solution is in this regard similar to that of medieval Europe: peace is maintained through the separation of claims and identities rather than through their resolution.

Yet the disastrous wars of the twentieth century illustrate perfectly what the problems are with such networks. Reflective, entrepreneurial and pluralistic though they may be it is often disastrous for the right hand not to know what the left hand is doing, and before long things will usually get out of hand completely. Without a central leadership there will be less accountability, less control, and less sense of responsibility on the part of the people ostensibly in charge. Come to think of it the failed efforts at political and economic reforms in the 1990s are an equally good illustration of the same shortcomings.

Part VIII

The future of modern society

20 The new politics of modernisation

A modern society, we began this book, is a society that always changes, and change here does not denote alteration or flux but instead a sense that things are being added to one another in a cumulative fashion and that as a result society as a whole is moving in some particular direction. Taking a cue from Aristotle we argued that change can be understood as the transformation of the potential into the actual; change happens when something that is not but which could be is transformed into something that is. While change thus understood can and does happen quite by itself, changes will be more frequent the more people reflect on the potentialities inherent in the world, the more they act on these potentialities, and the more easily conflicts between thoughts and actions are resolved.

All societies are reflective, entrepreneurial and pluralistic to some extent and there is no society where change is absent. Yet social changes are usually next to impossible to bring about. We all have a bias in favour of the status quo and this is particularly likely to be the case if the status quo protects a position of wealth or power. And yet in modern societies change takes place constantly, automatically and relentlessly, and the reason is that reflection, entrepreneurship and pluralism all are institutionalised. Instead of relying on the efforts, abilities and goodwill of individuals, change is brought about by institutional means. These institutions form a piece of social machinery – something akin to a perpetual motion machine – which always churns out new and unexpected results. As the inhabitants of modern societies we may have made these machines but we are not their masters and change just happens by itself whether we like it or not.

In this book we applied this model to the way in which Europe, China and Japan were modernised. As we saw both parts of the world were highly reflective, entrepreneurial and pluralistic from early on in their history. In both parts of the world there were also plenty of institutions charged with reflective, entrepreneurial and conflict resolving tasks. At the same time differences in institutionalisation explain the different paths the societies took. In some places the road to modern society was fairly smooth while in other places it was extraordinarily bumpy or temporarily blocked. In concluding this book let us briefly draw out some of the implications of this argument as it pertains both to societies in the process of modernisation and to societies that already call themselves modern.

Modernisation theory revisited

As we noted in the introductory chapters, modernisation was one of the most common buzzwords of the 1950s and 1960s. 'Modernise' was what countries in poor parts of the world had to do in order to 'catch up' with the countries of Europe and North America. Modernisation was good since it would allow these countries to provide better for their citizens; modernisation was good also since it would help save Africa, Asia and Latin America from the scourge of Soviet-led Communism. In addition the rhetoric helped to reinforce a hierarchical division of the world where some countries were seen as leaders and others as followers. Thus it did for the Europeans and North Americans what talk of 'civilisation' had done in the previous generation and talk of a 'Washington consensus' does for us today. In our hubris we have made it our business to tell others how to organise their societies and their lives, and in their desperation – or subjection – these others have often gone along with our suggestions.

And yet modernisation never seemed to work quite the way it was intended and despite strenuous efforts the stragglers never managed to catch up. European modernisers and domestic modernising elites were not always guided by the best of intentions but even when they were their efforts usually failed. They all had a vision of what a modern society was like and this vision was what they were hoping to implement, but social engineering is a difficult business under the best of circumstances and it is impossible when you have entirely the wrong blueprints.[1] The modernising visions were like horizons constantly receding before weary travellers. In the end of course modern society never corresponded to any particular vision; it was not an industrial society, an urbanised society, or a secularised, democratised or individualised society. It was not really any of these things, it only seemed that way to the innocent eye.

In our contemporary world many similar hopes are attached to processes of globalisation. To enthusiasts this is the opportunity which at long last will make it possible for the poor countries of the world to pull themselves up.[2] And there is certainly no doubt that all societies, rich and poor, can benefit from the expansion of markets and from increases in trade.[3] The problem is rather that the benefits are likely to be unevenly distributed. The reason is that societies still today, and most likely in the future, are modern to very different degrees. Consequently when societies open up to the global market they will begin to be transformed but the transformations will be exogenously rather than endogenously driven. Change is produced in some societies and then exported to other societies; some countries are the engines and others are pulled along by the engines. Not surprisingly the engines are the ones likely to draw disproportionate benefits. Those who are pulled along will benefit too but they will benefit less and they will continue to be at the mercy of developments that originate elsewhere. Globalisation will in this way help the poor while simultaneously reinforcing existing worldwide inequalities.

Consider Singapore as an early case of such market integration. By abolishing restrictions on foreign trade in goods and services and by creating a highly favourable environment for foreign corporations, Singapore was transformed in the span of less than 40 years from a colonial backwater into one of the richest countries in the world. By all accounts this is an extraordinary success story and surely the envy of modernisers everywhere. At the same time modernity Singapore-style continues to be seriously lopsided.[4] All the emphasis has been on institutions that support entrepreneurship and little or nothing has been on institutions that encourage reflection and pluralism. As a result repression in Singaporean society is equal only to its conformism and the boredom it induces. Importing change rather than generating it themselves Singaporean are always nervously looking behind their backs to see who is about to overtake them. This is not to say of course that proper modernisation could not happen in Singapore as well. It certainly could but it would require many additional institutional reforms.

One of the countries following the Singaporean example is China.[5] Today the country's economy is growing spectacularly but almost exclusively by assuming the role of a proletarian in the new international division of labour. The Chinese are putting together cheap consumer goods for European and North American markets but they are responsible for little by means of market creation, research or technological development. Meanwhile repressive labour laws and rules against political dissent and organisation make the country into an attractive proposition for international investors. This is surely a curious end for an erstwhile Communist regime. And yet reforms are under way and restrictions on political expression have recently been relaxed. The authorities have stopped controlling people's minds and now control only their bodies. As we saw above this solution to the problem of pluralism was employed also by the classical imperial state and it is still likely to be the cheaper and more efficient option. At the same time far more radical changes are required for China to properly modernise. The test is not whether the country can produce cheap gadgets for the world market but instead whether the country would continue to change even without such external support.

This is not a call for autarchy. Not at all. International trade and foreign direct investments are crucial sources of prosperity. The point is rather that real and long-term benefits only will accrue to societies that have made change into an internally derived rather than an imported process. Although change never can be controlled or directed, each society must set about the task of creating reflective, entrepreneurial and pluralistic institutions. The temporary windfalls produced by globalising markets may give less incentives for such reforms, and this in itself is a problem. The example of Argentina in the 1930s should serve as a warning.[6] For a while one of the most promising countries in the world, Argentina benefited greatly from the booming world market in agricultural products. For immigrants from Europe the country was at the time at least as attractive a destination as the United States. At the same time the institutional structure was never there. Argentina was not properly modern and as soon as the worldwide depression of the 1930s hit agricultural prices, the country was doomed. Somehow it never really recovered.

This book provided no alternative blueprint to the developmental models it rejected but it did provide an alternative point of view on the problem of modernisation itself. As we repeatedly argued, modernity is no particular thing, it has no particular content and it is not caused by any set of given causes. Instead modernity is best understood as a blank space which each society fills with ever-alternating images of itself. Paradoxically the only permanent feature, and the only viable foundation of a self-identity, is to be found in such endless changes.[7] Change is certainly associated with things like economic growth and technological development but economic growth and technological development too have a large number of disparate sources. All we can do in the end is to create a society that is open to new possibilities whatever they turn out to be. What we need to create is a permissive environment; an environment in which many different things are possible. In such an environment the possibility of change, driven by all kinds of causes, will be maximised. As long as we provide the mechanics, modernity will take care of itself.

This is not to say that there only is one development model or that successful modernisation must follow the examples set by societies in Europe and North America. On the contrary our alternative perspective shows that modernisation can happen in different and perhaps competing ways and that modern societies can be of many different kinds.[8] Indeed this explains why it has been possible for countries in East Asia to modernise quickly in the latter part of the twentieth century while at the same time maintaining much of their social and cultural distinctiveness. What matters is reflection, entrepreneurship and pluralism but these activities can be carried out in various ways and be institutionalised quite differently.

One lesson may indeed be that it is easier to work with what our own traditions have handed down to us than to slavishly mimic foreign models. This is a way to preserve one's character but due to the path-dependences and lag-times involved it might also simply be a more efficient way to modernise. It is not enough just to start importing foreign institutions since the institutions, once in place, often end up working in unexpected and perhaps perverse ways. As the chapters above have demonstrated, modernisation is a complex, drawn-out, and perilous process. Indeed at its most pessimistic the argument above might make us sceptical regarding the possibility regarding the feasibility of anything like a 'modernisation theory.'[9] Modern society has little to do with rational planning, we said, and it is only incidentally associated with the exercise of state power.[10] All we may be able to do in the end is to avoid the most blatant mistakes. We know far more about what works badly than about what works well.

At the same time there are a number of implications to be drawn from the analysis above. We now know quite a bit more about the nature of change and how it can be turned into a permanent feature of social life. We know more about the role played by reflection, entrepreneurship and pluralism, and why institutions and institutionalisation matter. But we also know that these activities can be carried out and institutionalised in many alternative ways. If none of this amounts to a policy recommendation or an easily applied prescription perhaps that is only for the best.

Modernity and post-modernity

Next let us turn to countries that already call themselves modern. One question here has been whether modernity really is worth it. In recent times doubts on this score have been associated with the notion of 'post-modernity.' The claim is that we have entered a post-modern era which in important respects is radically different from the modern era which preceded it. The 'modern' is here taken as equivalent with the Enlightenment of the eighteenth century and its blind faith in rationality and unending social progress, and it is this meta-narrative that we no longer are said to believe in.[11] The result is a loss of faith and a lingering sense of malaise; people in post-modern societies are increasingly sceptical regarding progress, meaning, and often also truth.

Part of this analysis is correct, part of it is not. It is no doubt true that our faith in rationality has taken a number of serious knocks. There are today exceedingly few people who would admit to a belief that society can be transformed according to some preconceived master-plan. Communism and the Holocaust buried that faith. There is also widespread scepticism regarding far more limited versions of social engineering. Generally speaking progress has been revealed as a rather mixed blessing. On the whole the benefits – medical advances and the like – only barely make up for drawbacks such as the degradations of our physical and social environment.

Under circumstances such as these it is not surprising that people have lost faith in politics. There seems to be little or nothing that politics can do in order to make our societies better, more equal or just. It is perhaps just as well that the forces of globalisation seem to be undermining the previously impressive powers of the state.[12] In this way our decreasing ambitions are pushed by our declining abilities into a downward spiral where politics eventually is emptied of all meaning. Today traditional political ideologies, cemented after the French Revolution, are gradually dissolving and all that remains is a diffuse kind of centrist politics focusing on administration and the implementation of best practices. Or, foreshadowing a future trend, politicians have given up on substance altogether and focus instead on symbolic issues and on ways to divide people from each other in order to rule them more securely. Responding to such signals from their leaders, voters have become increasingly passive-aggressive. Most of the time we glory in our political apathy but then we are suddenly mobilised to act against 'asylum seekers,' 'global capitalism' or the European Union.

Not that most of us actually mind. Today only the hopeless romantics remember a time when politics provided an opportunity to escape the idiocy of our private lives.[13] Having lost faith in the meta-narratives all we have left are the small narratives, the stories that we tell ourselves and others about our individual lives.[14] On the level of society as a whole such small-scale story-telling is endlessly recycled in celebrity gossip, daytime talk shows and reality soaps. Entertaining though such chatter may be it is completely devoid of social analysis. Today people have largely stopped making sense of the life of their communities and are instead content to make sense only of their own biographies. Meanwhile they are forgetting that without a social context also our individual biographies will become incomprehensible to us.

But as we said most of this loose talk of 'post-modernism' is quite beside the point. Or rather, while the analysis is based on a number of disturbing facts it has little or nothing to do with modernity as we have conceived of it in this book. It is revealing that discussions of post-modernism largely have taken place in the form of a dialogue between French and German philosophers, with occasional interventions by their North American exegetes.[15] It was in France above all that enlightenment rationalism and étatism came to define the modern project, and it was in Germany which lacked a unified state that the anti-modern backlash came to be defined as an anti-rationalistic project. Ever since discussions of the meaning of modernity have been pursued in these terms, with French and German philosophers occasionally turning on their respective traditions and thereby switching sides. Most recently the Germans have often been the rationalists and the French have been the anti-rationalists.

Yet the perspective of this book is quite different. Rather than listening to Franco-German philosophers we have invoked another tradition, less commonly elevated to the status of a philosophical system, which is based above all on the historical experiences of the countries around the North Sea. In the Dutch Republic, England, western Germany and Scandinavia modern society was not the result of the implementation of some meta-narrative or grand master plan and it was not a state-led project.[16] Instead of being guided by narratives, modernity was guided by institutions, and the institutions in question always made it possible for people to embrace many competing accounts of their lives. Properly modern societies were always filled with many small narratives rather than a few big ones. This is indeed why modernity happened largely behind the state's back and often in defiance of the dictates of rationality.

When seen from this perspective it is obvious that modernity is far from over. There is nothing 'post' about contemporary developments. On the contrary the end of traditional politics as we have known it from the French Revolution onward can be seen as a precondition for the creation of a truly modern society. The Enlightenment was a totalitarian project at its core. In its cult of rationalism and the state it denied the importance of genuine reflection, entrepreneurship and pluralism. The powers-that-be never really wanted people to think or act too freely and they usually did their utmost to stamp out genuine diversity. The totalitarian consequences of the French, the Russian, or any other modern revolution, can easily be deduced from these initial premises. Leaving this baggage behind is no loss. Far from living in a post-modern world, it is only now at the beginning of the twenty-first century that modern society really can come into its own. There are today no alternatives to modernity, no serious challenges, no viable opposition.

A new kind of radicalism

The question is only where this leaves politics and where it leaves the dream of creating a society that is more equitable and more just. Politics has indeed become more centrist, more boring, and the periodic oscillations between voter passivity and voter aggression are certainly frightening. The dearth of alternatives means that there no longer is a place for radical solutions that promise real improvements to people's lives. The problem here is the lack of a notion of a proper outside. Since there are no alternatives to modern society there are no external, extra-modern, standards by which modern society can be assessed. Radicalism has come to an end since there is no outside from which modernity can be seen. Instead we are forced to take the existing as given and the given as good.

In some ways this situation resembles the European Middle Ages when the lack of an outside made it possible for the Church to impose its vision of the world on the people of an entire continent. Or it resembles the situation in imperial China where ethnocentrism and xenophobia helped sustain the ideology of the Confucian elite. And yet as we know the hegemonies of the Church and the Confucian literati were never complete. Even during these periods – by subsequent generations labelled as times of 'darkness' – there was critique, indeed often of a very vigorous kind. If we today once again are about to enter such a period of ideological hegemony it is worth considering what it was that made these previous debates possible.

In previous eras as well as today the alternative to an external standard is an internal standard, that is, a standard derived from the world which the standard itself is employed in order to measure.[17] Lacking a proper notion of an outside the only alternative left is to explore the inside looking for inconsistencies and contradictions. It was through such creative readings of the official canon that criticism of authority was possible both in medieval Europe and in imperial China. Engaging in a similar enterprise today we would begin by standing up for modernity but then go on to insist that its principles be more fully and more consistently applied. The problem is not too much modernity in other words but not enough of it. If there is no alternative to a modern society, and there is not, this is the only kind of radical politics possible today and in the future.[18]

What such an internal critique could accomplish can be illustrated by briefly considering to what extent a country such as the contemporary United States can be regarded as a properly modern country. At first this might strike us as a perverse question since many would identify the United States as the most modern of all modern societies. But is this really the case? And even if it is, are there ways the country could become more modern than it currently is? What a further modernisation would entail is quite clear. It would mean that American society become more reflective, more entrepreneurial and more pluralistic, and that a proper balance be maintained between these three. Finally it would mean that the opportunities for reflection and entrepreneurship be more widely distributed among the population making genuine pluralism possible. The question is how contemporary United States compares with this internally-derived standard. Obviously very much needs to be said about this topic but in concluding this book consider only a few points.

Take reflection first of all. From its very inception the European colony in North America was conceived of as an alternative to the old continent. It was an outside from which Europe could be better observed and it was on the basis of these observations that the American political, economic and social system originally was established. But this is all in the past. For a long time already Americans have found little to learn from the rest of the world, and today the country is at least as self-sufficient and self-congratulatory as ever imperial China. The commercialisation of American society has further eroded the ability of Americans to reflect creatively. Public opinion is increasingly manipulated by commercial interest and for commercial gain. The reflective process has become commodified and reflection is commonly regarded as quite pointless unless it has commercial applications. People who simply sit there with their books, or who struggle for years with complicated works of art, are made to feel like fools when everyone around them is off making money.[19] In this way the traditional shields which protected reflective activities have broken down. The commodification of culture also means that most of us become passive consumers of the ideas, music and art which others produce. Reflection has become the prerogative of well-paid professionals. A further modernisation of American society would require a reversal of these trends. A more modern United States would spread reflective opportunities more widely and it would look for ways of protecting reflective activities from commercial pressure.

Take entrepreneurship next. The United States is often considered as a 'can-do' society and a high proportion of Americans think of themselves as entrepreneurs. The American dream of entrepreneurial success is alive and widely shared, not least among the most recent of immigrants.[20] At the same time this dream has become increasingly difficult to realise. American society has become dramatically more inegalitarian in the last couple of decades with a small elite hogging an ever-larger proportion of wealth, power and educational opportunities.[21] An aristocratisation of America is under way which is most evident among business tycoons and politicians. Obviously entrepreneurial success is far easier to attain for those who have access to the required resources already from birth. In addition also entrepreneurship has suffered from commercialisation. In contemporary United States economic activities are glorified while other kinds of activities atrophy. There is little space for new political, cultural or artistic movements. A further modernisation of American society would require a reversal also of these trends; a more modern United States would spread entrepreneurial opportunities more widely and provide more room for activities that make other than economic sense.

Finally consider pluralism. Ever since the founding of the country Americans have emphasised the importance of freedom of thought and expression and these rights were famously enshrined in the constitution. And yet the limitations on reflection and entrepreneurship mean that American society is not as diverse as it pretends to be or as diverse as it could be. There is an official public culture dominated by a small and homogeneous set of ideas, values and aspirations, and very few dissenting voices are actually expressed.[22] Many Americans have a fear of public confrontations and arguments are all too often reduced to expressions of emotions; people do not think differently, they feel differently. In contrast to arguments, feelings are taken to be more authentic and thereby as incontestable; feelings are private expressions without any public resolution. A more modern American society would deal with these shortcomings. It would be a more diverse society but also one where public conflicts were addressed publicly rather than privatised and emotionalised.

But it would be unfair to conclude with an anti-American rant. The United States has unique problems but it may still be that reflection, entrepreneurship and pluralism are in a better shape here than in other societies that call themselves modern. And it is certainly the case that the same factors that restrict reflection, entrepreneurship and pluralism in the United States operate also in Europe, China and Japan. In the end we all face the challenge of making our societies more modern than they currently are. This is a radical, transformative, project which should inspire us rather than to fill us with resignation or trepidation. Today as well as in the future modernity is all we have but it is also quite good enough.

Notes

1 The nature and origin of modern society

1 Lach and van Kley, 1993. On Ming China, see book 4, pp. 1563–610; on Tokugawa Japan, book 4, pp. 1828–88.
2 On China, see Schrecker, 1976, pp. 298–305. On Japan, see Westney, 1987, pp. 1–8.
3 To explain the gap between Europe and the rest of the world, says Braudel, 'is to tackle the essential problem of the history of the modern world.' Braudel, 1979/2002, II, p. 134.
4 Paz, 1974, pp. 19–37; Nauert, 1995, pp. 19–23.
5 Mommsen, 1942, pp. 226–42; Nauert, 1995, pp. 19–23.
6 Bacon, The Advancement of Learning, 1605, discussed in von Leyden, 1958, p. 488.
7 ibid.
8 Bury, 1920/1955; Koselleck, 1985, pp. 21–38.
9 Kant, 1784/1983, p. 41.
10 Hegel, 1821/1957, pp. 155–79 with additions, pp. 279–88.
11 Dunn, 1989, pp. 333–56; Arendt, 1963, pp. 43–5; Paz, 1974, pp. 6–7.
12 Burke, 1775/1852, p. 49.
13 Becker, 1932, pp. 119–68. Compare Scott, 1998.
14 Paz, 1974, pp. 26–31.
15 In this sense Popper's view of scientific progress is symptomatic of the modern outlook. See Popper, 1953/1965, pp. 33–65.
16 Marx and Engels writing about 'the bourgeoisie,' in Marx and Engels, 1848/1985, p. 84.
17 Schumpeter, 1942/1976, p. 124.
18 Abramovitz, 1989, pp. 3–79; Kuttner, 1997, pp. 191–224.
19 Kuznets, 1966, pp. 490–509; Mokyr, 1990, pp. 3–7.
20 Kuttner, 1997, pp. 24–8.
21 See, for example, Smith, 1776/1981, pp. 452–72.
22 Abramovitz, 1989, pp. 5–6.
23 Mill, 1848/1987, pp. 189–98.
24 Malthus, 1798/1982, pp. 73–92.
25 Mill, 1848/1987, pp. 192–3.
26 ibid., p. 191.
27 North, 1994, p. 367; Lau, 1996, pp. 63–91.
28 Kuttner, 1997, pp. 26–8; Schumpeter, 1989, pp. 221–71.
29 Schumpeter, 1942/1976, p. 132.
30 Abramovitz, 1989, pp. 13–15.
31 Mokyr, 1990, p. 81.
32 Mill, 1848/1987, p. 192.
33 Hacker, 1977, p. 54.

34 This is the case despite the marginal improvements provided by the so-called 'endogenous growth theory.' Lucas, 1988. For a critique, see Gilpin, 2001, pp. 108–28.
35 Abramovitz, 1989, p. 116.
36 The famous source is the monumental œuvre of Needham's, summarised in Ronan and Needham, 1979. Compare also Lin, 1995, pp. 278–85.
37 Thirsk, 1978, pp. 110–12; Kindleberger, 1993, pp. 187–8.
38 Hegel, 1830–31/1956, § 324.

2 The failure and success of East Asia

1 Landes, 1998, especially pp. 17–44; or Jones, 1987, pp. 225–38.
2 Spence, 1990/99, pp. 132–7.
3 The 'white and cultured' quote is from Valignano, 1580s/1965, p. 4.
4 Kennedy, 1993, p. 193.
5 Lieberman, 1997, especially pp. 497–507; Feuerwerker, 1992, pp. 757–69; Myers, 1991, pp. 604–28.
6 Mill, 1859/1985, pp. 136–7.
7 ibid., p. 136; Hegel, 1831/1956, pp. 116, 138.
8 See discussion in O'Leary, 1989, pp. 235–61.
9 Weber, 1922/1964, especially pp. 142–70.
10 Wittfogel discussed in O'Leary, 1989, pp. 235–61.
11 Wilkinson, 1991, pp. 110–19.
12 Hamilton, 1985, pp. 187–211; Wong, 1997, pp. 14–15; Jones, 1990, pp. 5–22; Pomeranz, 2000, pp. 16–24.
13 Pomeranz, 2000, pp. 31–107; Wong, 1997, pp. 13–32, 73–104; Jones, 1987, pp. 202–22.
14 Jones, 1987, pp. 22–41.
15 Pomeranz, 2000, pp. 36–41; Wong, 1997, pp. 22–7.
16 Wong, 1997, pp. 73–104. For a critique, see Vries, 2002, pp. 67–138.
17 Pomeranz, 2000, pp. 265–97; Goldstone, 2000, pp. 175–94.
18 Duyvendak, 1949, pp. 1–35.
19 Pomeranz, 2000, pp. 211–25. Compare Ringmar, Why Europe, 2002; Jones, 1987, pp. 70–84.
20 Elvin, 1973, p. 222.
21 Mehmet, 1995, pp. 55–90.
22 Hall, 1965, pp. 18–19.
23 Berger, 1987.
24 Henderson and Appelbaum, 1992, pp. 1–26.
25 Johnson, 1982, pp. 3–34; 305–24.
26 Wade, 1990, pp. 345–86.
27 Castells, 1992, pp. 33–70.
28 Solow, 2003, p. 50.
29 Paz, 1974, pp. 1–2.

3 The self-transforming machine

1 Čapek, 1967, pp. 78–9.
2 Dawkins, 1996, pp. 73–107.
3 Kolakowski, 1990, pp. 32–43.
4 Hayek, 1988, pp. 66–88.
5 Tocqueville, 1840/1945, pp. 104–5.
6 Jones, 1990, pp. 5–22.
7 North, 1990, p. 3; Hamilton, 1938.

8 This, at least, was Schumpeter's view of democracy. See Schumpeter, 1944/1975, pp. 269–302.
9 Ferguson, 1767/1995, pp. 172–9.
10 Compare Ferguson, 1767/1995, p. 174.
11 Sennett, 1998, pp. 68–70.
12 Mumford, 1964, pp. 204–7.
13 Skinner, 1989, pp. 90–131.
14 Compare Menger, 1981, pp. 257–85; Hamilton, 1938, p. 86.
15 Cohen, 1978, pp. 160–81; Elster, 1982, pp. 453–9.
16 Cameron and Patrick, 1967, pp. 2–3.
17 Bagehot, 1867/1997, p. 59; Ringmar, Institutionalisation, 2002, pp. 42–4.
18 Dawkins, 1996, pp. 138–97.

4 The discovery of distance

1 'Réfléchir,' Dictionnaire historique.
2 Mokyr, 1990, p. 71.
3 'Réfléchir,' Dictionnaire historique.
4 Mead, 1932/1964, pp. 144–64.
5 Compare the Bible, Qoh 8:17.29; 1 Cor 13:12.8.
6 Augustine, 397–8/1961, p. 242.
7 Scott, 1990, pp. 105–7.
8 Lovejoy, 1936, pp. 67–98.
9 Bakhtin, 1965/1984, pp. 59–144, 198–277.
10 ibid., pp. 74–90.
11 Huizinga, 1924/1989, pp. 31–56, 138–51; Bakhtin, 1965/1984, p. 73.
12 Scott, 1990, pp. 172–82.
13 Holdsworth, 1963, pp. 141–53; Le Goff, 1981/1986, pp. 107–22, 177–204.
14 Huizinga, 1924/1989, p. 223.
15 Cohn, 1970, pp. 71–98.
16 Huizinga, 1924/1989, pp. 200–14; Foucault, 1966/1973, pp. 17–44.
17 Veyne, 1983, pp. 118–19.
18 Cohn, 1970, pp. 82, 192.
19 ibid., p. 197.
20 Nauert, 1995, pp. 8–10; Grafton, 1988, pp. 767–91.
21 Hale, 1977, p. 275.
22 Baron, 1966, pp. 121–2; Rüegg, 1996, pp. 446–7.
23 Machiavelli, 1513/1961, p. 142.
24 Nauert, 1995, pp. 14–23, 197–8.
25 Yates, 1964, pp. 398–431.
26 Hale, 1977, pp. 232–41.
27 Grafton, 1988, p. 771.
28 Nauert, 1995, pp. 38–40.
29 Boorstin, 1983, pp. 116–289; Lach and van Kley, 1965, pp. 50–88, 230–334.
30 Boorstin, 1983, pp. 165–72.
31 Todorov, 1982, pp. 48–68.
32 Vespucci, 1497.
33 Todorov, 1982, pp. 141–2, 164.
34 Las Casas, 1552/1992, p. 124.
35 Pagden, 1987, pp. 79–98.
36 Todorov, 1982, pp. 193–212.
37 ibid.
38 Pagden, 1987, pp. 79–98.
39 Skinner, 1978, pp. 135–73.

40 ibid.
41 More, 1516/1965, pp. 38–9.
42 ibid., pp. 44–50; 86–7.
43 ibid., pp. 86–7. Compare Fenlon, 1974, pp. 120–32.
44 Rabelais, 1548/1991, books 4 and 5, pp. 415–732.
45 Swift, 1726/1992. Compare Ferguson, 1767/1995, pp. 186–7.
46 Montesquieu, 1721/1964.
47 Machiavelli, 1531/1983, p. 97.
48 Locke, 1690/1980, V:49, p. 29; on Rousseau, see Pagden, 1993, pp. 120–2.
49 Kuhn, 1957, pp. 134–84; Koestler, 1959/1989, pp. 431–517.
50 Quoted in Boorstin, 1983, pp. 319–20.
51 ibid., pp. 312–15.
52 Goldstone, 2000, pp. 175–94.
53 Koyré, 1957/1973, pp. 55–6.
54 ibid., pp. 157–88.
55 Pascal, 1662/1966, no. 68, p. 48.
56 Marejko, 1989, pp. 11–32, 58–76.
57 Jacob, 1988, pp. 43–5.
58 Quoted in Kuhn, 1957, p. 194.
59 Jacob, 1988, pp. 54–61.
60 Oakeshott, 1962/1991, pp. 5–42; Scott, 1998, pp. 316–33.

5 The face in the mirror

1 On the medievalism of Petrarca, see Kristeller, 1967, p. 126; on the mysticism of Copernicus, see Yates, 1964, pp. 153–5.
2 Haskins, 1927.
3 Boorstin, 1983, pp. 209–17.
4 Kuhn, 1957, pp. 115–19.
5 Goody, 1986, pp. 35–44.
6 Miller, 1998, pp. 143–55.
7 Gregory, 1998, pp. 47–65.
8 On mirrors in Holland, see Schama, 1987, p. 317.
9 Meyerhoff and Metzger, 1992, p. 344. On autobiographies, see Gurevich, 1995, pp. 110–55.
10 Hale, 1977, pp. 304–6.
11 Findlen, 2000, pp. 170–2.
12 Gurevich, 1995, pp. 196–9.
13 Eisenstein, 1983, especially pp. 3–11.
14 Anderson, 1983, p. 41.
15 Hale, 1977, p. 283.
16 Watt, 1957, p. 47.
17 Leys, 1998.
18 Eisenstein, 1983, pp. 148–86.
19 Grafton, 1988, pp. 767–91; Eisenstein, 1983, pp. 171–7.
20 Hobbes, 1651/1981, II:21, pp. 267–8.
21 Deutsch, 1953/1966.
22 Eisenstein, 1983, pp. 92–117.
23 Anderson, 1983, pp. 41–9; Eisenstein, 1983, pp. 92–107.
24 Anderson, 1983, p. 39.
25 Hellmuth, 1990, pp. 467–72; Harris, 1996, pp. 10–12.
26 Harris, 1996, p. 57.
27 Bödeker, 1990, pp. 423–45.
28 Compare Hellmuth, 1990, pp. 486–9.

29 On Britain, see Thomas, 1959, pp. 623–36; on France, see Harris, 1996.
30 Gunn, 1989, p. 251; Baker, 1990, p. 168; Habermas, 1962/1989, pp. 89–102.
31 Baker, 1990, p. 167.
32 Gunn, 1989, p. 249.
33 ibid., p. 251; Baker, 1990, p. 168.
34 Quoted in Bödeker, 1990, p. 425.

6 Institutions that reflect

1 Compare Schleiermacher, 1808/1991, pp. 2–3.
2 Other candidates are for example legal institutions and public bureaucracies which also formed at this time.
3 Haskins, 1927/1993, p. 369.
4 Baldwin, 1972, pp. 1–15.
5 Rüegg, Themes, 1996, pp. 16–17; Haskins, 1927/1993, pp. 368–97.
6 Verger, 1996, pp. 43–4.
7 Schleiermacher, 1808/1991, pp. 39–40.
8 Rüegg, Epilogue, 1996, pp. 448–52.
9 Ringmar, 1996, pp. 105–8.
10 Castiglione, 1528/1959, pp. 72–82.
11 Hale, 1977, pp. 294–7.
12 Nauert, 1995, pp. 124–36.
13 ibid., pp. 207–9.
14 Greenblatt, 1980, pp. 230–1.
15 Brockliss, 1996, pp. 616–18.
16 Schleiermacher, 1808/1991, p. 16.
17 ibid., pp. 66–80.
18 Yates, 1964, pp. 144–56.
19 French, 1972, pp. 126–59.
20 Jacob, 1988, pp. 46–7.
21 Yates, 1964, pp. 159–68.
22 Wallis, Origin.
23 Koerner, 1999, p. 106.
24 Cranston, 1967, pp. 238–9.
25 Bacon, 1627/1989, pp. 71–83.
26 Mumford, 1964, pp. 105–29.
27 Polanyi, 1962/1969, pp. 49–72; Schleiermacher, 1808/1991, p. 14.
28 Jacob, 1975, pp. 155–76; Cranston, 1967, p. 237.
29 Mumford, 1964, pp. 114–15.
30 Polanyi, 1962/1969, pp. 49–72.
31 Shapin, 1991, pp. 304–12. Compare the ironic version of Solomon's House which Gulliver discovers in Swift, 1726/1992.
32 Mill, 1861/1991, pp. 272–3, 283.
33 Bagehot, 1867/1997, p. 74.
34 Finer, II, 1999, pp. 1024–51; Harris, 1981, pp. 29–60; Graves, 1990, pp. 1–14.
35 Holt, 1981, pp. 5–6, 19–24; Bagehot, 1867/1997, pp. 74, 151–2.
36 Ringmar, 1996, pp. 129–32.
37 Finer, III, 1999, pp. 1307–74; Ertman, 1997, pp. 96–105.
38 Runeby, 1962, pp. 13–42.
39 Quoted in Bessette, 1994, p. 41.
40 Bagehot, 1867/1997, p. 90.
41 Mill, 1861/1991, pp. 341–4.
42 Bagehot, 1867/1997, p. 62.
43 Bessette, 1994, pp. 21–2.

44 Thomas, 1959, pp. 623–36; Bessette, 1994, pp. 222–8.
45 Bessette, 1994, pp. 156–9.
46 ibid., pp. 6–39.
47 Bessette, 1994, pp. 6–13.
48 Madison, Hamilton and Jay, 1788/1987, no. 42, p. 276.
49 Bessette, 1994, pp. 20–8.
50 Mill, 1861/1991, pp. 373–83.
51 Bessette, 1994, p. 18.

7 Origins of the entrepreneurial outlook

1 Ekelund and Hébert, 1997, pp. 520–3.
2 Kuttner, 1997, pp. 11–67.
3 Schumpeter, 1989, pp. 221–71.
4 Although the two functions no doubt are combined in most business leaders. Schumpeter, 1942/1976, pp. 111–20.
5 Mokyr, 1990, pp. 31–56.
6 Woodblock prints, engravings and book illuminations allowed for more artistic freedom. Ariès, 1973, pp. 327–31.
7 Gurevich, 1995, pp. 151–5.
8 Huizinga, 1924/1989, pp. 56–67.
9 Auerbach, 1953, pp. 123–42; Gurevich, 1995, pp. 19–88.
10 Gurevich, 1995, pp. 110–15.
11 Compare Mauss, 1938/1985, pp. 1–25, as well as the other contributions to this volume.
12 Aristotle, 350 BCE/1986, pp. 12–15.
13 Friedman, 1980, pp. 234–42.
14 Le Goff, 1990, pp. 9–32.
15 Ekelund and Hébert, 1996, pp. 115–30.
16 Pirenne, 1937, pp. 183–4.
17 Smith, 1776/1981, I:10, p. 141.
18 Compare Turner's concept of 'liminality,' in Turner, 1974, pp. 231–70.
19 Cohn, 1970, pp. 53–60.
20 ibid., pp. 61–70.
21 Lopez, 1976/1998, pp. 60–2.
22 Le Goff, 1990, pp. 35–8; see Deut, 23:20–1.
23 Lopez, 1976/1998, pp. 97–102, 113–19.
24 Lopez, 1976/1998, pp. 113–19.
25 Gurevich, 1995, pp. 38–61.
26 MacIntyre, 1985, pp. 125–7.
27 Gurevich, 1995, pp. 52–4. Berger, 1970/1973, pp. 83–96; Auerbach, 1953, pp. 123–42.
28 Huizinga, 1924/1989, p. 72.
29 Burckhardt, 1860/1958, I, p. 143; II, pp. 303–23. Compare Watt, 1997, pp. 120–5.
30 Cellini, 1558–66/1956; on Petrarca's autobiography, see Gurevich, 1995, pp. 234–6.
31 Ringmar, 1996, pp. 170–6.
32 Baron, 1966, pp. 106–13, 121–30; Hale, 1977, p. 280.
33 de Vries and van der Woude, 1997, pp. 255–7.
34 Schama, 1987, pp. 190–323.
35 Daston and Park, 1998, pp. 135–46; Burckhardt, 1860/1958, II, pp. 286–92.
36 Strong, 1984, pp. 42–62.
37 Mattingly, 1955/1988, p. 218; Ringmar, 1996, pp. 170–6.
38 Ekelund and Hébert, 1997, pp. 39–65.
39 Discussed in Todorov, 1982, pp. 15–18; Greenblatt, 1991, pp. 64–6.

40 Las Casas, 1552/1992, p. 13.
41 Pico della Mirandola, 1486/1948, pp. 223–54.
42 Quoted in Erikson, 1962, p. 193.
43 Long, 1991, pp. 882–3.
44 Pico della Mirandola, 1486/1948, p. 225.
45 Donaldson, 1988, pp. 7–11.
46 Watt, 1997, pp. 3–11.
47 Quoted in ibid., p. 7.
48 Compare the Latin American myths discussed in Taussig, 1980, especially pp. 13–38.
49 Watt, 1997, p. 15.
50 Luther, 1566/1995, pp. 275–98. Compare Erikson, 1962, pp. 243–50.

8 The age of the demiurge

 1 Schumpeter, 1942/1976, p. 132.
 2 Compare the discussion of Vico in Unger, 1987, pp. 84–7.
 3 Watt, 1957, pp. 60–92; Watt, 1997, pp. 141–92.
 4 Defoe, 1719/1985, p. 146. Compare Watt, 1957, pp. 89–92.
 5 Compare Tocqueville, 1840/1945, pp. 104–6.
 6 Kant, 1784/1983, pp. 41–6.
 7 Watt, 1957, pp. 67–74. Compare Taylor, 1989, pp. 159–75.
 8 Carruthers, 1996, pp. 127–94.
 9 Mackay, 1941/1932, pp. 46–88. Compare Galbraith, 1975/1995, pp. 31–3.
10 Ross, 1965, Introduction, p. 9.
11 Defoe, 1697/1889, p. 31. Compare Thirsk, 1978, pp. 9–10.
12 Defoe, 1697/1889, p. 45.
13 ibid.
14 ibid., pp. 32–3. See also Ferguson, 1767/1995, III:4, p. 138.
15 Defoe, 1719/1985, pp. 139; 240–1.
16 It was only after 23 of the 28 years on the island that Man Friday arrived. Defoe, 1719/1985, pp. 185–7.
17 Rousseau, 1762/1971, pp. 130–2. Compare Watt, 1997, pp. 172–7.
18 Compare, however, the life of Alexander Selkirk, the real-life inspiration for Robinson's adventure. Ross, 1965, Selkirk, pp. 301–10.
19 Olson, 1965, pp. 5–52.
20 On side-payments, see Olson, 1965, pp. 133–4; on trust, see Fukuyama, 1995, pp. 49–57.
21 Quoted in Ball, 1989, p. 173.
22 Compare Axelrod, 1994, pp. 306–18.
23 Braudel, 1979/2002, II, pp. 434–8.
24 ibid., p. 150; Goody, 1996, p. 193.
25 Goody, 1996, pp. 192–204.
26 Braudel, 1979/2002, II, p. 150.
27 ibid., pp. 154–60. For a general application of this argument, see Wintrobe, 1995, pp. 43–70.
28 Lopez, 1976/1998, pp. 73–4.
29 de Vries and van der Woude, 1997, pp. 382–96.
30 Maitland, 1900/1996, pp. xx–xxii.
31 Braudel, 1979/2002, II, pp. 448–9.
32 On the United States in this context, see Fukuyama, 1995, pp. 269–81.
33 Compare Rousseau, 1762/1971, p. 518.
34 For an eighteenth-century discussion, see McKendrick, 'Consumer Revolution,' 1982, pp. 29–31; de Vries, 1992, pp. 85–9. For a contemporary discussion, see Madrick, 2002, pp. 1–12; Solow, 2003.

35 See for example Mokyr, 1977, pp. 981–1008; Gilboy, 1932, pp. 620–39.
36 de Vries, 1992, pp. 110–11.
37 Thirsk, 1978, pp. 1–23.
38 McKendrick, 'Consumer Revolution,' 1982, p. 12.
39 ibid., p. 9.
40 ibid., p. 15.
41 Quoted in ibid., p. 17.
42 Burtt, 1992, pp. 128–49.
43 Smith, 1776/1981, II, p. 660. Compare McKendrick, 'Consumer Revolution,' 1982, p. 15.
44 de Vries, 1992, pp. 89–93. Although, as he points out, the data is both uncertain and contested.
45 ibid., pp. 100–1; 106–7.
46 ibid., pp. 107–15; McKendrick, 1974, p. 197.
47 The term is from de Vries, 1992, p. 107.
48 ibid., pp. 110–14.
49 Braudel, 1979/2002, II, pp. 316–21.
50 Polanyi, 1944, pp. 53–5.
51 Weber, 1920–21/1992, pp. 60–3.
52 Hobbes, 1651/1981, I:11, p. 161.
53 Quoted in McKendrick, 'Consumer Revolution,' 1982, p. 15.
54 With the obvious exception of the consumption of the feudal elite, see Gurevich, 1977, pp. 16–17.
55 Baudrillard, 1970/1999, pp. 77–8.
56 Burckhardt, 1860/1958, II, pp. 361–70.
57 Compare Chesterfield, 1750/1992, p. 200.
58 McKendrick, 'Consumer Revolution,' 1982, p. 12.
59 Smith, 1776/1981, volume V, II:4, pp. 869–70. Compare Ferguson, 1767/1995, III:4, pp. 137–8.

9 Institutions that get things done

1 North and Weingast, 1989, pp. 803–32; Kelly, 1992, pp. 229–32. Compare 'several property,' in Hayek, 1988, pp. 29–37; Lindblom, 2002, p. 53.
2 de Soto, 2000, pp. 32–59.
3 For the scholastic debates see Tuck, 1979, pp. 20–2, 28–9; for the common perceptions, see Gurevich, 1977, pp. 3–15.
4 Compare also Simmel, 1900/1997, pp. 351–4.
5 Pirenne, 1937, pp. 39–56.
6 Trakman, 1983, pp. 7–21.
7 ibid., pp. 9–10.
8 Braudel, 1979/2002, II, p. 53.
9 Hobbes, 1651/1981, II:24, p. 295.
10 Simmel, 1900/1997, pp. 285–86; 298–9.
11 Maitland, 1900/1996, p. xv. Hayek, 1988, pp. 31–3.
12 Tuck, 1979, pp. 60–1.
13 Locke, 1690/1980, chapter 5, §27, p. 19. On government, compare chapter 11, §138, p. 73; Hobbes, 1651/1981, I:14, p. 189.
14 Smith, 1776/1981, V:3, p. 910.
15 Trakman, 1983, pp. 24–7.
16 Norberg, 1994, pp. 276–98. Compare Elias, 1939/1978, pp. 421–39.
17 North and Weingast, 1989, pp. 803–32; Carruthers, 1996, p. 120; Sacks, 1994, pp. 56–64.
18 Caenegem, 1995, pp. 115–17.

19 Montesquieu, 1748/1964, III:5, p. 538.
20 Kelly, 1992, p. 291.
21 Lindblom, 2002, pp. 143–6, 165–6.
22 Huizinga, 1924/1989, pp. 31–56.
23 Hacking, 1975/1999, pp. 1–10.
24 Pascal, 1662/1966, p. 151. See Gigerenzer *et al.*, 1989, pp. 1–2.
25 Compare Defoe, 1697/1889, pp. 80–90.
26 Gorsky, 1998, pp. 499–507.
27 ibid., p. 507. Hacking gives the figure of 'one eighth of the whole population of the empire.' Hacking, 1990, p. 48.
28 de Vries and van der Woude, 1997, pp. 382–96.
29 Braudel, 1979/2002, I, p. 306; Kindleberger, 1993, p. 179.
30 Hacking, 1999, pp. 47–54.
31 Pirenne, 1937, p. 121.
32 de Vries and van der Woude, 1997, pp. 137–8.
33 Kindleberger, 1993, p. 180.
34 Hacking, 1975, pp. 111–21; de Vries and van der Woude, 1997, p. 115; Gigerenzer *et al.*, 1989, pp. 8, 20–1.
35 Hacking, 1990, n. 7, p. 49.
36 Compare, however, Hayek, Free Enterprise, 1948, pp. 113–14; Hayek, 1988, p. 36.
37 May, 2002, pp. 161–2; Sacks, 1994, p. 41.
38 Braudel, 1979/2002, II, pp. 416–21.
39 Schumpeter, 1942/1976, pp. 98–199. Compare Smith, 1776/1981, II, pp. 754–5; or Kuttner, 1997, pp. 24–8, 194–5.
40 Smith, 1776/1981, II, p. 641.
41 MacLeod, 1991, pp. 888–94.
42 Quoted in May, 2002, p. 162.
43 MacLeod, 1991, p. 889.
44 Compare Bagehot, 1873/1999, pp. 281–300.
45 Ritter *et al.*, 1997, pp. 137–45.
46 ibid., pp. 153–7.
47 de Vries and van der Woude, 1997, pp. 150–1.
48 On the initial stages of the Industrial Revolution as largely self-financed, see Kindleberger, 1993, pp. 187–8.
49 Cameron and Patrick, 1967, pp. 1–3.
50 Lopez, 1976/1998, p. 78.
51 Pirenne, 1937, p. 101; de Vries and van der Woude, 1997, p. 130.
52 Compare Bagehot, 1873/1999, pp. 75–100.
53 de Vries and van der Woude, 1997, pp. 84–9.
54 ibid., pp. 133–4.
55 ibid., pp. 147–58; Braudel, 1979/2002, II, pp. 100–1.
56 Dickson, 1967, pp. 3–35; Braudel, 1979/2002, II, p. 107.
57 Hoppit, 1990, pp. 308–9; Galbraith, 1975/1995, pp. 28–44.
58 Mackay, 1841/1932, pp. 52, 54.
59 Hoppit, 1990, pp. 305–22.
60 ibid., p. 315.
61 Quoted in ibid., p. 319.
62 Defoe, 1697/1889, p. 47.
63 Bentham, XIII, 1787.
64 On the Dutch War of Independence, see de Vries and van der Woude, 1997, pp. 100–18. On American War of Independence, Galbraith, 1975/1995, pp. 68–84.
65 Carruthers, 1996, pp. 3–4.
66 Compare, however, the failure of the Banque de France. Galbraith, 1975/1995, pp. 21–7.

10 A world in pieces

1 Sen argues strongly against this conclusion in Sen, 1999, pp. 3–17.
2 Koselleck, 1985, p. 6.
3 Mattingly, 1955/1988, pp. 16–22; Black, 1992, pp. 87–92.
4 Finer, II, pp. 935–49.
5 Kelly, 1992, pp. 120–3.
6 Ekelund and Hébert, 1996, pp. 17–82. On 'The Order of St. Benedict, Inc.' see Kantorowitz, 1951/1957, p. vii.
7 Black, 1992, pp. 42–116.
8 On the wealth of different languages spoken in France, see Weber, 1972, pp. 67–94.
9 Gurevich, 1995, pp. 176–95.
10 Compare Tocqueville, 1840/1945, pp. 239–41.
11 Lovejoy, 1936, pp. 67–98.
12 Kantorowitz,1951/1957, pp. 194–232; Gierke, 1881/1996, pp. 9–30.
13 Compare the 'farewell address' of the Swedish king Gustav II Adolf as he departed for the Thirty Years War in 1630. Ringmar, 1996, pp. 129–32.
14 Cohn, 1970, pp. 158–9.
15 Compare Nauert, 1995, pp. 173–9.
16 Anderson, 1983, pp. 41–2.
17 Genesis, 11:3–9.
18 One such provincial intellectual who insisted on using Latin was Carl Linnæus, see Koerner, 1999, p. 76.
19 Schulze, 1996, pp. 123–4.
20 Bozeman, 1960, pp. 485–98; Mattingly, 1955, pp. 78–86.
21 On Henri IV, see Toulmin, 1990, pp. 45–56.
22 Eco, 1995, pp. 238–59, 269–88.
23 Bull, 1992, pp. 80–3.
24 Toulmin, 1990, pp. 77–8. On the scepticism with which the Catholic church viewed the printing press, see Eisenstein, 1983, p. 160.
25 Hirschman, 1977, pp. 77–8.
26 Quoted in Klein, 1994, p. 162.
27 Hume, 1777/1985, Superstition, p. 74; Shaftesbury, 1711/1999, pp. 4–28.
28 Tocqueville, 1856/1955, pp. 10–13; Hume, 1777/1985, Parties, p. 60.
29 Burke, 1795/1949, p. 403.
30 Hume, 1777/1985, Parties, p. 60.
31 Parker, 1987, pp. 210–12. These figures revise earlier, exaggerated, estimates made by nineteenth-century historians.
32 Hobbes, 1651/1981, I:13, p. 186.
33 Machiavelli, 1532/1980, p. 92.
34 Bodin, 1576/1992, II:1, p. 92.
35 ibid., II:5, p. 120.
36 Koselleck, 1959/1988, pp. 23–31.
37 Hobbes, 1651/1981, II:29, p. 368.
38 ibid., I:13, pp. 227–8.
39 ibid., II:30, pp. 379–83.
40 ibid., II:30, p. 381.
41 Toulmin, 1990, pp. 46–62.
42 Schulze, 1996, p. 44.
43 Bérenger, 1990, pp. 159–65.
44 Ringmar, 1996, pp. 163–4.
45 Schulze, 1996, pp. 114–36.
46 *Readings*, 1635/1906.

47 On the idea of establishing an academy in England on the French model, see Defoe, 1697/1889, pp. 124–5.
48 On inter-state competition, see Landes, 1998, pp. 36–8; Jones, 1987, pp. 127–49.

11 The polite alternative

1 Koselleck, 1959/1988, pp. 62–75. Compare Habermas 1962/1989, pp. 56–73.
2 Klein, 1994, pp. 3–8.
3 Elias, 1939/1978, pp. 29–47.
4 Castiglione, 1528/1959.
5 Discussed in Elias, 1939/1978, pp. 42–7, 56–68.
6 Elias, 1939/1978, pp. 443–524.
7 Skinner, 1998, pp. 1–57.
8 Koselleck, 1959/1988, pp. 86–97.
9 Shaftesbury, 1711/1999, p. 56. Compare Gadamer, 1975/1989, pp. 24–5.
10 ibid., p. 53.
11 Compare the debate on the 'two Smiths' – the sociable author of *Theory of Moral Sentiments* and the utilitarian author of *The Wealth of Nations*. Montes, 2003, pp. 63–90.
12 ibid., on Hobbes, pp. 42–5; 55; on mechanical metaphors, p. 54.
13 Mayr, 1986, pp. 102–14. Compare Raeff, 1975, pp. 1221–43.
14 On how Hobbes integrates the body and the machine into a machine-body, a sort of robot, see Mayr, 1986, pp. 104–5.
15 Caenegem, 1995, pp. 135–7.
16 Mayr, 1986, p. 109.
17 Koselleck, 1959/1988, pp. 23–40.
18 Public actions, as Hobbes explained, were 'never without some restraint,' while private actions were 'in secret free.' Hobbes, 1651/1981, II:31, p. 402.
19 Shaftesbury, 1711/1999, pp. 72–5.
20 Koselleck, 1959/1988, pp. 138–57.
21 Compare Shapin, 1994, p. 45.
22 Koselleck, 1959/1988, pp. 138–57; Ringmar, 1998, pp. 540–2.
23 Klein, 1993, pp. 88–91. Compare Livingston, 1931, p. 619.
24 Swift, 1713. Compare Shapin, 1994, pp. 115–25.
25 Elias, 1939/1978, pp. 56–67.
26 For a Renaissance example, see Greene, 1979, pp. 173–86; for a general discussion, see Mead, 1932/1964, pp. 150–64, 364–84; Gadamer, 1975/1989, pp. 101–34.
27 Compare the conversational games played in Boccaccio, 1348/1972, or in Urbino, see Greene, 1979, pp. 173–86.
28 Gadamer, 1975/1989, pp. 19–30.
29 Shaftesbury, 1711/1999, 22–5; Klein, 1994, p. 162.
30 Although he also said that he was conversing 'even with God Himself by ejaculations,' Defoe, 1719/1985, p. 146.
31 Ross, 1965, Introduction, p. 8.
32 Klein, 1993, pp. 73–108.
33 Klein, 1994, pp. 175–94.
34 Shaftesbury, 1711/1999, pp. 356–65. On Shaftesbury's dislike of Hobbes, see ibid., pp. 42–5.
35 Klein, 1994, pp. 154–60.
36 On the withdrawal of polite society from popular culture, see Burke, 1978, pp. 273–6.
37 Elias, 1939/1978, pp. 507–12; on European 'civilisation' and the Crusades, see pp. 292–308.
38 Dagger, 1989, pp. 292–308.
39 Burke, 1790/1982, p. 171; Shaftesbury, 1711/1999, p. 33. Compare Klein, 1994, pp. 96–100.

40 Caenegem, 1995, pp. 125–42. Compare Skinner, 1998, pp. 59–99.
41 Montesquieu, 1748/1964, III:5, p. 538.

12 Institutions dealing with conflicts

1 Compare Shapin, 1994, pp. 65–125.
2 Fukuyama, 1995, pp. 149–52.
3 Mayr, 1986, pp. 181–9.
4 ibid., pp. 148–54.
5 Adam Smith, 1758/1982, p. 49.
6 Hume, 1777/1985, 'Balance of Trade,' pp. 312–13.
7 Subsequent quote in Koerner, 1999, p. 83.
8 Mayr, 1986, pp. 190–3.
9 ibid., p. 195; Mumford, 1964, p. 394.
10 Mayr, 1986, pp. 139–47.
11 Compare Hobbes' argument concerning 'the Foole,' who rationally prefers to break all conventions. Hobbes, 1651/1981, I:15, pp. 203–4. Discussed in Gauthier, 1986, pp. 160–70.
12 Mattingly, 1955/1988, pp. 82–3.
13 Compare Waltz, 1979/1986, pp. 115–29.
14 Quoted in Mayr, 1986, p. 142.
15 Aristotle, 350 BCE/1986, pp. 124–9; Polybius, 146 BCE, 'An Analysis of the Roman Government,' quoted in Mayr, 1986, p. 141.
16 Mayr, 1986, p. 141.
17 Quoted in ibid., p. 143.
18 Runeby, 1962, pp. 79–110.
19 Mayr, 1986, pp. 140–1.
20 ibid., pp. 156–7.
21 Ball, 1989, pp. 155–76; Gunn, 1974, pp. 301–28.
22 Both quoted in Hofstadter, 1969, pp. 2, 21.
23 Ball, 1989, p. 163.
24 Hofstadter, 1969, p. 17.
25 Quoted in ibid., p. 2.
26 Shaftesbury, 1711/1999, p. 53.
27 Washington's view on opposition parties is discussed in Hofstadter, 1969, pp. 91–102.
28 Shapin, 1994, pp. 74–86. On the connection between this lack of partisanship and 'civic virtue,' see Burtt, 1992, pp. 7–9.
29 Ball, 1989, p. 171.
30 Compare Kant on 'unsocial sociability,' in Kant, 1795/1983, p. 124.
31 Roberts, 1986, pp. 106–7.
32 Gunn, 1974, pp. 301–28.
33 Hofstadter, 1969, pp. 40–73.
34 See, for example, Dahl, 1986, pp. 127–52.
35 Hayek, Free Enterprise, 1948, pp. 107–10.
36 Lindblom, 2002, pp. 65–75.
37 Polanyi, 1962/1969, pp. 49–72.
38 Burtt, 1992, pp. 15–38.
39 Compare Montesquieu discussed in Hirschman, 1977, pp. 56–63; Burtt, 1992, pp. 150–64.
40 Burtt, 1992, pp. 128–49.
41 Mayr, 1986, pp. 164–80.
42 Hume, 1777/1985, Balance of Trade, pp. 311–12.
43 Ekelund and Hébert, 1997, pp. 69–75.

44 Quoted in Mayr, p. 169.
45 Smith, 1776/1981, I:2, p. 27.
46 ibid., IV:2, p. 456. Compare also Simmel, 1900/1997, p. 291.
47 Lindblom, 2002, pp. 98–9, 111–15.

13 Institutions and revolutions

1 Jones, 1987, pp. 104–26.
2 See also Ringmar, Institutionalisation, 2002, pp. 42–4.
3 Bagehot, 1867/1997, pp. 50–71. For a similar argument regarding the Dutch Republic, see de Vries, 1973, pp. 191–4.
4 Bagehot, 1867/1997, p. 59.
5 Quoted in Baker, 1990, p. 179.
6 North and Weingast, 1989, pp. 803–32.
7 On the formation of the English parliament, see Harris, 1981, pp. 29–60; on the emergence of the parliament as a reflective institution, see Graves, 1990, pp. 77–81.
8 Contrast Bagehot's verdict on the French parliament during the Second Empire in Bagehot, 1867/1997, p. 94.
9 Lubenow, 2002, pp. 220–1.
10 Hellmuth, 1990, pp. 467–501. Compare Habermas, 1962/1989, pp. 89–94.
11 North and Weingast, 1989, p. 819.
12 ibid., pp. 803–32; Sacks, 1994, pp. 56–64.
13 Shaftesbury, 1711/1999, pp. 57–8. Compare Klein, 1994, pp. 195–212.
14 Mayr, 1986, pp. 122–36.
15 On Holland, see de Vries, 1973, pp. 191–202. On Sweden, see Ringmar, Institutionalisation, 2002, pp. 24–47.
16 Compare Ruth, 1984, pp. 53–96.
17 On the Swedish constitution, see Koenigsberger, 1982, pp. 173–7; on the central bank, see Kindleberger, 1993, pp. 133–4; on the parliament, see Ringmar, 1996, pp. 129–32.
18 Although Swedish war-making to a large extent was financed also by spoils and by foreign loans. Carruthers, 1996, pp. 94–102.
19 Roberts, 1986, pp. 106–7.
20 Ringmar, 1996, pp. 110–44.
21 Ringmar, Institutionalisation, 2002, pp. 39–42.
22 Ruth, 1984, pp. 53–96.
23 Rabelais, 1548/1991, 2:10, pp. 167–78.
24 Harris, 1996, p. 53.
25 Darnton, 1979, pp. 39–57, 159–60; Harris, 1996, pp. 57–8, 65–8.
26 Darnton, 2000.
27 Baker, 1990, pp. 224–8; Koselleck, 1959/1988, pp. 15–22; Mettam, 1990, pp. 52–3.
28 Norberg, 1994, pp. 276–98.
29 Kindleberger, 1993, p. 181.
30 Tocqueville, 1856/1955, p. 193.
31 Compare the concerns of Dahl, 1970/1990, pp. 68–87.
32 Moore, 1966, pp. 467–79.
33 Compare the Soviet collectivisation and the Tanzanian villagisation discussed in Scott, 1998, pp. 193–261.
34 Francisco Goya, Quinta del Sordo: Saturn, 1820–3, Museo del Prado, Madrid.
35 Arendt, 1963, pp. 215–81; Scott, 1998, pp. 309–41.
36 Arendt, 1963, pp. 141–78.
37 ibid., pp. 43–7; Dunn, 1989, pp. 337–8.
38 Compare Bessette, 1994, pp. 13–26.
39 Caenegem, 1995, pp. 150–74.
40 This tension is explored in Hofstadter, 1955, pp. 23–59.

14 Reflection

1 Compare, for example, Lieberman, 1997, pp. 463–546. Pinyin transliterations of Chinese names and terms are used, except when the European usage is well-established, thus 'Confucius' rather than 'Kong Fūzi.'

2 A point made in for example Hamilton, 1985, pp. 187–211; Wong, 1997, pp. 14–15; Jones, 1990, pp. 5–22; Pomeranz, 2000, pp. 16–24.

3 Among many translations, see Wilhelm and Baynes, 1967; Ronan and Needham, 1979, pp. 127–90. For a contemporary discussion, see the contributions to Tu, 2004.

4 Chou Tun-i, 'An Explanation of the Diagram of the Great Ultimate,' in Chan, 1963, p. 463. Compare, for example, Tung Chung-shi, ibid., pp. 271–88.

5 Lao Tzu, 'The Natural Way of Lao Tzu,' in Chan, 1963, §42, p. 160.

6 Jullien, 1999, pp. 11–13.

7 Jullien, 1999, p. 32.

8 ibid., pp. 137–40.

9 ibid., pp. 151–4.

10 ibid., p. 133; Gernet, 1972/1999, p. 344.

11 Quoted in Cahill, 1982, p. 207. Compare Suzuki, 1956/1996, pp. 279–84.

12 A feature already noted by Max Weber. See Weber, 1922/1964, p. 155.

13 Jullien, 1999, p. 31. The pantheon of Chinese folk-religion constitutes a partial exception, see Eastman, 1988, pp. 42–8.

14 Compare, however, Spence, 1990/99, pp. 112–14.

15 Confucius, The Analects, 11:11, quoted in Chan, 1963, p. 36.

16 See, for example, 'The Natural Way of Lao Tzu,' in Chan, 1963, pp. 136–76; Ronan and Needham, 1979, pp. 85–113.

17 Cahill, 1982, pp. 91–6.

18 Jullien, 1999, pp. 92–3.

19 Ronan and Needham, 1979, pp. 107–10.

20 Jullien, 1999, p. 179.

21 One could even include the Falun Gong here although their social programme is less conspicuous. See Thornton, 2002, pp. 661–81.

22 Jullien, 1999, p. 202.

23 Cahill, 1982, p. 107. On the institutionalisation of this viewpoint, see Levenson, 1975, pp. 325–33.

24 Balazs, 1964, p. 237.

25 ibid.

26 Chan, 1963, pp. 588–653. On social and political implications of the doctrine, see de Bary, 1959, pp. 39–41.

27 Huang, 1981, pp. 42–9.

28 Eberhard, 1975, pp. 33–70. Compare Ronan and Needham, 1981, pp. 67–221.

29 Eberhard, 1975, p. 41.

30 ibid., p. 51.

31 On the problems this posed for the science of astronomy, see Ronan and Needham, 1981, pp. 77–9.

32 de Bary, 1975, pp. 42–4; Balazs, 1964, p. 202.

33 Balazs, 1964, pp. 129–49; Hucker, 1975, pp. 223–8.

34 The historical evidence is discussed in Hucker, 1975, pp. 22–6.

35 Cahill, 1982, pp. 36–7.

36 Pocock, 1989, pp. 71–2.

37 de Bary, 1959, pp. 34–5.

38 Confucius, The Analects, 2:11, quoted in Chan, 1963, p. 23.

39 Quoted in Li, 1996, p. 122. There is no reason to doubt this quote despite the otherwise dubious nature of this source.

40 For a general introduction, see Wood, 1995, pp. 55–78.

41 Wood, 1995, p. 55.
42 On the Song interpretation, see Wood, 1995, pp. 81–110; on the nineteenth-century interpretation, see ibid., pp. 165–70.
43 Ng, 2003, pp. 52–7. Compare Balazs, 1964, p. 158.
44 de Bary, 1975, pp. 163–203. Another example is the radical Confucian Wang An-shih of the eleventh century, see de Bary, 1959, pp. 35–6.
45 de Bary, 1975, p. 178.
46 ibid., pp. 186, 188.
47 For a damning account of the influence of Legalism on Chinese politics, see Fu, 1996, especially pp. 3–10.
48 Chan, 1963, p. 253. On the anti-historicism of the Legalist see also Hucker, 1975, pp. 93–4.
49 Quoted in Fu, 1996, p. 85.
50 Hucker, 1975, pp. 41–7.
51 Quoted in 'Sources of Chinese Tradition,' pp. 209–10.
52 On Mao's admiration for Qín Shi Huángdì, see Li, 1996, p. 122.
53 Jullien, 1999, pp. 220–1; Gernet, 1972/1999, p. 85; Hucker, 1975, pp. 71–2.
54 Elvin, 1973, pp. 180–1.
55 Compare Fei, 1947/1992, pp. 53–9; Goody, 1996, pp. 243–6.
56 Gernet, 1972/1999, pp. 83–5.
57 On the transfer of Chinese technology to the West, see Ronan and Needham, 1979, pp. 58–77.
58 Gregory, 1998, pp. 50–4.
59 Suzuki, 1956/1996, pp. 66–80.
60 Balazs, 1964, p. 133.
61 Clunas, 1997, pp. 113–14.
62 Cahill, 1982, p. 106.
63 ibid., p. 211; Levenson, 1975, pp. 325–33.
64 Clunas, 1997, pp. 41–55.
65 ibid., p. 135.
66 ibid., p. 33.
67 Gernet, 1972/1999, pp. 332–7.
68 Elvin, 1973, pp. 114–18.
69 Examples include 'Pictures and Poems on Husbandry and Weaving' by Lou Shou; 'Treatise on Agriculture' by Ch'en Fu, and 'Essential Techniques for the Common People,' a reprinted classic from the sixth century. See Elvin, 1973, pp. 114–16.
70 ibid., p. 134; Hucker, 1966, p. 67.
71 Hucker, 1966, p. 67.
72 Yang, 1959, pp. 146–56.
73 Compare the phrase *wairu neifa*, 'outside Confucian, inside Legalist.' Fu, 1996, p. 126.
74 Fei, 1947/1992, pp. 71–9.
75 On Mèngzi, or Mencius, see in Chan, 1963, pp. 49–3; on Xunzi, or Hsün Tzu, ibid., pp. 115–35 and Dong Zhongshu, or Tung Chung-shu, ibid., pp. 271–88.
76 Hartwell, 1971, pp. 299–304; Gernet, 1972/1999, pp. 304–5.
77 Finer, 1999, II, 1999, p. 810.
78 ibid., p. 819.
79 Hucker, 1975, p. 321.
80 ibid., pp. 335–6.
81 de Bary, 1975, p. 178.
82 Hucker, 1975, pp. 318–19; Huang, 1981, pp. 18–24, 42–74.
83 Huang, 1981, p. 44.
84 Meskill, 1969, pp. 150–3.
85 ibid., pp. 153–5, 163–8, 171–4.

86 Hucker, 1966, pp. 41–2; Finer, 1999, II, pp. 817–26.
87 For an extensive discussion, see Hucker, 1966; Hucker, 1975, pp. 150–3, 161–3.
88 Huang, 1981, p. 58.
89 Hucker, 1975, p. 306; Finer, 1999, II, p. 836.
90 For a summary, see Finer, 1999, II, pp. 832–7.
91 ibid., p. 837.
92 ibid., pp. 830–1.
93 Hucker, 1966, pp. 44–5.
94 Jullien, 1999, pp. 47–50; Fu, 1996, pp. 40–4.
95 On similar tactics employed by Mao during the Hundred Flowers Campaign in 1957. See Li, 1996, pp. 197–202.

15 Entrepreneurship

1 Jullien, 1999, p. 40.
2 ibid., pp. 177–218.
3 ibid., pp. 34–5.
4 For Sun Zi, see ibid., pp. 25–38; Jullien, 2000, pp. 35–53; Wing, 1988. For a bastardised version, see for example Michaelson, 2001.
5 Jullien, 1999, p. 29. Or, in the image of Hanfeizi, it was like floating a boat down a river. Fu, 1996, p. 89.
6 Chan, 1963, p. 139.
7 Quoted in Chan, 1963, p. 167.
8 Fu, 1996, p. 89.
9 Jullien, 1999, pp. 42–4; 47–54.
10 ibid., pp. 47–54; Fu, 1996, pp. 60–1, 75–7.
11 Fu, 1996, pp. 59–60.
12 Gernet, pp. 110–17.
13 Elvin, 1973, pp. 47–8.
14 Quoted in Chan, 1963, p. 43.
15 Hucker, 1975, pp. 55–6, 81, 100; Chan, 1963, pp. 528, 599.
16 Compare the pleads to activism of Xunzi, 'On Nature,' in Chan, 1963, p. 122.
17 Elvin, 1973, pp. 179–99.
18 Ng, 2003, pp. 52–7.
19 On the worldview of the imperial state, see Fairbank and Teng, 1960/1967, pp. 106–7; Spence, 1990/99, pp. 118–19.
20 Gernet, 1972/1999, pp. 195–201.
21 ibid., pp. 326–39; Lo, 1955, pp. 489–93; Duyvendak, 1949, pp. 16–17.
22 Duyvendak, 1949, p. 17; Lo, 1955, p. 499.
23 Duyvendak, 1949, pp. 27–35. Compare also Boorstin, 1983, pp. 186–201.
24 Duyvendak, 1949, pp. 27–8.
25 ibid., p. 27. On the emperor's harem, see Huang, 1981, pp. 28–9.
26 Huang, 1981, pp. 13–20; Finer, 1999, II, pp. 826–9.
27 Willets, 1964/1967, pp. 13–14.
28 Elvin, 1973, p. 217.
29 ibid., p. 218. See also Myers and Wang, 2002, p. 565.
30 Elvin, 1973, p. 220.
31 Duyvendak, 1939/1967, pp. 86–9; Willetts, 1964/1967, pp. 89–91. See also Spence, 1990/99, pp. 119–20.
32 Quoted in Duyvendak, 1939/1967, p. 88.
33 Myers and Wang, 2002, p. 607.
34 ibid., pp. 592–604.
35 ibid., pp. 576, 632–3.
36 ibid., pp. 594–6.

37 ibid., pp. 563–75; Elvin, 1973, pp. 268–84.
38 Pomeranz, 2000, pp. 114–65; Adshead, 1997, on the consumerism of dress, see pp. 67–101; Myers and Wang, 2002, p. 577.
39 Myers and Wang, 2002, p. 629.
40 ibid., pp. 591, 609.
41 ibid., p. 642.
42 ibid., p. 607.
43 Generally on the family, see Eastman, 1988, pp. 15–40. For a contemporary illustration, see Oxfeld, 1993, pp. 211–40; Hamilton, 1998, pp. 41–77.
44 Fukuyama on how this still is true in Taiwan. Fukuyama, 1995, p. 72.
45 Myers and Wang, 2002, p. 644.
46 Greenhalgh, 1994, pp. 746–51.
47 Eastman, 1988, pp. 24–8; on corporal punishment of children, see p. 22.
48 Fukuyama, 1995, pp. 79, 345; Myers and Wang, 2002, pp. 586, 590.
49 On the the the art of networking, see Yang, 1994, pp. 47–145. See also Fei, 1947/1992, pp. 71–9; Yang, 1965, pp. 291–309.
50 Eastman, 1988, pp. 237–9; Myers and Wang, 2002, p. 631.
51 Balazs, 1964, p. 159. On the Taiping Rebellion, see Spence, 1990/99, pp. 171–80.
52 Spence, 1990/99, pp. 110–16.

16 Pluralism

1 Lach and van Kley, 1993, pp. 1563–93.
2 Compare O'Leary, 1989, pp. 235–61.
3 Spence, 1990/99, pp. 118–22, 147–50.
4 'Demographics of China,' at www.thefreedictionary.com.
5 Huang, 1981, pp. 58–9; Yang, 1959, pp. 156–63.
6 Finer, 1999, II, pp. 826–32.
7 Huang, 1981, p. 58.
8 Watson, 1993, p. 100.
9 The seminal work is Rotours, 1963.
10 Sutton, 1995, pp. 136–72; Yi, 1996.
11 Wood, 1995, p. 1.
12 Gernet, 1972/1999, p. 94.
13 Fu, 1996, pp. 37–77; Chan, 1963, pp. 251–61.
14 Fu, 1996, p. 107.
15 ibid., p. 92.
16 Confucius, The Analects, 12:2, quoted in Chan, 1963, p. 39.
17 Fei, 1947/1992, pp. 71–9.
18 Confucius, The Analects, 12:17, quoted in Chan, 1963, p. 40.
19 This is the overarching theme of Jullien, 2000, see especially pp. 93–115.
20 ibid., pp. 35–53.
21 Compare Pocock, 1989, pp. 49–50.
22 Confucius, The Analects, 12:17, quoted in Chan, 1963, p. 40.
23 Gernet, 1972/1999, p. 78.
24 Pocock, 1989, pp. 54–9.
25 ibid., p. 57.
26 The Daoist Zhuang-zi, or Chuang Tzu, quoted in ibid., p. 58.
27 Confucius, The Analects, 12:17, quoted in Chan, 1963, p. 40. Xunzi on how falsification of terms was similar to the falsification of credentials or measurements. Chan, 1963, p. 124.
28 Xunzi quoted in Chan, 1963, p. 126.
29 Confucius, The Analects, 13:6, quoted in Chan, 1963, p. 41.
30 Jullien, 2000, pp. 15–18.

31 For an apologia, see for example Li *et al.*, 2002, pp. 95–140.
32 Jullien, 2000, pp. 15–34. On the use of ambiguity as a resistance strategy, see Thornton, 2002, pp. 661–81.
33 Spence, 1990/99, p. 108. On the contradictions between Buddhism and Confucianism, see Wing-tsit Chan quoted in Wood, 1995, p. 47.
34 C. K. Yang, 1975, p. 280. For a similar discussion regarding Korea, see Kim, 1996, p. 204.
35 C. K. Yang, 1975, p. 282.
36 ibid.,; Eastman, 1988, pp. 52–3.
37 Gernet, 1972/1999, p. 346.
38 C. K. Yang, p. 283. On the persecution of Buddhists in the ninth century, see Gernet, 1972/1999, pp. 294–6.
39 de Bary, 1959, pp. 29–30.
40 Fei, 1947/1992, pp. 94–100; Watson, 1993, p. 81. On the role of ritual in the writings of the Neo-Confucian Chu Hsi, see de Bary, 1959, pp. 37–8.
41 Watson, 1993, p. 94.
42 C. K. Yang, p. 276.
43 Huang, 1981, pp. 46–7.
44 Confucius, Analects, 1:12, quoted in Chan, 1963, p. 21. Compare Fei, 1947/1992, pp. 94–100.
45 Huang, 1981, pp. 4–6; Finer, 1999, II, 1999, p. 822.
46 Pocock, 1989, p. 46; Gernet, 1972/1999, p. 84.
47 Hsun Tzu quoted in Pocock, 1989, p. 46.
48 ibid., p. 46; Jullien, 2000, pp. 117–40.
49 On the two kinds of caps, see Confucius, Analects, 9:3 and 1:12, in Chan, 1963, p. 35.
50 Gernet, 1972/1999, p. 63.
51 These two points deal with the concerns raised in de Vries, 2002, pp. 67–75.
52 Gernet, 1972/1999, p. 62; Finer, 1999, I, pp. 450–66.
53 Fu, 1996, pp. 38–40.
54 Gernet, 1972/1999, pp. 67–9.
55 ibid., pp. 69–72.
56 Jullien, 2000, p. 124.
57 Gernet, 1972/1999, pp. 300–51; Wood, 1995, pp. 81–110.
58 On the Yürchen, see Gernet, 1972/1999, pp. 356–9.
59 Gernet, 1972/1999, pp. 330–48.
60 Ronan and Needham, 1979, pp. 50–4; Lo, 1955, p. 501.
61 Spence, 1990/99, pp. 271–83.
62 ibid., pp. 300–8.
63 ibid., pp. 267–9.

17 Europe and China compared

1 Jullien, 1999, pp. 211–12. Compare qualifications in Watson, 1993, pp. 16–17.
2 Paz, 1974, pp. 1–5; Koselleck, 1985, pp. 21–38.
3 Karl Löwith, 'Meaning in History,' 1949, discussed in Ng, 2003, pp. 37–9.
4 Jullien, 1999, pp. 211–12.
5 Although the Manchus in particular also maintained a number of their indigenous customs. See Rawski, 1998, pp. 4–5, 60.
6 See the examples provided in Wood, 1995, pp. 8–11.
7 For a closely related argument, see de Bary, 1959, pp. 48–9.
8 Mokyr, 1990, p. 233.
9 Huang, 1981, p. 52.
10 Balazs, 1964, p. 44.
11 Watson, 1993, p. 96.

12 Compare Jullien, 2000, pp. 15–34.
13 Elvin, 1973, pp. 187–8.
14 ibid., pp. 190–1.
15 ibid., pp. 198–9.
16 Jones, 1990, pp. 5–22; Hamilton, 1985, pp. 187–211.
17 Elvin, 1973, pp. 203–34.
18 Lin, 1995, pp. 278–85.
19 Elvin, 1973, p. 194.
20 Jullien, 2000, pp. 124–5.
21 Much the same applies in the legal system, see Hucker, 1966, p. 24.
22 Jullien, 1999, p. 69.
23 Finer, 1999, II, pp. 835–6.
24 Mokyr, 1990, p. 234.
25 ibid., p. 209.
26 A point ignored by Pomeranz, 2000, but emphasised by Wong, 1997, p. 133.
27 Jullien, 2000, pp. 44–5.
28 These points should answer the concerns of Vries, 2002, pp. 67–138.
29 Hacker, 1977, p. 47.
30 Wong, 1997, p. 102.

18 Foreign challenges, Japanese responses

1 Spence, 1990/99, pp. 118–21.
2 Quoted in ibid., pp. 122–3.
3 Jansen, 2000, pp. 1–4; 21–5.
4 Spence, 1990/99, pp. 154–66.
5 ibid., pp. 142–3.
6 Watson, 1992, pp. 50–1.
7 Toby, 1977; Jansen, 2000, pp. 1–41.
8 Jansen, 1980/1995, pp. 43–4; Jansen, 1992, pp. 71–6.
9 Quoted in Jansen, 1992, p. 101. Throughout Japanese names are given with the family name first.
10 Dore, 1965, p. 100.
11 Hibbett, 1959, pp. 36–64; Jansen, 2000, pp. 175–86.
12 Jansen, 2000, pp. 166–7.
13 ibid., p. 246.
14 Harootunian, 1980, pp. 14–15.
15 ibid., pp. 24–5.
16 ibid., pp. 18–29; Jansen, 2000, pp. 204–10.
17 Jansen, 2000, pp. 206–9. On the Daoist influences on this alleged native tradition, see Harootunian, 1980, p. 20; Jansen, 1975/1995, pp. 13, 26.
18 Harootunian, 1980, pp. 18–19.
19 Harootunian, 1970, pp. 47–128.
20 Hirakawa, 1989, pp. 435–48; Jansen, 2000, pp. 208–15. *Ran* from 'Horanda' combined with *gaku* meaning 'learning.'
21 ibid., pp. 3–4.
22 Jansen, 1975/1995, pp. 33–9.
23 Totman, 1980, pp. 6–8; Craig, 1986, p. 39.
24 Altman, 1986, pp. 232–3; Totman, 1980, pp. 7–8.
25 Totman, 1980, pp. 12–13.
26 ibid., pp. 17–18.
27 Wood, 1995, pp. 159–65.
28 Totman, 1980, pp. 17–18.
29 Jansen, 1986, pp. 68–9; Craig, 1986, p. 42; Wood, 1995, p. 160.

30 Totman, 1980, pp. 17–18.
31 Jansen, 1975/1995, pp. 43–51.
32 Levy, 1955, pp. 515–16.
33 A feature emphasised by the first European travellers to the country, see Cooper, 1965, pp. 53–71.
34 Compare 'The Tale of Forty-Seven Ronin,' discussed in Levy, 1955, p. 519.
35 Jansen, 2000, pp. 237–56; Schrecker, 1976, pp. 96–106.
36 Jansen, 2000, pp. 247–56.
37 Hirakawa, 1989, pp. 455–61; Ericson, 1979, p. 383; Jansen, 1975/1995, pp. 43–51.
38 A policy referred to as *kôbu gattai* – the 'union of court and camp.'
39 Jansen, 1986, pp. 68–9; Craig, 1986, p. 42.
40 Lockwood, 1956, p. 43.
41 Craig, 1986, p. 38; van Wolferen, 1990, pp. 36–7.
42 Watson, 1992, pp. 35, 42.
43 ibid., p. 36.
44 When the Tokugawa delegate arrived at the Bank of England, for example, he suspiciously noted down all previous Japanese visitors who had made entries in the guestbook. Ericson, 1979, pp. 401–4.
45 Craig, 1986, pp. 45–6.
46 Jansen, 1986, p. 82.
47 ibid., pp. 76–81.
48 This is the theme of the articles collected in Vlastos, 1998. Compare Hobsbawm and Ranger, 1983.
49 Craig, 1986, pp. 49–52.
50 Jansen, 1992, pp. 94–5; Itô, 1998, pp. 42–4. On the persecution of Buddhists, see Keetelar, 1990, especially pp. 43–86.
51 Jansen, 1986, pp. 70–1.
52 Itô, 1998, pp. 45–6.
53 Jansen, 2000, pp. 69–70.

19 Japan and China in a modern world

 1 Jansen, 1980/1995, p. 42.
 2 ibid., pp. 64, 69.
 3 Hirakawa, 1989, pp. 463–6; Jansen, 1980/1995, pp. 53–68.
 4 Hirakawa, 1989, pp. 434–35, 464; Jansen, 1980/1995, pp. 58–61.
 5 On the Itô mission, see Hirakawa, 1989, pp. 433–5.
 6 ibid., p. 465.
 7 ibid., p. 465.
 8 Altman, 1986, pp. 237–47.
 9 ibid., pp. 231–2.
10 Ambaras, 1998, pp. 8–10.
11 Hirakawa, 1989, pp. 460–2; Jansen, 1980/1995, pp. 48, 52.
12 Altman, 1986, p. 240; Hirakawa, 1989, pp. 470–2.
13 Hirakawa, 1989, pp. 477–87.
14 Yamamura, 1997, pp. 294–352.
15 Jansen, 1986, pp. 78–9.
16 Crawcour, 1974, p. 119; Crawcour, 1997, pp. 56–8; Yamamura, 1997, pp. 307–8.
17 On corporate forms, see Yamamura, 1997, pp. 322–42.
18 Totten, 1974/1999, p. 401.
19 Nakamura, 2000, pp. 197–202. Numbers for manufacturing output on p. 194. Although as Crawcour, 1997, points out the numbers are uncertain, see p. 42.
20 On trade unions see Totten, 1974/1999, p. 401; on farmers, see Ambaras, 1998, pp. 4–13.

21 Gordon, 1998, pp. 19–36; Yamamura, 1999. On the strike activity and the origin of the Japanese employment system see Weiss, 1993, p. 328.
22 Gordon, 1998, p. 24.
23 Hirakawa, 1989, pp. 487–9.
24 Altman, 1986, p. 241.
25 Quoted in Hirakawa, 1989, p. 496. Compare Jansen, 1980/1995, pp. 70–1.
26 Ono Seiichiro, 1938, quoted in Itô, 1998, p. 46.
27 Totten, 1974/1999, p. 400; Gordon, 1998, pp. 27–8.
28 For a similar argument, see Crawcour, 1974, p. 113; Westney, 1987, pp. 210–24. Compare also Smith, 1988.
29 Dore, 1965, p. 100.
30 As powerfully argued in Upham, 1998, pp. 48–64. Compare Hirakawa, 1989, pp. 472–7.
31 Crawcour, 1974, p. 119.
32 Lockwood, 1956, p. 40.
33 Spence, 1990/99, pp. 145–9.
34 ibid., pp. 197–208.
35 ibid., pp. 192–7.
36 Wood, 1995, p. 165–70.
37 Quoted in Spence, 1990/99, p. 196.
38 ibid., pp. 167–80.
39 ibid., pp. 142–3. See also Grasso, Corrin and Kort, 1997, pp. 59–62; Young, 1970, pp. 157–65; Kwong, 2000, pp. 663–96.
40 Spence, 1990/99, pp. 271–89; Young, 1970, pp. 165–75; Grasso, Corrin and Kort, 1997, pp. 72–97.
41 For one damning account, see Potter and Potter, 1990/97, pp. 59–95.
42 Lockwood, 1956, p. 42.
43 Hacker, 1977, pp. 54–5.
44 van Wolferen, 1990, p. 39.
45 ibid., p. 37.
46 For a rational choice interpretation see Ramseyer and Rosenbluth, 1998, especially pp. 15–40.
47 Baba and Imai, 1992, pp. 141–51.
48 See the issue of *Japan Forum* on the topic of factionalism, especially Stockwin, 1989, pp. 161–71.
49 One example concerns the choice of video format discussed in Baba and Imai, 1992, pp. 148–9.
50 Compare Dissanayake, 1996, pp. 193–8.

20 The new politics of modernisation

1 On the importance of practical knowledge see Scott, 1998, pp. 309–41.
2 See for example Legrain, 2003, p. 24.
3 Lindblom, 2002, pp. 98–9, 111–15.
4 Compare, for example, Buruma, 1995 with Yew, 1998. Historically speaking city-states have of course often been highly creative. It is revealing to compare Singapore with Florence.
5 Yew, 1998, pp. 714–32. Although Singapore was a model for Chinese development mainly during the Deng years.
6 Compare the discussion in Dahl, 1971, pp. 132–41.
7 See, once again, Paz, 1974, pp. 26–31.
8 Compare Wittrock, 2000, pp. 31–60 as well as other articles in the same volume.
9 Compare Hirschman, 1981.
10 Scott, 1998, pp. 81–3.

11 Lyotard, 1979.
12 Whether this actually is happening is itself a contested issue. For a sceptical view, see Micklethwait and Wooldridge, 2000, pp. 143–63.
13 Arendt, 1958/1998, 38–49; Fukuyama, 1992, pp. 300–12.
14 On modernity as a belief in *metarécits*, see Lyotard, 1979, pp. 7–9.
15 Berlin, 1994, pp. 26–71.
16 Compare Jacob, 1988, pp. 52–4.
17 Walzer, 1983, pp. xiv.
18 Unger, 1987, pp. 36–7, 200–2.
19 This was recently vividly illustrated by the euphoria of the dot.com bubble. See Cassidy, 2002, pp. 25–36.
20 For one recent account, see Talwar, 2002.
21 Phillips, 2002, pp. 293–401; Luttwak, 1998, pp. 1–53.
22 This is the constant theme of Chomsky's political writings. For an overview, see Chomsky, 1988/2002.

Bibliography

Abramovitz, Moses. 'Thinking about Growth,' in his *Thinking about Growth: And Other Essays on Economic Growth and Welfare* (Cambridge: Cambridge University Press, 1989), pp. 3–79.

Adshead, S. A. M. *Material Culture in Europe and China, 1400–1800: The Rise of Consumerism* (Basingstoke: Macmillan, 1997).

Altman, Albert A. 'The Press,' in *Japan in Transition: From Tokugawa to Meiji*, edited by Marius B. Jansen and Gilbert Rozman (Princeton: Princeton University Press, 1986).

Ambaras, David R. 'Social Knowledge, Cultural Capital, and the New Middle Class in Japan, 1895–1912,' *Journal of Japanese Studies*, 24:1, 1998, pp. 1–33.

Anderson, Benedict. *Imagined Communities: Reflections on the Origins and Spread of Nationalism* (London: Verso, 1983).

Appadurai, Arjun. 'Introduction: Commodities and the Politics of Value,' in *The Social Life of Things: Commodities in Cultural Perspective* (Cambridge: Cambridge University Press, 1986).

Arendt, Hannah. [1958], *The Human Condition* (Chicago: University of Chicago Press, 1998).

—— *On Revolution* (Harmondsworth: Penguin, 1963).

Ariès, Philippe. *Centuries of Childhood: A Social History of Family Life* (Harmondsworth: Penguin, 1973).

Aristotle. [350 BCE] *The Politics* (Buffalo: Prometheus, 1986).

Auerbach, Erich. *Mimesis: The Representation of Reality in Western Literature* (Princeton: Princeton University Press, 1953).

Augustine, Saint. [397–98], *Confessions* (Harmondsworth: Penguin, 1961).

Axelrod, Robert. 'The Emergence of Cooperation,' *American Political Science Review*, 75, 1994, pp. 306–18.

Baba, Yasunori and Ken-ichi Imai, 'Systematic Innovation and Cross-Border Networks: The Case of the Evolution of the VCP Systems,' in *Entrepreneurship, Technological Innovation and Economic Growth*, edited by F. M. Scherer and Mark Perlman (Ann Arbor: University of Michigan Press, 1992).

Bacon, Francis. [1627], *The New Atlantis and The Great Instauration* (Wheeling: Crofts Classics, 1989).

Bagehot, Walter. [1867], *The English Constitution* (Brighton: Sussex Academic Press, 1997).

—— [1873], *Lombard Street: A Description of the Money Market* (New York: John Wiley, 1999).

Baker, Keith Michael. 'Public Opinion as Political Invention,' in his *Inventing the French*

Revolution: Essays on French Political Culture in the Eighteenth Century (Cambridge: Cambridge University Press, 1990).

Bakhtin, Mikhail. [1965], *Rabelais and His World* (Bloomington: Indiana University Press, 1984).

Balazs, Étienne. *Chinese Civilization and Bureaucracy: Variations on a Theme* (New Haven: Yale University Press, 1964).

Baldwin, John W. 'Introduction,' in *Universities in Politics: Case Studies from the Late Middle Ages and Early Modern Period*, edited by John W. Baldwin and Richard A. Goldthwaite (Baltimore: Johns Hopkins University Press, 1972).

Ball, Terence. 'Party,' in *Political Innovation and Conceptual Change*, edited by Terence Ball, James Farr and Russell L. Hanson (Cambridge: Cambridge University Press, 1989) pp. 155–76.

Baron, Hans. *Crisis of the Early Italian Renaissance: Civic Humanism and Republican Liberty in an Age of Classicism and Tyranny* (Princeton: Princeton University Press, 1966).

Baudrillard, Jean. [1970], *The Consumer Society: Myths and Structures* (London: Sage, 1999).

Baumer, F. L. 'The Conception of Christendom in Renaissance England,' *Journal of the History of Ideas*, vol. 6, 1945.

Becker, Carl L. *The Heavenly City of the Eighteenth-Century Philosophers* (New Haven: Yale University Press, 1932).

Bentham, Jeremy. *Defence of Usury*, 1787, available at http://socserv2.socsci. mcmaster.ca/~econ/ugcm/3ll3/bentham/usury.

Bérenger, Jean, 'The Austrian Lands: Habsburg Absolutism under Leopold I,' in *Absolutism in Seventeenth Century Europe*, edited by John Miller (London: Macmillan, 1990).

Berger, Peter L. [1970], 'On the Obsolescence of the Concept of Honor,' in *The Homeless Mind: Modernization and Consciousness*, Peter L. Berger, Brigitte Berger and Hansfried Kellner (New York: Vintage, 1973).

—— 'East Asian Capitalism: A Second Case,' in his *The Capitalist Revolution: Fifty Propositions about Prosperity, Equality and Liberty* (Aldershot: Gower, 1987).

Berlin, Isaiah. 'European Unity and Its Vicissitudes,' in his *The Crooked Timber of Humanity* (Princeton: Princeton University Press, 1990).

—— *The Magus of the North: J. G. Hamann and the Origins of Modern Irrationalism* (London: Fontana, 1994).

Bessette, Joseph M. *The Mild Voice of Reason: Deliberative Democracy and American National Government* (Chicago: University of Chicago Press, 1994).

Black, Antony. *Political Thought in Europe, 1250–1450* (Cambridge: Cambridge University Press, 1992).

Boccaccio, Giovanni. [1348], *The Decameron* (Harmondsworth: Penguin, 1972).

Bödeker, Hans Erich. 'Journals and Public Opionion: The Politicization of the German Enlightenment in the Second Half of the Eighteenth Century,' in *The Transformation of Political Culture: England and Germany in the Late Eighteenth Century*, edited by Eckhart Hellmuth (Oxford: Oxford University Press, 1990).

Bodin, Jean. [1576], *On Sovereignty*, edited by Julian H. Franklin (Cambridge: Cambridge University Press, 1992).

Boorstin, Daniel J. *The Discoverers: A History of Man's Search to Know His World and Himself* (New York: Vintage Books, 1983).

Bozeman, Adda B. *Politics and Culture in International History* (Princeton: Princeton University Press, 1960).

Braudel, Fernand. [1979], *Civilization and Capitalism, 15th–18th Century: Volume I. The Structures of Everyday Life* (London: Phoenix, 2002).

—— [1979], *Civilization and Capitalism, 15th–18th Century: Volume II. The Wheels of Commerce* (London: Phoenix, 2002).

Brockliss, Laurence. 'Curricula,' in *A History of the University in Europe: vol II, Universities in Early Modern Europe (1500–1800)*, edited by Hilde de Ridder-Symoens (Cambridge: Cambridge University Press, 1996).

Bull, Hedley. 'The Importance of Grotius,' in *Hugo Grotius and International Relations*, edited by Hedley Bull, Benedict Kingsbury and Adam Roberts (Oxford: Clarendon, 1992).

Burckhardt, Jacob. [1860], *The Civilization of the Renaissance in Italy*, translated by (New York: Harper & Row, 1958).

Burke, Edmund. 'Speech on Conciliation with America,' 1775, in *The Works and Correspondence of the Right Honourable Edmund Burke: Volume 3* (London: 1852).

—— [1790], *Reflections on the Revolution in France* (Harmondsworth: Penguin, 1982).

—— [1795], 'Thoughts on French Affairs,' in *Edmund Burke's Politics: Selected Writings and Speeches of Edmund Burke on Reform, Revolution, and War*, edited by Ross J. S. Hoffman and Paul Levack (New York: Knopf, 1949).

Burke, Peter. *Popular Culture in Early Modern Europe* (London: Temple Smith, 1978).

Burtt, Shelley. *Virtue Transformed: Political Argument in England, 1688–1740* (Cambridge: Harvard University Press, 1992).

Buruma, Ian. 'The Singapore Way', *The New York Review of Books*, 42:16, October 19, 1995.

Bury, J. B. [1920], *The Idea of Progress* (New York: Dover, 1955).

Caenegem, R. C. van. *An Historical Introduction to Western Constitutional Law* (Cambridge: Cambridge University Press, 1995).

Cahill, James. *The Compelling Image: Nature and Style in Seventeenth-Century Chinese Painting* (Cambridge: Belknap Press, 1982).

Cameron, Rondo and Hugh T. Patrick, 'Introduction,' in *Banking in the Early Stages of Industrialization*, edited by Rondo Cameron *et al.* (Oxford: Oxford University Press, 1967).

Čapek, Milič. 'Change,' *The Encyclopedia of Philosophy* (New York: Macmillan, 1967).

Carruthers, Bruce G. *City of Capital: Politics and Markets in the English Financial Revolution* (Princeton: Princeton University Press, 1996).

Cassidy, John. *Dot.con: The Greatest Story Ever Told* (London: Allen Lane, 2002).

Castells, Manuel. 'Four Asian Tigers with a Dragon Head: A Comparative Analysis of the State, Economy, and Society in the Asian Pacific Rim,' in *States and Development in the Asian Pacific Rim*, edited by Richard P. Appelbaum and Jeffrey Henderson (Newbury Park: Sage, 1992), pp. 33–70.

Castiglione, Baldesar. [1528], *The Book of the Courtier*, translated by Charles S. Singleton (New York: Doubleday, 1959).

Cellini, Benvenuti. [1558–66], *Autobiography* (Harmondsworth: Penguin, 1956).

Chan, Wing-tsit. *A Sourcebook in Chinese Philosophy* (Princeton: Princeton University Press, 1963).

Chesterfield, Lord 'Letter to His Son, 25 January, 1750,' in *Lord Chesterfield's Letters* (Oxford: Oxford University Press, 1992).

Chomsky, Noam. [1988], *Manufacturing Consent: The Political Economy of the Mass Media* (New York: Pantheon, 2002).

Chou Tun-i. 'An Explanation of the Diagram of the Great Ultimate,' in *A Sourcebook in*

Chinese Philosophy, edited by Wing-tsit Chan (Princeton: Princeton University Press, 1963).

Clunas, Craig. *Pictures and Visuality in Early Modern China* (London: Reaktion Books, 1997).

Cohen, G. A. *Karl Marx's Theory of History: A Defence* (Princeton: Princeton University Press, 1978).

Cohn, Norman. *The Pursuit of the Millennium: Revolutionary Millenarians and Mystical Anarchists of the Middle Ages* (London: Pimlico, 1970).

Confucius, *The Analects*, in *A Sourcebook in Chinese Philosophy*, edited by Wing-tsit Chan (Princeton: Princeton University Press, 1963).

Cooper, Michael. ed. *They Came to Japan: An Anthology of European Reports on Japan, 1543–1640* (Berkeley: University of California Press, 1965).

Craig, Albert M. 'The Central Government,' in *Japan in Transition: From Tokugawa to Meiji*, edited by Marius B. Jansen and Gilbert Rozman (Princeton: Princeton University Press, 1986).

Cranston, Maurice. 'Bacon, Francis,' *Encyclopædia of Philosophy* (New York: Macmillan, 1967).

Crawcour, Sydney E. 'The Tokugawa Period and Japan's Preparation for Modern Economic Growth,' *Journal of Japanese Studies*, 1:1, 1974, pp. 113–25.

—— 'Economic Change in the Nineteenth Century,' in *The Economic Emergence of Modern Japan*, edited by Kozo Yamamura (Cambridge: Cambridge University Press, 1997).

Dagger, Richard. 'Rights,' in *Political Innovation and Conceptual Change*, edited by Terence Ball, James Farr and Russell L. Hanson (Cambridge: Cambridge University Press, 1989).

Dahl, Robert A. [1970], *After the Revolution?: Authority in a Good Society* (New Haven: Yale University Press, 1990).

—— *Polyarchy: Participation and Opposition* (New Haven: Yale University Press, 1971).

—— 'On Removing Certain Impediments to Democracy in the United States,' in his *Democracy, Liberty, and Equality* (Oslo: Norwegian University Press, 1986).

Darnton, Robert. *The Business of Enlightenment: A Publishing History of the Encyclopédie, 1775–1800* (Cambridge: Belknap Press, 1979).

—— 'Paris: The Early Internet,' *New York Review of Books*, June 29, 2000.

Daston, Lorraine and Katherine Park, *Wonders and the Order of Nature, 1150–1750* (New York: Zone Books, 1998).

Dawkins, Richard. *Climbing Mount Improbable* (New York: W. W. Norton, 1996).

de Bary, Wm. Theodore. 'Some Common Tendencies in Neo-Confucianism,' in *Confucianism in Action*, edited by David S. Nivison and Arthur F. Wright (Stanford: Stanford University Press, 1959).

—— 'Chinese Despotism and the Confucian Ideal: A Seventeenth Century View,' in *Chinese Thought and Institutions*, edited by John K. Fairbank (Chicago: University of Chicago Press, 1975).

de Soto, Hernando. *The Mystery of Capital: Why Capitalism Triumphs in the West and Fails Everywhere Else* (London: Bantam, 2000).

de Vries, Jan. 'On the Modernity of the Dutch Republic,' *Journal of Economic History*, 33:1, 1973, pp. 191–202.

—— 'Between Purchasing Power and the World of Goods: Understanding the Household Economy in Early Modern Europe,' in *Consumption and the World of Goods*, edited by John Brewer and Roy Porter (London: Routledge, 1992), pp. 85–132.

—— and Ad van der Woude. *The First Modern Economy: Success, Failure, and Persever-ance of the Dutch Economy, 1500–1815* (Cambridge: Cambridge University Press 1997).

de Vries, P. 'Governing Growth: A Comparative Analysis of the Role of the State in the Rise of the West,' *Journal of World History*, 13:1, 2002, pp. 67–138.

Defoe, Daniel. [1697], 'An Essay upon Projects,' reprinted in *The Earlier Life and Chief Earlier Works of Daniel Defoe*, edited by Henry Morley (London: George Routledge, 1889).

—— [1719], *The Life and Adventures of Robinson Crusoe* (Harmondsworth: Penguin, 1985).

Deutsch, Karl. [1953], *Nationalism and Social Communication: An Inquiry into the Founda-tion Nationality* (Cambridge: MIT Press, 1966).

Dickson, P. G. M. 'The Financial Revolution,' in his *The Financial Revolution in England: A Study in the Development of Public Debt, 1688–1756* (London: Macmillan, 1967), pp. 3–35.

Dictionnaire historique de la langue française (Paris: Robert, 1993).

Dissanayake, Wimal. 'Self, Agency, and Cultural Knowledge: Reflections on Three Japanese Films,' in *Narratives of Agency: Self-Making in China, India, and Japan*, edited by Wimal Dissanayake (Minneapolis: University of Minnesota Press, 1996).

Donaldson, Peter S. *Machiavelli and Mystery of State* (Cambridge: Cambridge University Press, 1988).

Dore, Ronald. 'The Legacy of Tokugawa Education,' in *Changing Japanese Attitudes toward Modernization*, edited by Marius B. Jansen (Princeton: Princeton University Press, 1965), pp. 99–132.

Dunn, John. 'Revolution,' in *Political Innovation and Conceptual Change*, edited by Terence Ball, James Farr and Russell L. Hanson (Cambridge: Cambridge University Press, 1989).

Duyvendak, J. J. L. [1939], 'The True Dates of the Chinese Maritime Expeditions in the Early Fifteenth Century,' reprinted in *European Expansion and the Counter-Example of Asia, 1300–1600*, edited by Joseph R. Levenson (Englewood Cliffs: Prentice-Hall, 1967).

—— *China's Discovery of Africa* (London: Probsthain, 1949).

Eastman, Lloyd E. *Family, Fields, and Ancestors: Constancy and Change in China's Social and Economic History* (New York: Oxford University Press, 1988).

Eberhard, Wolfram. 'The Political Function of Astronomy and Astronomers in Han China,' in *Chinese Thought and Institutions*, edited by John K. Fairbank (Chicago: Uni-versity of Chicago Press, 1975).

Eco, Umberto. *The Search for the Perfect Language* (Oxford: Blackwell, 1995).

Eisenstein, Elizabeth L. *The Printing Revolution in Early Modern Europe* (Cambridge: Cambridge University Press, 1983).

Ekelund, Robert B. and Robert F. Hébert, *A History of Economic Theory and Method* (New York: McGraw-Hill, 1997).

—— Robert F. Hébert *et al.*, *Sacred Trust: the Medieval Church as an Economic Firm* (Oxford: Oxford University Press, 1996).

Elias, Norbert. [1939], *The Civilizing Process: The History of Manners and State Formation and Civilization* (Oxford: Blackwell, 1994).

Elster, Jon. 'Marxism, Functionalism, Game Theory: A Debate,' *Theory and Society*, 11:4, 1982.

Elvin, Mark. *The Pattern of the Chinese Past: A Social and Economic Interpretation* (Stanford: Stanford University Press, 1973).

Ericson, Mark D. 'The Bakufu Looks Abroad: the 1865 Mission to France,' *Monumenta Nipponica*, 34:4, 1979, pp. 383–407.

Erikson, Erik H. *Young Man Luther: A Study in Psychoanalysis and History* (New York: W. W. Norton, 1962).

Ertman, Thomas. *Birth of the Leviathan: Building States and Regimes in Medieval and Early Modern Europe* (Cambridge: Cambridge University Press, 1997).

Fairbank, John K. and S. Y. Teng, [1960], 'Ch'ing Administration: Three Studies,' reprinted in *European Expansion and the Counter-Example of Asia, 1300–1600*, edited by Joseph R. Levenson (Englewood Cliffs: Prentice-Hall, 1967).

Fei Xiaotong. [1947], *From the Soil: The Foundations of Chinese Society*, translated by Gary G. Hamilton and Wan Zheng (Berkeley: University of California Press, 1992).

Fenlon, D. B. 'England and Europe: Utopia and Its Aftermath,' *Transaction of the Royal Historical Society*, 1974, pp. 120–32.

Ferguson, Adam. [1767], *An Essay on the History of Civil Society* (Cambridge: Cambridge University Press, 1995).

Feuerwerker, Albert. 'Presidential Address: Questions about China's Early Modern Economic History that I Wish I Could Answer,' *Journal of Asian Studies*, 51:4, 1992.

Findlen, Paula. 'The Modern Muses: Renaissance Collecting and the Cult of Remembrance,' in *Museums and Memory*, edited by Susan A. Crane (Stanford: Stanford University Press, 2000).

Finer, S. E. *The History of Government* (Oxford: Oxford University Press, 1999).

Foucault, Michel. [1966], *The Order of Things: An Archeology of the Human Sciences* (New York: Vintage, 1973).

French, Peter. *John Dee: The World of an Elizabethan Magus* (New York: Dorset, 1972).

Friedman, David D. 'In Defense of Thomas Aquinas and the Just Price,' in *History of Political Economy*, 12:2, 1980, pp. 234–42.

Fu, Zhengyuan. *China's Legalists: The Earliest Totalitarians and Their Art of Ruling* (Armonk: M. E. Sharpe, 1996).

Fukuyama, Francis. *The End of History and the Last Man* (Harmondsworth: Penguin, 1992).

—— *Trust: The Social Virtues and the Creation of Prosperity* (Harmondsworth: Penguin, 1995).

Gadamer, Hans-Georg. [1975], *Truth and Method* (London: Sheed & Ward, 1989).

Galbraith, John Kenneth. [1975], *Money: Whence It Came, Where It Went* (Harmondsworth: Penguin, 1995).

Gauthier, David. *Morals by Agreement* (Oxford: Clarendon, 1986).

Gernet, Jacques. [1972], *A History of Chinese Civilization* (Cambridge: Cambridge University Press, 1999).

Gierke, Otto. [1881], *Political Theories of the Middle Ages*, translated by F. W. Maitland (Bristol: Thoemmes Press, 1996).

Gigerenzer, Gerd, Zeno Swijtink, Theodore Porter, Lorraine Daston, John Beatty and Lorenz Krüger, *The Empire of Chance: How Probability Changed Science and Everyday Life* (Cambridge: Cambridge University Press, 1989).

Gilboy, E. W. 'Demand as a Factor in the Industrial Revolution,' in *Facts and Factors in Economic History*, edited by A. H. Cole (Cambridge: Harvard University Press, 1932), pp. 620–39.

Gilpin, Robert. *Global Political Economy: Understanding the International Political Order* (Princeton: Princeton University Press, 2001).

Goldstone, Jack A. 'The Rise of the West – or Not?: A Revision to Socio-Economic History,' *Sociological Theory*, 18:2, 2000, pp. 175–94.

Goldthwaite, Richard. 'The Empire of Things: Consumer Demand in Renaissance Italy,' in *Patronage, Art, and Society in Renaissance Italy*, edited by F. W. Kent and Patricia Simons (Oxford: Clarendon Press, 1987), pp. 153–75.

Goody, Jack. *The Logic of Writing and the Organization of Society* (Cambridge: Cambridge University Press, 1986).

—— *The East in the West* (Cambridge: Cambridge University Press, 1996).

Gordon, Andrew. 'The Invention of Japanese-Style Labor Management,' in *Mirror of Modernity: Invented Traditions of Modern Japan*, edited by Stephen Vlastos (Berkeley: University of California Press, 1998).

Gorsky, Martin. 'The Growth and Distribution of English Friendly Societies in the Early Nineteenth Century,' *Economic History Review*, 51:3, 1998, pp. 489–511.

Grafton, Anthony. 'The Availability of Ancient Works,' in *The Cambridge History of Renaissance Philosophy*, edited by Charles B. Schmitt, Quentin Skinner and Eckhard Kessler (Cambridge: Cambridge University Press, 1988), pp. 767–91.

Grasso, June, Jay Corrin and Michael Kort, *Modernization and Revolution in China* (Armonk: M. E. Sharpe, 1997).

Graves, Michael A. R. *Early Tudor Parliaments, 1485–1558* (London: Longman, 1990).

Greenblatt, Stephen. *Marvellous Possessions: The Wonder of the New World* (Oxford: Clarendon Press, 1991).

—— Stephen. *Renaissance Self-Fashioning: From More to Shakespeare* (Chicago: University of Chicago Press, 1980).

Greene, Thomas M. 'Il Cortegiano and the Choice of a Game,' *Renaissance Quarterly*, 32: 1979, pp. 173–86.

Greenhalgh, Susan. 'De-Orientalizing the Chinese Family Firm,' *American Ethnologist*, vol. 21, no. 4, 1994, especially pp. 746–51.

Gregory, Richard. *Mirrors in Mind* (Harmondsworth: Penguin, 1998).

Gunn, J. A. W. 'Public Opinion,' in *Political Innovation and Conceptual Change*, edited by Terence Hall, James Farr and Russel L. Hanson (Cambridge: Cambridge University Press, 1989).

Gunn, J. A. W. 'Interests Will Not Lie: A Seventeenth-Century Political Maxim,' *Journal of the History of Ideas*, vol. 29, no. 4, 1968.

—— 'Influence, Parties and the Constitution: Changing Attitudes, 1783–1832,' *The Historical Journal*, 17:2, 1974, pp. 301–28.

Gurevich, Aaron. 'Representations of Property during the High Middle Ages,' *Economy & Society*, 6:1, 1977, pp. 1–30.

—— *The Origins of European Individualism* (Oxford: Blackwell, 1995).

Habermas, Jürgen. [1962], *The Structural Transformation of the Public Sphere: An Inquiry into a Category of Bourgeois Society* (Cambridge: MIT Press, 1989).

Hacker, Barton C. 'The Weapons of the West: Military Technology and Modernization in Nineteenth Century China and Japan,' *Technology and Culture*, 18, 1977, pp. 43–55.

Hacking, Ian. *The Taming of Chance* (Cambridge: Cambridge University Press, 1990).

—— [1975], *The Emergence of Probability: A Philosophical Study of Early Ideas about Probability, Induction and Statistical Inference* (Cambridge: Cambridge University Press, 1999).

Hale, J. R. *Renaissance Europe: Individual and Society, 1480–1520* (Berkeley: University of California Press, 1977).

Hall, John Whitney. 'Changing Conceptions of the Modernization of Japan,' in *Changing Japanese Attitudes toward Modernization*, edited by Marius B. Jansen (Princeton: Princeton University Press, 1965).

Hamilton, Gary G. 'Why No Capitalism in China: Negative Questions in Comparative Historical Sociology,' *Journal of Developing Societies*, 2: 1985, pp. 187–211.

—— 'Culture and Organization in Taiwan's Market Economy,' in *Market Cultures: Society and Morality in the New Asian Capitalisms*, edited by Robert W. Hefner (Boulder: Westview, 1998), pp. 48–9.

Hamilton, Walton H. 'Institution,' *International Encyclopaedia of the Social Sciences*, 1938.

Harootunian, Harry D. *Toward Restoration: The Growth of Political Consciousness in Tokugawa Japan* (Berkeley: University of California Press, 1970).

—— 'The Functions of China and Tokugawa Japan,' in *The Chinese and the Japanese*, edited by Akira Iriye (Princeton: Princeton University Press, 1980).

Harris, Bob. *Politics and the Rise of the Press: Britain and France, 1620–1800* (London: Routledge, 1996).

Harris, G. L. 'The Formation of Parliament,' in *The English Parliament in the Middle Ages*, edited by R. G. Davies and J. H. Denton (Manchester: Manchester University Press, 1981).

Hartley, Harold. *The Royal Society: Its Origins and Founders* (London: Royal Society, 1991).

Hartwell, Robert M. 'Financial Expertise, Examinations, and the Formulation of Economic Policy in Northern Song China,' *Journal of Asian Studies*, 30, 1971, pp. 281–314.

Haskins, Charles Homer. *The Renaissance of the Twelfth Century* (Cambridge: Harvard University Press, 1927).

Hayek, Friedrich A. 'The Meaning of Competition,' and '"Free" Enterprise and Competitive Order,' both in his *Individualism and Economic Order* (Chicago: University of Chicago Press, 1948).

—— *Fatal Conceit: The Errors of Socialism* (London: Routledge, 1988).

Hegel, G. W. F. [1821], *Hegel's Philosophy of Right*, translated by T. M. Knox (New York: Oxford University Press, 1957).

—— [1830–31], *The Philosophy of History*, translated by J. Sebree (New York: Dover, 1956).

Hellmuth, Eckhart. 'The Palladium of All Other English Liberties: Reflections on the Liberty of the Press in England during the 1760s and 1770s,' in *The Transformation of Political Culture: England and Germany in the Late Eighteenth Century*, edited by Eckhart Hellmuth (Oxford: Oxford University Press, 1990).

Henderson, Jeffrey and Richard P. Appelbaum, 'Situating the State in the East Asian Development Process,' in *States and Development in the Asian Pacific Rim*, edited by Richard P. Appelbaum and Jeffrey Henderson (Newbury Park: Sage, 1992), pp. 1–26.

Hibbett, Howard. *The Floating World in Japanese Fiction* (Boston: Tuttle, 1959).

Hirakawa, Sukehiro. 'Japan's Turn to the West,' in *The Cambridge History of Japan: Volume 5, The Nineteenth Century*, edited by Marius B. Jansen (Cambridge: Cambridge University Press, 1989).

Hirschman, Albert O. *The Passions and the Interests: Political Arguments for Capitalism before Its Triumph* (Princeton: Princeton University Press, 1977).

—— 'The Rise and Fall of Development Economics,' in his *Essays in Trespassing: Economics to Politics and Beyond* (Cambridge: Cambridge University Press, 1981).

Hobbes, Thomas. [1651], *Leviathan* (Harmondsworth: Penguin, 1981).

Hobsbawm, Eric J. and Terence O. Ranger, eds, *The Invention of Tradition* (Cambridge: Cambridge University Press, 1983).

Hofstadter, Richard. *The Age of Reform: From Bryan to F.D.R.* (New York: Vintage, 1955).

—— *The Idea of a Party System: The Rise of Legitimate Opposition in the United States, 1780–1840* (Berkeley: University of California Press, 1969).

Holdsworth, C. J. 'Visions and Visionaries in the Middle Ages,' *History*, vol. 48, 1963.

Holt, J. C. 'The Prehistory of Parliament,' in *The English Parliament in the Middle Ages*, edited by R. G. Davies and J. H. Denton (Manchester: Manchester University Press, 1981).

Hoppit, Julian. 'Attitudes to Credit in Britain, 1680–1790,' *The Historical Journal*, 33:2, 1990, pp. 305–22.

Huang, Ray. *1587, a Year of No Significance: The Ming Dynasty in Decline* (New Haven: Yale University Press, 1981).

Hucker, Charles O. *The Censorial System of Ming China* (Stanford: Stanford University Press, 1966).

—— *China's Imperial Past: An Introduction to Chinese History and Culture* (Stanford: Stanford University Press, 1975).

Hugo Grotius and International Relations, edited by Hedley Bull, Benedict Kingsbury and Adam Roberts (Oxford: Clarendon, 1990).

Huizinga, Johan. [1924], *The Waning of the Middle Ages* (New York: Doubleday, 1989).

Hume, David. [1777], 'Of Balance of Trade,' 'Of Civil Liberty,' 'Of Superstition and Enthusiasm,' and 'Of Parties in General,' in his *Essays: Moral, Political, and Literary* (Indianapolis: Liberty Fund, 1985).

Itô, Kimio. 'The Invention of War and the Transformation of the Image of Prince Shotoku in Modern Japan,' in *Mirror of Modernity: Invented Traditions of Modern Japan*, edited by Stephen Vlastos (Berkeley: University of California Press, 1998).

Jacob, J. R. 'Restoration, Reformation and the Origins of the Royal Society,' *History of Science*, 13, 1975, pp. 155–76.

Jacob, Margaret C. *The Cultural Meaning of the Scientific Revolution* (New York: McGraw-Hill, 1988).

Jansen, Marius B. [1975], *Japan and Its World: Two Centuries of Change* (Princeton: Princeton University Press, 1995).

—— 'The Ruling Class,' in *Japan in Transition: From Tokugawa to Meiji*, edited by Marius B. Jansen and Gilbert Rozman (Princeton: Princeton University Press, 1986), pp. 68–90.

—— *China in the Tokugawa World* (Cambridge: Harvard University Press, 1992).

—— *The Making of Modern Japan* (Cambridge: Belknap Press, 2000).

Johnson, Chalmers. *MITI and the Japanese Miracle: The Growth of Industrial Policy, 1925–1975* (Stanford: Stanford University Press, 1982).

Jones, Eric L. *The European Miracle: Environments, Economies and Geopolitics in the History of Europe and Asia* (Cambridge: Cambridge University Press, 1987).

—— 'The Real Question about China: Why Was the Song Economic Achievement Not Repeated?' *Australian Economic History Review*, vol. 30, no. 2, 1990, pp. 5–22.

Jullien, François. *The Propensity of Things: Toward a History of Efficacy in China* (New York: Zone Books, 1999).

—— *Detour and Access: Strategies of Meaning in China and Greece* (New York: Zone Books, 2000).

Kant, Immanuel. [1784], 'An Answer to the Question: What is Enlightenment?' in Immanuel Kant, *Perpetual Peace and Other Essays on Politics, History and Morals*, translated by Ted Humphrey (Indianapolis: Hackett, 1983).

Kantorowitz, Ernst. [1951], *The King's Two Bodies* (Princeton: Princeton University Press, 1957).

Keetelar, James E. *Of Heretics and Martyrs in Meiji Japan: Buddhism and Its Persecution* (Princeton: Princeton University Press, 1990).

Kelly, J. M. *A Short History of Western Legal Theory* (Oxford: Oxford University Press, 1992).

Kennedy, Paul M. *Preparing for the Twenty-First Century* (New York: Random House, 1993).

Kim, Kwang-Ok. 'The Reproduction of Confucian Culture in Contemporary Korea: An Anthropological Study,' in *Confucian Traditions in East Asian Modernity: Moral Education and Economic Culture in Japan and the Four Mini-Dragons*, edited by Tu Wei-Ming (Cambridge: Harvard University Press, 1996).

Kindleberger, Charles P. *A Financial History of Western Europe* (Oxford: Oxford University Press, 1993).

Klein, Lawrence E. 'The Political Significance of "Politeness" in Early Eighteenth-Century Britain,' in *Cicero, Scotland, and 'Politeness'*, edited by N. T. Phillipson, ed. (The Folger Shakespeare Library, 1993), pp. 73–108.

—— *Shaftesbury and the Culture of Politeness: Moral Discourse and Cultural Politics in Early Eighteenth-Century England* (Cambridge: Cambridge University Press, 1994).

—— 'Politeness and the Interpretation of the British Eighteenth Century,' *Historical Journal*, 45:2, 2002.

Koenigsberger, H. G. 'From Contractual Monarchy to Constitutionalism,' in *Neostoicism and the Early Modern State*, edited by Gerhard Oestreich, Brigitta Oestreich and H. G. Koenigsberger (Cambridge: Cambridge University Press, 1982).

Koerner, Lisbet. *Linnaeus: Nature and Nation* (Cambridge: Harvard University Press, 1999).

Koestler, Arthur. [1959], *The Sleepwalkers: A History of Man's Changing Vision of the Universe* (Harmondsworth: Penguin, 1989).

Kolakowski, Leszek. 'The Intellectuals,' in his *Modernity on Endless Trial* (Chicago: University of Chicago Press, 1990).

Koselleck, Reinhart. [1959], *Critique and Crisis: Enlightenment and the Pathogenesis of Modern Society* (Oxford: Berg, 1988).

—— *Futures Past: On the Semantics of Historical Time*, translated by Keith Tribe (Cambridge: Cambridge University Press, 1985).

Koyré, Alexandre. [1957], *Du monde clos à l'univers infini*, translated by Raissa Tarr (Paris: Gallimard, 1973).

Kristeller, Paul Oskar. 'Petrarch,' *The Encyclopedia of Philosophy* (New York: Macmillan, 1967).

Krugman, Paul R. 'The Myth of Asia's Miracle,' *Foreign Affairs*, 73:6, 1994, pp. 62–78.

Kuhn, Thomas S. *The Copernican Revolution: Planetary Astronomy in the Development of Western Thought* (Cambridge: Harvard University Press, 1957).

Kuttner, Robert. 'Markets, Innovation, and Growth,' in his *Everything for Sale: The Virtues and Limits of Markets* (New York: Knopf, 1997), pp. 191–224.

Kuznets, Simon. 'Characteristics of Modern Economic Growth,' in his *Modern Economic Growth: Rate, Structure, and Spread* (New Haven: Yale University Press, 1966).

Kwong, L. S. K. 'Chinese Politics at the Crossroads: Reflections on the Hundred Days Reform of 1898,' *Modern Asian Studies*, 34:3, 2000, pp. 663–96.

Lach, Donald and Edwin J. van Kley, *Asia in the Making of Europe: Volume I. The Century of Discovery* (Chicago: University of Chicago Press, 1965).

—— *Asia in the Making of Europe: Volume III. A Century of Advance* (Chicago: University of Chicago Press, 1993).

Landes, David S. *The Wealth and Poverty of Nations: Why Some Are So Rich and Some So Poor* (New York: Norton, 1998).

Lao Zi, 'The Natural Way of Lao Zi,' in *A Sourcebook in Chinese Philosophy*, edited by Wing-tsit Chan (Princeton: Princeton University Press, 1963).

Las Casas, Bartolomé de. [1552], *A Short Account of the Destruction of the Indies* (Harmondsworth: Penguin, 1992).

Lau, Lawrence J. 'The Sources of Long-Term Economic Growth: Observations from the Experience of Developed and Developing Countries,' in *The Mosaic of Economic Growth*, edited by Ralph Landau, Timothy Taylor and Gavin Wright (Stanford: Stanford University Press, 1996), pp. 63–91.

Le Goff, Jacques. [1981], *The Birth of Purgatory*, translated by Arthur Goldhammer (Chicago: University of Chicago Press, 1986).

—— *Your Money or Your Life: Economy and Religion in the Middle Ages* (New York: Zone Books, 1990).

Legrain, Philippe. *Open World: The Truth about Globalisation* (London, Abacus 2003).

Levenson, Joseph R. 'The Amateur Ideal in Ming and Early Ch'ing Society: Evidence from Painting,' in *Chinese Thought and Institutions*, edited by John K. Fairbank (Chicago: University of Chicago Press, 1975).

Levy, Marion J. 'Contrasting Factors in the Modernization of China and Japan,' in *Economic Growth: Brazil, India, Japan*, edited by Simon Kuznets, Wilbert E. Moore and Joseph J. Spengler (Durham: Duke University Press, 1955), pp. 496–536.

Leyden, W. von. 'Antiquity and Authority: A Paradox in the Renaissance Theory of History,' *Journal of the History of Ideas*, vol. 19, no. 4, 1958.

Leys, Simon. 'The Imitation of Our Lord Don Quixote,' *New York Review of Books*, 45:10, June 11, 1998.

Li, Deshun *et al.*, 'Special Issue: Marxism and Contemporary China,' *Social Sciences in China*, 23:3, 2002, pp. 95–140.

Li, Zhisui. *The Private Life of Chairman Mao* (London: Arrow, 1996).

Lieberman, Victor. 'Transcending East–West Dichotomies: State and Culture Formation in Six Ostensibly Disparate Areas,' *Modern Asian Studies*, 31, 1997, pp. 463–546.

Lin, Justin Yifu. 'The Needham Puzzle: Why the Industrial Revolution Did Not Originate in China,' *Economic Development and Cultural Change*, 43:2, 1995, pp. 269–92.

Lindblom, Charles E. *The Market System: What It Is, How It Works, and What to Make of It* (New Haven: Yale University Press, 2002).

Livingston, Arthur. 'Gentleman, Theory of the,' *Encyclopedia of the Social Sciences*, vol. 6, 1931.

Lo, Jung-Pang. 'The Emergence of China as a Sea Power during the Late Song and Early Yüan Periods,' *Far Eastern Quarterly*, 14:4, 1955, pp. 489–503.

Locke, John. [1690], *An Essay Concerning Human Understanding* (Oxford: Clarendon, 1975).

—— [1690], *Second Treatise of Government* (Indianapolis: Hackett, 1980).

Lockwood, William W. 'Japan's Response to the West: The Contrast with China,' *World Politics*, 9:1, 1956.

Long, P. O. 'Invention, Authorship, "Intellectual Property", and the Origin of Patents: Notes toward a Conceptual History.' *Technology and Culture*, 32:4, 1991.

Lopez, Robert S. [1976], *The Commercial Revolution of the Middle Ages, 950–1350* (Cambridge: Cambridge University Press, 1998).

Lovejoy, Arthur O. *The Great Chain of Being: A Study of the History of an Idea* (Cambridge: Harvard University Press, 1936).

Lubenow, William C. 'Making Words Flesh: Changing Roles of University Learning and the Professions in 19th Century England,' *Minerva*, 40: 2002, pp. 217–34.

Lucas, Robert E. 'On the Mechanics of Economic Development,' *Journal of Monetary Economics*, 22:1, 1988.

Luther, Martin. [1566], *Table Talk* (New York: HarperCollins, 1995).

Luttwak, Edward. *Turbo Capitalism: Winners & Losers in the Global Economy* (London: Orion, 1998).

Lyotard, Jean-François. *La condition postmoderne* (Paris: Éditions Minuit, 1979).

Machiavelli, Niccolò. 'Letter to Francesco Vettori, December 10, 1513,' in *The Letters of Machiavelli*, translated by Allan Gilbert (Chicago: University of Chicago Press, 1961).

—— [1531], *Discourses on the First Ten Books of Titus Livy* (Harmondsworth: Penguin, 1983).

—— [1532], *The Prince*, translated by Luigi Ricci (New York: New American Library, 1980).

MacIntyre, Alasdair. *After Virtue: A Study in Moral Theory* (London: Duckworth, 1985).

Mackay, Charles. [1841], *Extraordinary Popular Delusions and the Madness of Crowds* (New York: Farrar, Straus & Giroux, 1932).

McKendrick, Neil. 'Home Demand and Economic Growth: A New View of the Role of Women and Children in the Industrial Revolution,' in *Historical Perspectives: Studies in English Thought and Society in Honour of J. H. Plumb* (London, Europa, 1974).

—— 'The Consumer Revolution of Eighteenth-century England,' and 'The Commercialization of Fashion,' both in Neil McKendrick, John Brewer and J. H. Plumb, *The Birth of a Consumer Society: The Commercialisation of Eighteenth-Century England* (London: Europa, 1982).

MacLeod, Christine. 'The Paradoxes of Patenting: Invention and Its Diffusion in 18th- and 19th-Century Britain, France, and North America,' *Technology and Culture*, 32:4, 1991, pp. 885–910.

Madison, James, Alexander Hamilton and John Jay, [1788], *The Federalist Papers* (Harmondsworth: Penguin, 1987).

Madrick, Jeff. *Why Economies Grow: The Forces that Shape Prosperity and How to Get Them Working Again* (New York: Basic Books, 2002).

Maitland, Frederic W. [1900], 'Translator's Introduction,' to Otto Gierke, [1881], *Political Theories of the Middle Ages*, translated by F. W. Maitland (Bristol: Thoemmes Press, 1996).

Malthus, Thomas. [1798], *An Essay on the Principle of Population* (Harmondsworth: Penguin, 1982).

Marejko, Jan. *Cosmologie et politique: L'influence de la révolution scientifique sur la formation des régimes politiques modernes* (Lausanne: l'Age d'Homme, 1989).

Marx, Karl and Friedrich Engels, [1848], *Communist Manifesto* (Harmondsworth: Penguin, 1985).

Mattingly, Garrett. *Renaissance Diplomacy* (London: Cape, 1955).

Mauss, Marcel. 'A Category of the Mind,' in *The Category of the Person: Anthropology, Philosophy, History*, edited by Michael Carrithers, Steven Collins and Steven Lukes (Cambridge: Cambridge University Press, 1985).

May, Christopher. 'The Venetian Moment: New Technologies, Legal Innovation and the Institutional Origins of Intellectual Property,' *Prometheus*, 20:2, 2002, pp. 159–79.

Mayr, Otto. *Authority, Liberty & Automatic Machinery in Early Modern Europe* (Baltimore: Johns Hopkins University Press, 1986).

Mead, George H. [1932], *Mind, Self, and Society: From the Standpoint of A Social Behaviorist* (Chicago: University of Chicago Press, 1964).

Mehmet, Ozay. *Westernizing the Third World: The Eurocentricity of Economic Development Theory* (London: Routledge, 1995).

Menger, Carl. 'The Theory of Money,' in his *Principles of Economics*, translated and edited by James Dingwall and Bert F. Hoselitz (New York: New York University Press, 1981), pp. 257–85.

Meskill, John. 'Academies and Politics in the Ming Dynasty,' in *Chinese Government in Ming Times: Seven Studies*, edited by Charles O. Hucker (New York: Columbia University Press, 1969).

Mettam, Roger 'France,' in *Absolutism in Seventeenth Century Europe*, edited by John Miller (Basingstoke: Macmillan, 1990).

Meyerhoff, Barbara and Deena Metzger, 'The Journal as Activity and Genre,' in Barbara Meyerhoff, *Remembered Lives: The Work of Ritual, Storytelling, and Growing Older* (Ann Arbor: University of Michigan Press, 1992).

Michaelson, Gerald A. *Sun Tzu: The Art of War for Managers* (Avon: Adams Media Corporation, 2001).

Micklethwait, John and Adrian Wooldridge, *A Future Perfect: The Challenge and Hidden Promise of Globalization* (London: Heinemann, 2000).

Mill, John Stuart. [1848], *Principles of Political Economy* (Fairfield: Augustus M. Kelley, 1987).

—— [1861], 'Considerations on Representative Government,' in *On Liberty and Other Essays* (Oxford: Oxford University Press, 1991).

—— [1859] *On Liberty* (Harmondsworth: Penguin, 1985).

Miller, Jonathan. *On Reflection* (London: National Gallery Publications, 1998).

Modernity History Sourcebook: Dr. John Wallis, The Origin of The Royal Society, 1645–1662, available at http://www.fordham.edu/halsall/mod/1662royalsociety.html.

Mokyr, Joel. 'Demand vs. Supply in the Industrial Revolution,' *Journal of Economic History*, 37, 1977, pp. 981–1008.

—— *The Lever of Riches: Technological Creativity and Economic Progress* (Oxford: Oxford University Press, 1990).

Mommsen, Theodor E. 'Petrarch's Conception of the "Dark Ages",' *Speculum*, 17:2, 1942, pp. 226–42.

Montes, Leonidas. '*Das Adam Smith Problem:* Its Origins, the Stages of the Current Debate, and One Implication for Our Understanding of Sympathy,' *Journal of the History of Economic Thought*, 25:1, 2003, pp. 63–90.

Montesquieu, [1721], *Lettres persanes* (Paris: Flammarion, 1964).

—— [1748], *De l'Ésprit des lois*, in *Œuvres complètes* (Paris: Seuil, 1964).

Moore, Barrington, Jr. *Social Origins and Dictatorship and Democracy: Lord and Peasant in the Making of the Modern World* (Boston: Beacon, 1966).

More, Thomas. [1516], *Utopia* (Harmondsworth: Penguin, 1965).

Mumford, Lewis. *The Pentagon of Power: Volume II. The Myth of the Machine* (New York: Harvest, 1964).

Myers, Ramon H. 'How Did the Modern Chinese Economy Develop?,' *Journal of Asian Studies*, 50:3, 1991, pp. 604–28.

—— and Yeh-chien Wang, 'Economic Developments, 1644–1800,' *The Cambridge History of China: Volume 9, Part 1, The Ch'Ming Empire to 1800* (Cambridge: Cambridge University Press, 2002).

Nakai, Nobuhiko and James L. McClain, 'Commercial Change and Urban Growth in Early Modern Japan,' in *The Japanese Economy in the Tokugawa Era, 1600–1868*, edited by Michael Smitka (New York: Garland, 1998).

Nakamura, Naofumi. 'Meiji-Era Industrialization and Provincial Vitality: The Significance of the First Enterprise Boom of the 1880s,' *Social Sciences Japan*, 3:2, 2000, pp. 187–205.

Nauert, Charles G. *Humanism and the Culture of Renaissance Europe* (Cambridge: Cambridge University Press, 1995).

Ng, On-Cho. 'The Epochal Concept of "Early Modernity" and the Intellectual History of Late Imperial China,' *Journal of World History*, 14:1, 2003, pp. 37–61.

Ng, Wai-Ming. *The I Ch'ing in Tokugawa Thought and Culture* (Honolulu: University of Hawai'i Press, 2000).

Norberg, Kathryn, 'The French Fiscal Crisis of 1788 and the Financial Origins of the Revolution of 1789,' in *Fiscal Crises, Liberty, and Representative Government, 1450–1789*, edited by Philip T. Hoffman and Kathryn Norberg (Stanford: Stanford University Press, 1994).

North, Douglass C. *Structure and Change in Economic History* (New York: Norton, 1981).

—— *Institutions, Institutional Change and Economic Performance* (Cambridge: Cambridge University Press, 1990).

—— 'Economic Performance through Time,' *American Economic Review*, 84, 1994.

—— and Barry W. Weingast, 'Constitutions and Commitment: The Evolution of Institutions Governing Public Choice in 17th Century England,' *Journal of Economic History*, vol. 49, 1989, pp. 803–32.

Oakeshott, Michael. [1962], 'Rationalism in Politics,' in his *Rationalism in Politics and Other Essays* (Indianapolis: Liberty Fund, 1991).

O'Leary, Brendan. *The Asiatic Mode of Production: Oriental Despotism, Historical Materialism and Indian History* (Oxford: Basil Blackwell, 1989).

Olson, Mancur. *The Logic of Collective Action: Public Goods and the Theory of Groups* (Cambridge: Harvard University Press, 1965).

Oxfeld, Ellen. *Blood, Sweat, and Mahjong: Family and Enterprise in an Overseas Chinese Community* (Ithaca, Cornell University Press, 1993).

Pagden, Anthony. 'Dispossessing the Barbarians: the Language of Spanish Thomism and the Debate over the Property Rights of the American Indians,' in *The Languages of Political Theory in Early-Modern Europe*, edited by Anthony Pagden (Cambridge: Cambridge University Press, 1987).

—— *European Encounters with the New World: From Renaissance to Romanticism* (New Haven: Yale University Press, 1993).

Parker, Geoffrey. *The Thirty Years War* (New York: Military Heritage Press, 1987).

Pascal, Blaise. [1662], *Pensée*, translated by A. J. Krailsheimer (Harmondsworth: Penguin, 1966), no. 68.

Paz, Octavio. *The Children of the Mire: Modern Poetry from Romanticism to the Avant-Garde* (Cambridge: Harvard University Press, 1974).

Phillips, Kevin. *Wealth and Democracy: A Political History of the American Rich* (New York: Broadway Books, 2002).

Pico della Mirandola, Giovanni. [1486], 'On the Dignity of Man,' in *The Renaissance*

Philosophy of Man, edited by Ernst Cassirer, Paul Oskar Kristeller and John Herman Randall (Chicago: University of Chicago Press, 1948), pp. 223–54.

Pirenne, Henri. *Economic and Social History of Medieval Europe* (San Diego: Harcourt, Brace, 1937).

Pocock, J. G. A. 'Ritual, Language, Power: An Essay on the Apparent Meanings of Ancient Chinese Philosophy,' in his *Politics, Language and Time: Essays on Political Thought and History* (Chicago: University of Chicago Press, 1989).

Polanyi, Karl. *The Great Transformation: The Political and Economic Origins of Our Time* (Boston: Beacon, 1944).

Polanyi, Michael. [1962], 'The Republic of Science: Its Political and Economic Theory,' in his *Knowing and Being* (Chicago: University of Chicago Press, 1969), pp. 49–72.

Polybius. 'An Analysis of the Roman Government,' in *Rome at the End of the Punic Wars*, available at http://www.fordham.edu/halsall/ancient/polybius6.html.

Pomeranz, Kenneth. *The Great Divergence: China, Europe, and the Making of the Modern World Economy* (Princeton: Princeton University Press, 2000).

Popper, Karl R. [1953], 'Science: Conjectures and Refutations,' in his *Conjectures and Refutations: The Growth of Scientific Knowledge* (New York: Harper Torchbooks, 1965).

Potter, Sulamith Heins and Jack M. Potter, [1990], *China's Peasants: The Anthropology of a Revolution* (Cambridge: Cambridge University Press, 1997).

Rabelais, François. [1548], 'Five Books of the Lives, Heroic Deeds and Sayings of Gargantua and his Son Pantagruel,' in *The Complete Works of François Rabelais*, translated by Donald M. Frame (Berkeley: University of California Press, 1991).

Raeff, Marc. 'The Well-Ordered Police State and the Development of Modernity in Seventeenth- and Eighteenth-Century Europe: An Attempt at a Comparative Approach,' *American Historical Review*, vol. 80, 1975, pp. 1221–43.

Ramseyer, J. Mark and Frances M. Rosenbluth, *The Politics of Oligarchy: Institutional Choice in Imperial Japan* (Cambridge: Cambridge University Press, 1998).

Rawski, Evelyn S. *The Last Emperors: A Social History of Qing Imperial Institutions* (Berkeley: University of California Press, 1998).

Readings in European History, 'Letters Patent Establishing the French Academy in 1635,' edited by J. H. Robinson (Boston: Ginn, 1906) vol. 2, pp. 271–2. Available at http://history.hanover.edu/texts/facademy.htm.

Readings in European History, edited by J. H. Robinson, 'Letters Patent Establishing the French Academy in 1635' (Boston: Ginn, 1906) vol. 2, pp. 271–2.

Revel, Jacques. 'The Uses of Civility,' in *A History of Private Life: Volume III. Passions of the Renaissance*, edited by Roger Chartier (Cambridge: Belknap Press, 1989), pp. 167–205.

Ringmar, Erik. *Identity, Interest and Action: A Cultural Explanation of Sweden's Intervention in the Thirty Years War* (Cambridge: Cambridge University Press, 1996).

—— 'Nationalism: The Idiocy of Intimacy,' *British Journal of Sociology*, 49:4, 1998, pp. 534–49.

—— 'The Institutionalization of Modernity: Shocks and Crises in Germany and Sweden,' in *Culture and Crisis: The Case of Germany and Sweden*, edited by Nina Witoszek and Lars Trägårdh (New York: Berghahn, 2002).

—— 'Why Europe was First,' *Journal of Social Science* (Thailand), no. 2, 2002.

Ritter, Lawrence S., William L. Silber and Gregory F. Udell, *The Principles of Money, Banking and Financial Markets* (Reading: Addison-Wesley, 1997).

Roberts, Michael. 'Swedish Liberty: In Principle and in Practice,' in his *The Age of Liberty: Sweden, 1719–1772* (Cambridge: Cambridge University Press, 1986).

Ronan, Colin A. and Joseph Needham, *The Shorter Science and Civilisation in China: Volume 1* (Cambridge: Cambridge University Press, 1979).

—— *The Shorter Science and Civilisation in China: Volume 2* (Cambridge: Cambridge University Press, 1981).

Ross, Angus. [1965], 'Introduction,' and 'Appendix: Alexander Selkirk,' both in Daniel Defoe, [1719], *The Life and Adventures of Robinson Crusoe* (Harmondsworth: Penguin, 1985), pp. 7–21; 301–10.

Rotours, Robert des. *Quelques notes sur l'anthropophagie en Chine* (Leiden: Brill, 1963).

Rousseau, Jean-Jacques. [1762], 'Du Contrat Social,' in *Œuvres Complètes: II* (Paris: Seuil, 1971).

—— [1762], *Émile ou De l'éducation* in *Œevres Complètes* (Paris: Seuil, 1971).

Rüegg, Walter. 'Themes,' and 'Epilogue: The Rise of Humanism,' in *A History of the University in Europe: vol I, Universities in the Middle Ages*, edited by Hilde de Ridder-Symoens (Cambridge: Cambridge University Press, 1996).

Runeby, Nils. *Monarchia Mixta: Maktfördelingsdebatt i Sverige under den tidigare stormaktstiden* (Uppsala: Studia Historica Upsaliensia, 1962).

Ruth, Arne. 'The Second New Nation: The Mythology of Modern Sweden,' *Daedalus*, 113, 1984, pp. 53–96.

Sacks, David Harris, 'The Paradox of Taxation: Fiscal Crises, Parliament, and Liberty in England, 1450–1640,' in *Fiscal Crises, Liberty, and Representative Government, 1450–1789*, edited by Philip T. Hoffman and Kathryn Norberg (Stanford: Stanford University Press, 1994).

Sandel, Michael J. *Democracy's Discontent: America in Search of a Public Philosophy* (Cambridge: Harvard University Press, 1996).

Schama, Simon. *The Embarrassment of Riches: An Interpretation of Dutch Culture in the Golden Age* (London: Fontana, 1987).

Schleiermacher, Friedrich. [1808], *Occasional Thoughts on Universities in the German Sense*, translated and edited by Terrence N. Tice and Edwina Lawler (San Francisco: EMText, 1991).

Schneider, Laurence A. *A Madman of Ch'u: The Chinese Myth of Loyalty and Dissent* (Berkeley: University of California Press, 1980).

Schrecker, John E. 'The Reform Movement of 1898 and the *Ching-i* Reform as Opposition,' in *Reform in Nineteenth-Century China*, edited by Paul A. Cohen and John E. Schrecker (Cambridge: Harvard University Press, 1976).

Schulze, Hagen. *States, Nations and Nationalism: From the Middle Ages to the Present* (Oxford: Blackwell, 1996).

Schumpeter, Joseph A. [1942], *Capitalism, Socialism and Democracy* (New York: Harper, 1976).

—— 'The Creative Response in Economic History,' in his *Essays: On Entrepreneurs, Innovations, Business Cycles, and the Evolution of Capitalism*, edited by Richard V. Clemence (New Brunswick: Transaction Publishers, 1989).

Scott, James C. *Domination and the Art of Resistance: Hidden Transcripts* (New Haven: Yale University Press, 1990).

—— *Seeing Like a State: How Certain Schemes to Improve the Human Condition Have Failed* (New Haven: Yale University Press, 1998).

Sen, Amartya. 'Democracy as a Universal Value,' *Journal of Democracy*, 10:3, 1999, pp. 3–17.

Sennett, Richard. *The Corrosion of Character: The Personal Consequences of Work in the New Capitalism* (New York: W. W. Norton, 1998).

Shaftesbury, Anthony Ashley Cooper, Third Earl of. *Characteristics of Men, Manners, Opinions, Times*, edited by Lawrence E. Klein (Cambridge: Cambridge University Press, 1999).

Shaowen, Z. 'Adam Smith in China,' in *Adam Smith: International Perspectives*, edited by Hiroshi Mizuta (Basingstoke: Macmillan, 1993).

Shapin, Steven. '"A Scholar and a Gentleman": The Problematic Identity of the Scientific Practitioner in Early Modern England,' *History of Science*, 29: 1991, pp. 279–327.

—— *A Social History of Truth: Civility and Science in Seventeenth-Century England* (Chicago: University of Chicago Press, 1994).

Simmel, Georg. [1900], *The Philosophy of Money* (London: Routledge, 1997).

Skinner, Quentin. *The Foundations of Modern Political Thought, vol. II: The Age of Reformation* (Cambridge: Cambridge University Press, 1978).

—— 'The State,' in *Political Innovation and Conceptual Change*, edited by Terence Hall, James Farr and Russel L. Hanson (Cambridge: Cambridge University Press, 1989), pp. 90–131.

—— *Liberty before Liberalism* (Cambridge: Cambridge University Press, 1998).

Smith, Adam [1758], 'The History of Astronomy,' *Essays on Philosophical Subjects* (Indianapolis: Liberty Fund, 1982).

—— [1776], *An Inquiry into the Nature and Causes of the Wealth of Nations* (Indianapolis: Liberty Fund, 1981).

Smith, Thomas C. *Native Sources of Japanese Industrialization, 1750–1920* (Berkeley: University of California Press, 1988).

Solow, Robert M. 'Mysteries of Growth,' *New York Review of Books*, 50:11, 2003.

Sources of Chinese Tradition, edited by William T. de Bary *et al.* (New York: Columbia University Press, 1960).

Spence, Jonathan D. [1990], *The Search for Modern China* (New York: W. W. Norton, 1999).

Stockwin, J. A. A. 'Factionalism in Japanese Political Parties,' *Japan Forum*, 1:2, 1989, pp. 141–50.

Strong, Roy. *Art and Power: Renaissance Festivals, 1450–1650* (Woodbridge: Boydell Press, 1984).

Sutton, Donald S. 'Consuming Counterrevolution: The Ritual and Culture of Cannibalism in Wuxuan, Guangxi, China, May to July 1968,' *Comparative Studies in Society and History*, 37:1, 1995, pp. 136–72.

Suzuki, D. T. [1956], *Zen Buddhism: Selected Writings of D. T. Suzuki* (New York: Doubleday, 1996).

Swift, Jonathan. [1713], 'Hints towards an Essay on Conversation,' *Modern History Sourcebook*, available at http://www.fordham.edu/halsall/mod/1713swift-conversation. html.

—— [1726], *Gulliver's Travels* (Ware: Wordsworth Classics, 1992).

Taira, Koji. 'Japan: Labour,' in *The Economic Emergence of Modern Japan*, edited by Kozo Yamamura (Cambridge: Cambridge University Press, 1997).

Talwar, Jennifer P. *Fast Food, Fast Track: Immigrants, Big Business, and the American Dream* (Cambridge: Westview, 2002).

Taussig, Michael T. *Devil and Commodity Fetishism in Latin America* (Chapel Hill: University of North Carolina Press, 1980).

Taylor, Charles. *Sources of the Self: The Making of the Modern Identity* (Cambridge: Harvard University Press, 1989).

Thirsk, Joan. *Economic Policy and Projects: The Development of a Consumer Society in Early Modern England* (Oxford: Clarendon, 1978).

Thomas, Peter D. G. 'The Beginning of Parliamentary Reporting in Newspapers, 1768–1774,' *English Historical Review*, vol. 74, 1959, pp. 623–36.

Thornton, Patricia M. 'Framing Dissent in Contemporary China: Irony, Ambiguity and Metonymy,' *China Quarterly*, 171: 2002, pp. 661–81.

Toby, Ronald P. 'Reopening the Question of *Sakoku*: Diplomacy in the Legitimation of the Tokugawa Bakufu,' *Journal of Japanese Studies*, 3:2, 1977.

Tocqueville, Alexis de. [1840] *Democracy in America: Volume II* (New York: Vintage, 1945).

—— [1856], *The Old Regime and the French Revolution*, translated by Stuart Gilberg (New York: Doubleday, 1955).

Todorov, Tzvetan. *La conquête de l'Amérique: la question de l'autre* (Paris: Seuil, 1982).

Totman, Conrad. 'From *Sakoku* to *Kaikoku*: The Transformation of Foreign-Policy Attitudes, 1853–1868,' *Monumenta Nipponica*, 35:1, 1980, pp. 1–19.

Totten, George O. [1974], 'Japanese Industrial Relations at the Crossroads: the Great Noda Strike of 1927–1928,' in *Japan in Crisis: Essays on Taishō Democracy*, edited by Bernard S. Silberman and H. D. Harootunian (Ann Arbor: University of Michigan, 1999).

Toulmin, Stephen. *Cosmopolis: The Hidden Agenda of Modernity* (Chicago: University of Chicago Press, 1990).

Trakman, Leon E. *The Law Merchant: The Evolution of Commercial Law* (Littleton: Rothman, 1983).

Tu, Ching-I. *Interpretation and Intellectual Change: Chinese Hermeneutics in Historical Perspective* (New Brunswick: Transaction Publishers, 2004).

Tuck, Richard. *Natural Rights Theories: Their Origin and Development* (Cambridge: Cambridge University Press, 1979).

Turner, Victor. *Dramas, Fields and Metaphors: Symbolic Action in Human Society* (Chicago: University of Chicago Press, 1974).

Unger, Roberto Mangabeira, *Social Theory: Its Situation and Its Task* (Cambridge: Cambridge University Press, 1987).

Upham, Frank K. 'Weak Legal Consciousness as Invented Tradition,' in *Mirror of Modernity: Invented Traditions of Modern Japan*, edited by Stephen Vlastos (Berkeley: University of California Press, 1998).

Valignano, Alessandro. 'Poor and Barren,' *They Came to Japan: An Anthology of European Reports on Japan, 1543–1640*, edited by Michael Cooper (Berkeley: University of California Press, 1965).

van Wolferen, Karel. [1988], *The Enigma of Japanese Power: People and Politics in a Stateless Nation* (New York: Vintage, 1990).

Verger, Jacques. 'Patterns,' in *A History of the University in Europe: vol I, Universities in the Middle Ages*, edited by Hilde de Ridder-Symoens (Cambridge: Cambridge University Press, 1996).

Vespucci, Amerigo. 'Letter of Amerigo Vespucci to Pier Soderini, Gonfalonier of the Republic of Florence,' *Modern History Sourcebook: Account of His First Voyage, 1497*. Available at http://www.fordham.edu/halsall/mod/1497vespucci-america.html.

Veyne, Paul. *Did the Greeks Believe in Their Myths?: An Essay on the Constitutive Imagination*, translated by Paula Wissing (Chicago: University of Chicago Press, 1983).

Vlastos, Stephen. ed. *Mirror of Modernity: Invented Traditions of Modern Japan* (Berkeley: University of California Press, 1998).

Vries, P. H. H. 'Governing Growth: A Comparative Analysis of the Role of the State in the Rise of the West,' *Journal of World History*, 13:1, 2002, pp. 67–138.

Wade, Robert. *Governing the Market: Economic Theory and the Role of Government in East Asian Industrialization* (Princeton: Princeton University Press, 1990).

Waltz, Kenneth N. [1979], 'Theory of International Politics,' reprinted in Neorealism and Its Critics, edited by Robert O. Keohane (New York: Columbia University Press, 1986).

Walzer, Michael. *Spheres of Justice: A Defense of Pluralism and Equality* (New York: Basic Books, 1983).

Watson, James L. 'Rites or Beliefs: The Construction of a Unified Culture in Late Imperial China,' in *China's Quest for National Identity*, edited by Lowell Dittmer and Samuel S. Kim (Ithaca: Cornell University Press, 1993).

Watt, Ian. *The Rise of the Novel: Studies in Defoe, Richardson and Fielding* (Berkeley: University of California Press, 1957).

—— *Myths of Modern Individualism: Faust, Don Quixote, Don Juan, Robinson Crusoe* (Cambridge: Cambridge University Press, 1997).

Weber, Eugen. *Peasants into Frenchmen: The Modernisation of Rural France, 1870–1914* (Stanford: Stanford University Press, 1972).

Weber, Max. [1906], 'Protestant Sects and the Spirit of Capitalism,' in *From Max Weber: Essays in Sociology*, edited by H. H. Gerth and C. Wright Mills (London: Routledge, 1991).

—— [1920–21], *The Protestant Ethic and the Spirit of Capitalism* (London: Routledge, 1992).

—— [1922], *The Religion of China: Confucianism and Daoism*, translated by Hans H. Gerth (New York: Free Press, 1964).

Weiss, Linda. 'War, the State, and the Origins of the Japanese Employment System,' *Politics and Society*, vol. 21, no. 3, 1993.

Westney, D. Eleanor. *Imitation and Innovation: The Transfer of Western Organizational Patterns to Meiji Japan* (Cambridge: Harvard University Press, 1987).

Wilhelm, Richard and Vary F. Baynes, translators, *I Ching or The Book of Changes* (Princeton: Princeton University Press, 1967).

Wilkinson, Endymion. *Japan versus the West: Image and Reality* (Harmondsworth: Penguin, 1991).

Willetts, William. [1964], 'The Maritime Adventures of Grand Eunuch Ho,' reprinted in *European Expansion and the Counter-Example of Asia, 1300–1600*, edited by Joseph R. Levenson (Englewood Cliffs: Prentice-Hall, 1967).

Wilson, George M. *Patriots and Redeemers in Japan: Motives in the Meiji Restoration* (Chicago: University of Chicago Press, 1992).

Wing, R. L. *The Art of Strategy: A New Translation of Sun Zi's Classic The Art of War* (New York: Broadway Books, 1988).

Wintrobe, Ronald. 'Some Economics of Ethnic Capital Formation and Conflict,' in *Nationalism and Rationality*, edited by André Breton *et al.* (Cambridge: Cambridge University Press, 1995).

Wittrock, Björn. 'Modernity: One, None, or Many? European Origins and Modernity as a Global Condition,' *Daedalus*, 129:1, 2000, pp. 31–60.

Wong, R. Bin. *China Transformed: Historical Change and the Limits of European Experience* (Ithaca: Cornell University Press, 1997).

Wood, Alan T. *Limits to Autocracy: From Sung Neo-Confucianism to a Doctrine of Political Rights* (Honolulu: University of Hawai'i Press, 1995).

Yamamura, Kozo. 'Entrepreneurship, Ownership, and Management in Japan,' in *The Economic Emergence of Modern Japan*, edited by Kozo Yamamura (Cambridge: Cambridge University Press, 1997).

—— 'The Japanese Economy, 1911–30,' in *Japan in Crisis: Essays on Taishō Democracy*, edited by Bernard S. Silberman and H. D. Harootunian (Ann Arbor: University of Michigan, 1999).

Yang, C. K. 'Some Characteristics of Chinese Bureaucratic Behavior,' in *Confucianism in Action*, edited by David S. Nivison and Arthur F. Wright (Stanford: Stanford University Press, 1959).

—— 'The Functional Relationship between Confucian Thought and Chinese Religion,' in *Chinese Thought and Institutions*, edited by John K. Fairbank (Chicago: University of Chicago Press, 1975).

Yang, Lien-Sheng. 'The Concept of *Pao* as a Basis for Social Relations in China,' in *Chinese Thought and Institutions*, edited by John K. Fairbank (Chicago: University of Chicago Press, 1975).

Yang, Mayfair Mei-hui. *Gifts, Favors and Banquets: The Art of Social Relationships in China* (Ithaca: Cornell University Press, 1994).

Yates, Frances A. *Giardano Bruno and the Hermetic Tradition* (Chicago: University of Chicago Press, 1964).

Yew, Lee Kuang. *The Singapore Story: Memoirs of Lee Kuang Yew* (Singapore: Singapore Press Holdings, 1998).

Yi, Zheng. *Scarlet Memorial: Tales of Cannibalism in Modern China* (Boulder: Westview, 1996).

Young, Ernst P. 'Nationalism, Reform, and Republican Revolution: China in the Early Twentieth Century,' in *Modern East Asia: Essays in Interpretation*, edited by James Crowley (New York: Harcourt, Brace & World, 1970).

Index

absolutism: abolition of parliaments and 56–7; civil rights and 117; European and Chinese compared 175; limits to Chinese 149, 162; repression and 106–7

academies: distance created by scientific 55; in France 108; organisation of 54–5; publications of 55; private Chinese 149; reflection and scientific 53–5; scientific method of 54

alchemy: Daoists and 142; entrepreneurship and 71–2; scientific academies and 53; statecraft and 72

Ancients, the: compared with the Moderns 4–6; conversations of Humanists with 33; entrepreneurship in China and 153–4; Hobbes on 45; reflection in China and 143–6; universities and 50

astronomical observations: *arcanum imperium* and 173; Confucians and 143; in Europe 37–9; rationalism and 38–9; reflection and 37–9, 143; by renegade Daoist monks 143; statecraft and 173

Bank of England 75, 92–3, 94, 131

banks: Italian 70, 78, 91; financial revolution and 75

Beurs (Amsterdam): futures markets and 91; as insurance broker 89; stock-market 92

Buddhism: Chan and landscape painting 147; in Japan 186; mirror as metaphor in 146; potentiality and 140

bullionism 70–1; Hume on fallacy of 125

bureaucracy: academies and Chinese 149; examination system and 147–8; factionalism within Chinese 162–3; reflection and Chinese 147–8, 150

canon: astronomical observations and 38–9; break-up of medieval 33–4; Chinese conception of 144–6, 148–9; Chinese and European conceptions of compared 17; creativity of Chinese conception of 144–5; in European Middle Ages 30–1, 65–6; examination system and 148

capital: financial markets and 91–4; futures 90–1; markets in 85

capitalism: functionalism and 23–4; as source of social development 6–9

Censorate, Chinese: as reflective institution 150–1, 177

censorship: in China 177; in Europe 45; in Japan 185

Ch'ing dynasty: consumer culture of 158–9; Huang Zongxi and 144–5

chaos: advantages of 168–70; cannibalism and 163; Cultural Revolution and 163; fear of 163–5; ritualism as a way of dealing with 167–8

China: alleged stagnation of 144; art in 146–7; economic growth in 9; entrepreneurship in 152–61; ethnocentrism of 156; European visitors on 139; examination system in 148–9; explanation for failure of development in 11–13; explanation for success of development in 14–15; failure of development in 10–11, 198; historical reflection in 143–6; institutions that reflect 148–51; Japanese developments compared with 200; Japanese reactions to development in 185; parallelisms with Europe 139–40, 171–82; political entrepreneurship in 160–1; reflection in 139–51; revolutions of 198–201; social development compared with Europe 10–15, 139–40; technological